Margaret Oliphant:
Critical Essays
on a Gentle Subversive

Margaret Oliphant:
Critical Essays
on a Gentle Subversive

Edited by
D. J. Trela

Selinsgrove: Susquehanna University Press
London: Associated University Presses

© 1995 by Associated University Presses, Inc.

All rights reserved. Authorization to photocopy items for internal or personal use, or the internal or personal use of specific clients, is granted by the copyright owner, provided that a base fee of $10.00, plus eight cents per page, per copy is paid directly to the Copyright Clearance Center, 222 Rosewood Drive, Danvers, Massachusetts 01923. [0-945636-72-5/95 $10.00 + 8¢ pp, pc.]

Associated University Presses
440 Forsgate Drive
Cranbury, NJ 08512

Associated University Presses
25 Sicilian Avenue
London WC1A 2QH, England

Associated University Presses
P.O. Box 338, Port Credit
Mississauga, Ontario
Canada L5G 4L8

Library of Congress Cataloging-in-Publication Data

Margaret Oliphant : critical essays on a gentle subversive / edited by D.J. Trela.
  p. cm.
  Includes bibliographical references and index.
  Contents: The paradoxes of Oliphant's reputation / John Stock Clarke—The subversion of literary cliches in Oliphant's fiction / Margarete Rubik——The female bildungsroman / Linda Peterson—The haunted interpreter in Oliphant's supernatural fiction / Esther Schor—The making of a novelist / Joanne Shattock—Absolute commonplaces: Oliphant's theory of autobiography / Laurie Langbauer —Freed by necessity, trapped by the market: the editing of Oliphant's Autobiography / Elisabeth Jay—The cry that binds: Oliphant's theory of domestic tragedy / Dale Kramer—Feminist or anti-feminist? Oliphant and the woman question / Merryn Williams.
  ISBN 0-945636-72-5 (alk. paper)
  1. Oliphant, Mrs. (Margaret), 1828–1897—Criticism and interpretation. 2. Women and literature Scotland—History—19th century. I. Trela, D. J. (Dale J.)
PR114.M37 1995
823'.8—dc20   94-19751
                                                                  CIP

The paper used in this publication meets the requirements
of the American National Standard for Permanence of Paper
for Printed Library Materials Z39.48-1984.

PRINTED IN THE UNITED STATES OF AMERICA

Contents

Acknowledgments	7
List of Frequently Cited Sources and Abbreviations	9
Introduction: Discovering the Gentle Subversive D. J. TRELA	11

Part 1: Fiction

The Paradoxes of Oliphant's Reputation JOHN STOCK CLARKE	33
The Subversion of Literary Cliches in Oliphant's Fiction MARGARETE RUBIK	49
The Female *Bildungsroman:* Tradition and Subversion in Oliphant's Fiction LINDA PETERSON	66
The Haunted Interpreter in Oliphant's Supernatural Fiction ESTHER SCHOR	90

Part 2: Nonfiction

The Making of a Novelist: Oliphant and John Blackwood at Work on *The Perpetual Curate* JOANNE SHATTOCK	113
Absolute Commonplaces: Oliphant's Theory of Autobiography LAURIE LANGBAUER	124
Freed by Necessity, Trapped by the Market: The Editing of Oliphant's *Autobiography* ELISABETH JAY	135

The Cry That Binds: Oliphant's Theory of Domestic Tragedy
  DALE KRAMER   147

Feminist or Antifeminist? Oliphant and the Woman Question
  MERRYN WILLIAMS   165

List of Contributors   181
Index   183

Acknowledgments

THIS collection—the culmination of nearly a decade of planning, research, writing, and scholarly heartache—would not have been possible without the support of many stalwart friends and colleagues.

The project for a book of essays on Margaret Oliphant grew out of a special session on her at the 1988 Midwest Modern Language Association Conference in St. Louis. Had a forum for the study of an obscure Scottish woman writer not been provided, this book would have been a more difficult project to launch. I am grateful to MMLA for its initial support.

A constant source of constructive criticism of this project was Robert Colby, co-author, with his wife Vineta Colby, of *The Equivocal Virtue: Mrs. Oliphant and the Victorian Literary Market Place* (1966). Unable to contribute to the collection himself, Bob commented judiciously and thoughtfully on the essays in it. While he and I did not always agree, his suggestions improved the book while his encouragement sustained the editor. Both Bob and Vineta exemplify disinterested and thorough scholarship and a generosity of spirit that is all too rare in academia nowadays.

I also wish to acknowledge the support of G. B. Tennyson, an early reader and encourager of the project.

Before the collection was accepted for publication by Susquehanna University Press it had been accepted by two scholarly presses. The first shut down operations in 1989 and cancelled existing contracts; the second, after contracting for the book, determined the financial loss would be too great to proceed and also cancelled the agreement. Neither raised any objection to the subject or scholarship of the work. It is unfortunate that financial considerations now must enter so strongly into academic publishing decisions, for we certainly are deprived of a great deal of significant scholarship as a result. Had either of these first two agreements held, this book would include essays by additional authors: Deborah Morse, Betty Richardson, Helene Roberts, Barbara Quinn Schmidt and Malcolm Woodfield. I thank them for their support of this project and wish their individual essays a speedy publication in other venues. Again, had the first agreement held, this book would have appeared in 1990 and there would have been no need to reprint Esther H. Schor's essay from *Women's Studies* or to reprint portions of Elisabeth Jay's essay from the 'Introduction' to *The Autobiography of Margaret Oliphant: The Complete Text*. I am necessarily extremely grateful to the contributors to this collection for their loyalty to a project that seemed "star-cross'd," and their good-hearted incorporation of my editorial suggestions.

I offer thanks to Roosevelt University for a semester leave that allowed me to formulate the final version of the collection.

My faith in this project has been rewarded of late as I have noted with pleasure many more scholars investigating and studying the writings of Margaret Oliphant. This year should see publication of critical studies of her by Elisabeth Jay and Margarete Rubik; a secondary bibliography co-authored by John Stock Clarke and me is in progress; a number of recent doctoral dissertations have dealt in part or in whole with her writings; and articles on her are now appearing more frequently. Scholars are finding that her voluminous output contains much that is original, significant or noteworthy. This is truly a happy development that could be made more joyous if publishers would risk returning more of Oliphant's fiction to print.

Finally, I must thank my wife, Janet Boden, not only for her support of me and this project, but for having introduced me to the writings of Margaret Oliphant in the first place. She is the author of this work in a true sense. I wish also to acknowledge my parents, Ruby and Anthony Trela, for their constant, loving support of my educational aspirations. To these three I jointly dedicate this work.

D.J.T.
Chicago
March, 1994

Frequently Cited Sources and Abbreviations

NLS	National Library of Scotland
Colby	Robert and Vineta Colby, *The Equivocal Virtue: Margaret Oliphant and the Victorian Literary Marketplace*. Hamden, CT: Archon, 1966.
Williams	Merryn Williams. *Margaret Oliphant: A Critical Biography*. New York: St. Martin's, 1986.
A&L	*The Autobiography and Letters of Mrs. M. O. W. Oliphant*. Mrs. Harry Coghill, ed. Edinburgh: Blackwood, 1898. The volume was reprinted with an introduction by Q. D. Leavis in 1974 by Leicester University Press while only the autobiography with an introductory essay by Laurie Langbauer was reprinted in 1988 by the University of Chicago Press. These editions are photographic reproductions; pagination of the autobiography and letters is the same.
A	*The Autobiography of Margaret Oliphant: The Complete Text*, ed. Elisabeth Jay. Oxford University Press, 1990.

The following works of fiction currently in print are referred to by page in the text. Other more obscure editions are noted by the contributors.

Miss Marjoribanks	Introduction by Penelope Fitzgerald. Harmondsworth: Penguin/Virago, 1988. There is another edition (London: Zodiac, 1969) with a critical introduction by Q. D. Leavis. Pagination for the novel in both editions is the same.
Phoebe, Junior	Introduction Penelope Fitzgerald. Harmondsworth: Penguin/Virago, 1988.
The Perpetual Curate	Introduction by Penelope Fitzgerald. Harmondsworth: Penguin//Virago, 1987.
Salem Chapel	Introduction Penelope Fitzgerald. Harmondsworth: Penguin/Virago, 1986.

The Doctor's Family and Other Stories	Introduction by Merryn Williams. Oxford UP, 1986.
The Beleaguered City and Other Stories.	Introduction Merryn Williams. Oxford UP, 1988.
Hester	Introduction by Jennifer Uglow. London: Virago, 1985.
Kirsteen	Introduction by Merryn Williams. London: Everyman, 1984.

Introduction: Discovering the Gentle Subversive

D. J. TRELA

> Our own opinion is that every artist finds the natural conditions of his working, and that in doing what he has to do according to his natural lights he is doing the best which can be got from him. But it is hopeless to expect from the reader either the same attention or the same faith for twenty or thirty literary productions which he gives to four or five. The instinct of nature is against the prolific worker. In this way a short life, a limited period of activity, are much the best for art; and a long period of labour, occupied by an active mind and fertile faculties, tell against, and not for, the writer. It is a sort of foregone conclusion that the man who does little is likely to do that little better than the man who does much.[1]

MARGARET Oliphant wrote these words in her obituary of Anthony Trollope in 1883. While she praised the brilliance of Trollope's Barsetshire, comparing him favorably to Thackeray and Austen, she recognized that his industry was now, after his death, telling against him in popular opinion. While admitting that not all his fiction deserved to "live," she asserted all of it had provided honest, workmanlike entertainment. Yet Oliphant found it puzzling that the regular application of time, energy, and skill that would be viewed as laudable in nearly any endeavor or profession should, in literature generally and now in Trollope's particular case, be viewed apologetically or even contemptuously. "He has been discussed since his death with a certain condescension and careless praise, as if the industry and regularity which were so conspicuous in him, and which are so meritorious in a moral point of view, were his chief qualities." In other words, in the popular critical mind, industry does not imply real talent; while "regularity" may suggest an absence of the romantic quality of "inspiration" commonly thought necessary for truly great work.

Whether or not Oliphant had any thoughts of herself as she wrote this brief appreciation is uncertain, yet the parallels are obvious. By 1883 she was fifty-five, only twelve years younger than Trollope at his death, but she had already written more than he had: fifty-seven of her eventual ninety-eight novels—compared to his total of forty-seven. Her biographies, popular histories, short stories, and critical articles already numbered in the hundreds and her regularity, industry, and reliability were proverbial. Her support of her family through her writing was certainly "meritorious in a moral point of view," yet this meeting of necessity seemed to overshadow the quality and range of much of the work she had published. While family obligations and the desire to maintain a comfortable lifestyle kept her writing steadily, her comment about writers finding the "natural conditions of [their] working" suggests that her own steadiness was a characteristic she was not interested in or capable of altering, or that what she produced would have been all that different had her circumstances been different.

Although Oliphant has been largely overlooked in literary studies of the Victorian period, the contributors to this volume believe that a selective reappraisal of her writing is in order. The process tentatively began in the mid-1960s with Robert and Vineta Colby's pioneering biography *The Equivocal Virtue,* and continued with Q. D. Leavis's glowing assessments of the *Autobiography and Letters* and *Miss Marjoribanks* and more recently with the newly edited *Autobiography* by Elisabeth Jay, the 1986 biography by Merryn Williams, and scattered critical articles by John Stock Clarke, Margarete Rubik, Penelope Fitzgerald, and others.[2]

One of the keynotes of the contributions to this volume comes in the use of the term *gentle subversive* in the subtitle. It may seem a paradoxical expression, but it is chosen for good reasons. The first is that Oliphant simply is a better writer than she is generally given credit for, many recent critics having unhesitatingly called her "great." In this sense, her actual work subverts the common scholarly impression of it, which is reasonably well expressed by the dismissive tone of Trevor Royle in *Precipitous City.* Oliphant, he says, "soon found that hack writing was a reasonable means of financial independence. From her house in Fettes Row [in Edinburgh] articles, biographies, novels, and reviews flowed from her pen, mostly for the formidable John Blackwood . . . . Today most of Mrs. Oliphant's work is forgotten. She wrote too much too quickly and with too little intellectual equipment to do her work justice." To this is added her success in supporting her family.³ The "hack" status accorded her is still a sadly typical epithet. J. M. Barrie, a good friend of Oliphant's in her last decade, suggested by contrast that her intellect was so alive one could scarcely imagine that she slept. Lord Jeffrey wrote in praise of Oliphant's first, anonymously published novel in 1849, Robert Louis Stevenson claimed to have "wept" over the beauty of *A Beleaguered City,* Thomas and Jane Carlyle praised Oliphant's biography of Edward Irving. Henry James, Anne Thackeray Ritchie, and others all offered varying degrees of praise for her work, not simply admiration or respect for her industry, or sympathy for the personal tragedies she endured.

Second, Oliphant's views on issues of overriding importance to critics nowadays—women's rights and, more generally, a woman's role or position in society—are much more complex and, generally speaking, more progressive than she is generally given credit for. Again, the "common" scholarly understanding of Oliphant as part of the conservative *Blackwood's* stable of writers is subverted by examination of the facts. A few practical examples are perhaps in order.

Possibly the words most harmful to her current reputation she wrote in her late essay "The Anti-Marriage League," where she lacerated Hardy's *Jude the Obscure* and showed herself (so received opinion goes) prudish, squeamish about honest representations of sex, and a middling talent unable to recognize great writing. The truer picture, as Merryn Williams and Dale Kramer suggest, is considerably more complicated. Oliphant clearly recognized Hardy's ability, calling him one of the most important late-Victorian novelists. For a brief time, the two writers cautiously admired each other although their interests as novelists and critics were clearly not complementary.⁴ She had given a fairly favorable review to *Tess of the D'Urbervilles,* but thought Hardy's contrived plotting and illogical characterization marred his story, particularly when Tess, the "pure woman," ends up as Alec's mistress.

In her review of *Jude the Obscure* (*Blackwood's* 159, [January 1896] 135-49) she did find his sexual honesty repellent because she felt the foregrounding of sex a contrivance, a distortion of the way she believed most people really lived and acted. Since she herself was married only seven years and never seriously contemplated remarriage, her attitude certainly makes some sense. The voluptuous Arabella, the ascetic Sue both struck her as incredible characters[5] whose conduct was designed to wreak destruction on men. She hints at a certain misogyny in Hardy by his choosing to represent men as "passive, suffering, rather good than otherwise" and women as temptresses. She was hardly unique in her disapproval of Hardy's frankness. Further, she suggested that the loosening of restraints on the passions carried with it immense problems in an age before widespread birth control, in unwanted or uncared for children, once personal gratification had run its course. Hardy, she felt, in the brutal murder-suicide of the children dealt with this issue in an exceptionally clumsy and unconvincing way.

A second area where Oliphant has run into trouble from modern readers comes in her apparent opposition to women's rights, in part expressed in a comment in a private letter noting John Stuart Mill's "mad notion" about the vote for women and her early essays in opposition to suffrage. Marion Shaw, in "Victorian Women Prose Writers" in *The Victorians,* baldly asserts that "Margaret Oliphant . . . was no supporter of women's suffrage or the women's movement at all, as her articles for *Blackwood's Magazine* in the late 1850s and 1860s testify." While Shaw limits this observation to the 1860s, she does not document the evolution Oliphant's thought underwent in succeeding decades.[6] By 1880, when she published "The Grievances of Women" in the radical *Westminster Review* she openly acknowledged the patriarchal devaluation of women's work and "women's sphere," had grown increasingly frustrated at her inability to find regular, salaried work as an editor in a male-dominated profession, and had more than twenty years' painful experience of the incapacity of most of the men in her own family. This article, and later letters support votes for women, property rights, professional and university education, female doctors and the like. In another private letter Oliphant wrote, probably in the 1890s to Lady Frances Balfour she says, "I am not opposed to the suffrage for women, but only indifferent and averse to agitation of all kinds, and hopelessly old fashioned and out of date."[7] Oliphant repeatedly maintained political rights would mean little without corresponding changes in male attitudes—a view now paradoxically close to Mill's own. While she can perhaps be faulted for not recognizing that personal attitudes can be altered through the state's coercive powers, from about the midpoint of her career she can be characterized as what Merryn Williams calls an "Old Feminist."

This clear evolution in her political and social attitudes toward the role of women in society is also evident in her fiction. Indeed, it has been a frequent observation among Oliphant's more thoughtful critics that her fictional representation of women was more radical than her public political views. While there is no question that Oliphant represents women primarily in the domestic sphere, she often very sensitively suggests the physical and psychological toll they endured and equally often shows women operating in an empowered and emboldened domestic space, and, less often, as empowered in a man's world.

A third general assumption about Oliphant is somewhat more complex. It grows out of the image of the long-suffering, hard-working mother writing primarily to support her children and extended family. It also grows out of the common gloss on her fiction as "wholesome"—one of the more frequent and misguided of nineteenth century reviewers' characterizations. This image—for which Oliphant herself is partly responsible—is presented most clearly in the *Autobiography and Letters* published by her niece and cousin the year after her death. As Elisabeth Jay has shown in the complete text of the *Autobiography* published in 1990, this document's first editors consciously chose to foreground the mothering, nurturing, self-denying side of Oliphant. They chose to represent, in their own words, her "exquisite womanliness" whatever the tragedies of her life might be (A:ix). They chose, rather ironically, to represent Oliphant as the unempowered center of a domestic sphere, and not as the accomplished famous novelist, critic, traveler, historian, and biographer that she was.

The actual words Oliphant wrote in this document, and not the editorial gloss put on them by her niece and cousin, through their commentary, omissions and highly subjective selection of correspondence to supplement the *Autobiography*, suggest a much more cutting and incisive observer of people and events, a more committed experimenter with the form of autobiography, and a more serious questioner of the truths of her religious faith.

What does all this have to do with the presumed "wholesomeness" of Oliphant's fiction? Like the mistaken gloss given to her *Autobiography*, the fiction also has generally been misrepresented. Because it is primarily set in the domestic sphere and because it often appears to be resolved with a wedding, it seems to "fit" with conventional patterns so often used at that time. The truth again is considerably more complex. In general, while Oliphant worked within societal conventions, she was constantly testing the limits of those conventions, pointing out the hidden, unseemly side of the domestic role women were forced into and the abuses of power that men frequently engaged in. While readers can have little or no doubt about the "perfect happiness" of the unions with which Jane Austen's novels conclude, Oliphant leaves much greater room for doubt.

As an early example of this, the novel *Harry Muir* (1853), contains one of the most convincing descriptions of the self-destructive tendencies of an alcoholic in this period of fiction. Harry is an amiable man, devoted to his wife, family, and unmarried sisters when sober, but totally incapable of steadiness when drinking, and, despite his good intentions, incapable of helping himself. Yet this is a "domestic" novel, largely unnoticed by critics except for its apparent appropriation of Oliphant's real-life alcoholic brother Willie into the plot. On the surface the novel is "happily" resolved when the title character is killed in a fall from a horse while inebriated. His widow, sisters, and infant son, by taking on the management of the estate, bring prosperity where Harry had brought near-ruin. The final irony is that Harry's surviving family members gradually delude themselves about his true character and end by hallowing the memory of a weak, self-destructive individual. Similarly, the much later novel *Hester*, now generally considered one of Oliphant's best, ends ironically with the title character having the choice of two capable but dull men as husband, when what she really wants and is equipped for, but is denied, is the management of her Aunt Catherine's bank. In both works Victorian conventions are upheld, or outwardly respected. A dead husband's memory is hallowed; a young women may marry respectably. Yet the upheld conventions are implicitly questioned. What the contributors to this collection suggest is that this questioning or subverting of convention is more typical of Oliphant than the wholesome reverence toward convention attributed to her.

A final reason for Oliphant's critical eclipse is that to the casual observer she was a borderline penny-a-liner who churned out reams of hackwork to maintain herself and her family. There is no disputing that her work is uneven in quality. However, there is also an integrity and consistency to much of her work, as well as a level of experimentation with form and theorizing about genre that mark her as a genuine artist. The essays included here suggest particular ways in which Oliphant's writing deserves further attention. Laurie Langbauer and Elisabeth Jay suggest that Oliphant thought carefully and deeply about the nature of autobiography, and, by extension, biography. Linda Peterson sees Oliphant as a transitional figure in the writing of the female *Bildungsroman*. Dale Kramer shows an incisive literary critic who developed a consistent and convincing theory of domestic tragedy that rejected still prevalent classical models. John Stock Clarke, Margarete Rubik, and Esther Schor isolate recurrent themes in Oliphant's fiction that stress her questioning and challenging of society's expectations of men, women, and their commonly understood roles. Merryn Williams shows Oliphant's evolving attitude toward the woman question. Joanne Shattock explores Oliphant's unsubmissive working relationship with John Blackwood while writing *The Perpetual Curate*. The themes here explored more accurately represent the quality of work of which Oliphant was capable and the views she actually developed rather than those frequently attributed to her.

Margaret Oliphant Wilson was born 4 April 1828 at Wallyford, Scotland, now a suburb of Edinburgh. Her father was a minor civil servant and bank clerk, apparently a morose and bad-tempered man. Her mother "was a great raconteur" who "passed on everything she knew to her daughter"[8] including English and Scottish literature, the Bible, and Scots Presbyterianism, family and Scottish history. Margaret Wilson was the most important feminine influence on her daughter Margaret, an influence that one may perhaps trace in the strong women in much of her fiction. Though she spent many of her formative years and most of her adult life in England or in travel on the continent, she remembered her Scottish heritage, was proud of it and often recalled it in her fiction and nonfiction.

She was the youngest of three surviving children and the only girl. Whether she had any formal schooling is uncertain, but clearly her mother took pains with her education. She was an eager reader and a precocious child, as a recollection one tentatively dates to 1835 attests:

> I was a very small child, indeed seven or eight, but already a confirmed novel-reader, devouring everything that came in the way, as was the habit of my family, when "Ernest Maltravers" ended, breaking off in the middle of the story with a promise of a sequel, for which sequel I persecuted the proprietor of the nearest accessible circulating library, which in those days was an institution to be found everywhere, Mudie being not as yet. The old lady was first amazed and then shocked that so small a reader should be so eager for such a book, and discoursed to me most seriously on the subject, ending the lecture by bringing forth "Fatherless Fannie," an improving work of the period. All being fish that came to my net, I devoured "Fatherless Fannie" without being less eager for the other works.[9]

The family was religious, supporting in 1843 the breakaway Free Church that emerged from the Scottish Disruption. Many years later Oliphant noted the "loftiness" and "splendour" of the idealism of the ministers and parishoners who left the Church of Scotland in this schism, adding that they "carried away many fervid imaginations" including a "then very youthful writer."[10] Although she fell away from the rigorous tenets of this Protestant sect, as her stories of the supernatural and her meditations on her children's deaths in her *Autobiography* attest, she maintained a firm, if somewhat unorthodox theism throughout her life. Her biographies of religious leaders as well as religious themes in her histories also underscore her interest in such issues.

Exactly when she started writing fiction is uncertain. A probable point is 1845 when her mother was ill and Margaret had to sit by silently as nurse. She occupied the time by working on her first novel, not published until 1856 as *Christian Melville*. She continued to write in her spare time and in 1849 gave her brother Willie the manuscript of *Passages in the Life of Mistress Margaret Maitland* to take to London in search of a publisher. Henry Colburn accepted the book. The surviving contract is dated 24 August, and sets payment to "Miss Wilson" of one hundred and fifty pounds.[11] Thus Margaret became a published author at twenty-one and began a fifty-year career.

Eighteen fifty-two proved an important year for her. After having refused his proposal several years before, she married her cousin, the painter and stained-glass artist Frank Oliphant on 4 May. In July she began her formal relationship with *Blackwoods*, with the serialization of her novel *Katie Stewart*, the first of 267 separate articles or works of fiction that would appear there. Oliphant's introduction to the *Blackwood's* set had come a year earlier when, on a visit to her Wilson relatives in Edinburgh, she was introduced to Major William Blackwood and his brother John. As she recalled many years later, she was impressed by "the aspect of the mild and courteous soldier," his fairness, "consideration and gentleness."

> It was through the Major that I sent with trembling in the spring of 1852 my little story called "Katie Stewart" . . . hoping, I suppose, as young people do, that something wonderful might happen, yet scarcely expecting to be admitted to the honours of the Magazine at the first flight (though I was already at twenty-four the author, in youthful presumption, of three or four novels). I had, indeed, I believe, attempted that flight before in the case of "Margaret Maitland," my first production, respecting which I wrote a letter full of the sickness of hope deferred, which had so touched the heart of Mr. John Blackwood, who took it for the pathetic effusion of an old, sad, and disappointed writer, that he had nearly accepted my lucubrations out of pity, never suspecting that the pathos of that appeal came from a girl of twenty, who did not then know what disappointment meant. I presume it must have been the Major's gentle counsels which turned the scale in the case of "Katie Stewart," the first proofs of which, "for the Magazine"! I received on the morning of my wedding day—not exactly a moment when the glory and excitement of such a second event could have the appreciation which was its due.[12]

To round out the eventful year, Margaret's brother Willie, who had become a Presbyterian minister but was unable to control his drinking, was forced to leave the church quietly to avoid public exposure of his illness. He was fetched back to the family home, made little effort to find work, and later copied some of his sister's novels (at her request) that were published under his name and gave him a feeling of some accomplishment. In 1860 he settled in Rome where he probably relied on his sister for financial support, and where he died on 23 May 1885.

Relatively little is known about Margaret and Frank's marriage. Biographers have speculated it was not particularly happy and that Frank was too much his wife's intellectual inferior. Oliphant does not touch on her feelings for her husband in her *Autobiography;* much of the evidence of friction or unhappiness is taken from passages in her novels of this period and later. Such evidence must, of course, be treated with caution. Yet Frank and his mother-in-law do not seem to have gotten along well, Margaret lost several babies during these years, the couple were not financially astute and so were plagued with money worries even though they seem to have had an annual income of about six hundred pounds, and after several years of marriage it became clear Frank was gravely ill with tuberculosis. Any one of these concerns would be a source of stress to most couples; combined it is perhaps more wonder Margaret and Frank were so relatively content. They had three children who survived infancy, a girl Margaret, and Cyril, known as Tiddy, and Francis, born after his father's death, and nicknamed Cecco.

Throughout the 1850s Margaret continued to write fiction for *Blackwood's*. By 1854 she was able to convince her editors to let her try her hand as critic—an occupation that paid her somewhat less than her fiction, but which carried with it greater prestige. Though initially limited to writing on fiction, she gradually expanded her range of subjects and clearly gained the confidence of the Blackwoods in her ability. While still in her twenties, she wrote on Mary Russell Mitford, Dickens, Bulwer, Thackeray, and Macaulay; on women's rights; and on "Light Literature" concerning theology, science, history, and travel.[13]

While clearly her work was important as a creative outlet for her talents, it augmented the family's uncertain income. She seems to have provided at least half the earnings. Financial necessity thus was a spur to keep her writing; it too becomes a recurring, at times dominating theme in her correspondence with the Blackwoods as "personal embarrassments" forced her regularly to request advances. Her family's needs and her own often spendthrift ways both contributed to the indifferent quality and unevenness of some of the work she produced during her career.

After their marriage Frank and Margaret settled in London where her parents later joined them. Her mother died apparently of a rectal disease in 1854, and her father four years later. Initially Frank did a good business, getting a commission for windows at Ely Cathedral, among others, but the expense of his studio was a drain, he was not an orderly manager and his health began to fail in mid–1857. He possibly knew he was dying when he, Margaret, and their children traveled to Italy in the vain hope the change of climate would help, in January of 1859. He steadily deteriorated that spring and summer and when he died in Rome on 20 October, Margaret was alone and seven months pregnant.

After Cecco was born in January she returned to Britain and settled in Scotland briefly. It was a particularly difficult winter as she was in mourning, one thousand pounds in debt to the Blackwoods, had had a string of articles rejected by them, feared she might be losing her talent to write, and had her children to support. Her breakthrough came when, as she later recalled, after having another proposal for a novel for *Blackwood's* rejected by the Major and John Blackwood, she fought back her tears as she left their offices, returned to her lodgings in Fettes Row on the fringe of the Edinburgh New Town and wrote "The Executor," the first story of what became the "Chronicles of Carlingford," her most successful and famous novels, and among her best work. "I sat up nearly all night in a passion of composition, stirred to the very bottom of my mind. The story was successful, and my fortune, comparatively speaking, was made" she later wrote.[14]

There followed in the next five years *The Doctor's Family, Salem Chapel, The Perpetual Curate, Miss Marjoribanks,* and, a decade later, *Phoebe, Junior* plus articles and non-Carlingford fiction. These books boosted her popularity and income and gave her the financial breathing space to attempt an ambitious work of biography, based on original research, of Edward Irving, a charismatic Presbyterian minister excommunicated for heresy who had died in 1834. He had also tutored Jane Welsh and been the close friend of Thomas Carlyle, a connection that emboldened Margaret to appeal to both for anecdotes and information. Though Thomas was not particularly helpful, Margaret and Jane became fast friends. This biography, published by Hurst and Blackett, appeared in mid-1862. It is probably her finest work in this genre, and even earned praise from the usually critical Carlyle.

Throughout her career Oliphant worked primarily with Hurst and Blackett, William Blackwood and Sons, and Macmillan, although she appeared under the imprint of several other houses including Chapman & Hall, Methuen, Hutchinson, F. V. White, Longmans, Harper & Brothers, and Smith, Elder. Aside from magazines, her fiction was also serialized in provincial newspapers and reprinted with or without her approval in America. Normally she worked on several projects simultaneously and could scarcely finish one piece without starting almost immediately on the next. Her rate of production averaged about two novels per year, ten articles (not counting those rejected, about which little is known), a short story, and perhaps a single volume of nonfiction. Her voluminous output depressed demand for certain of her novels and at times seemed to make some publishers wary of accepting her material.

Perhaps because of her constant jumping from publisher to publisher, her rapid production, and her gender, she was never able to gain long-term salaried employment either as a reader of manuscripts or as an editor, which she most definitely sought to ease her financial worries. Yet even the Blackwoods, with whom she had a forty-five year affiliation, and to whom she became something like family, made her no guarantees, even though they appreciated her reliability and range. One letter to Oliphant from John Blackwood (26 December 1865) suggests this hybrid relationship combined business and friendship.

> Your proof did not get back to me until Sunday and as the printers were clamorous for upmaking on Saturday I made up without "Miss M[arjoribanks]," which I was sorry for when I saw your note. It may be a satisfaction to you to know that I had a horrible nightmare last night and dreamed that the Magazine had all been made up wrong. Mr. Hutchison, the manager of the printing office having unaccountably gone and printed papers that had been used before, and I still more unaccountably never having discovered the mess until my copy of the complete No. reached Randolph Crescent. I awoke swearing furiously and demanding of the terrified Hutchison how cancels could be managed in time. It was an Editor's dream with a vengeance, and whether the Christmas mince-pies or the leaving out of "Miss M." had most to do with it I know not. I wish I could venture on a double number of the Magazine, and so get myself out of the fix in which I am. I used to pique myself upon the sort of instinctive skill with which I balanced my quantities, never having to reject a good article for lack of space or to accept an indifferent one to fill up. I am half inclined to tell you to do the paper upon the religious or irreligious movement in Scotland. My objection to the movement is that it unsettles the creed of old women of both sexes to no purpose, as I do not see that any of the new lights either do or can offer any substitute. Do you think you could do any good?[15]

There is a curious mixture of genial friendship, deference, and intimacy coupled with pride and exercise of authority in this letter. It is a relationship that defies easy generalization. Though unwilling to guarantee accepting her work, they were nearly always willing to advance her money on faith of future writing they would accept. While they did not consistently trust her in an editorial capacity, they had no doubt about her gifts as a writer. Thus well into her sixties in the 1890s, Oliphant had no settled income except for a small pension from the Queen, no guaranteed employment, her niece and cousin to support, and financial anxieties that she alone could relieve. Among her last letters are some attempting to settle her financial affairs to the advantage of her heirs.

Oliphant's financial difficulties were compounded by the tragic pattern of untimely deaths and disabilities of her relatives. For aside from Willie's alcoholism and her husband's early death, her daughter Margaret died suddenly of fever in Rome early in 1864. Her brother Frank suffered a nervous illness in 1868, was unemployed for some time and only got work in rural Hungary. When his wife died in 1870, he collapsed; from then until his death in 1875 he became Margaret's financial responsibility, as did his two young daughters while his son Frank Jr. had already been supported by his aunt Margaret for two years. Frank was educated as an engineer but died suddenly in India in 1879. Her own sons she sent to Eton and Oxford. Though talented they were unambitious and often unwell. Their gentlemen's education seems to have made them unwilling to exert themselves overmuch. Also, Cyril probably suffered from alcoholism as his uncle had. He died suddenly in November of 1890, shortly after completing a brief biography of de Musset that had taken him eight years to write and which his mother had arranged for him to do as part of the "Foreign Classics for English Readers" series she edited for the Blackwoods.

She took her remaining son Cecco, himself ill with tuberculosis, to Switzerland that winter. A letter to her friend, Edward Pigott, sums up her own poignant feelings, her devotion to her remaining child, and her need to continue writing.

> About myself I have not very much to say. I was twenty-eight when my Cyril was born, and now I am sixty-two—and all that time he has never been out of my thoughts for a day—at first with what hope and pride, latterly with anxiety almost more engrossing—and now a blank until I shall go to him—which I dare not for the sake of my other children even pray or desire may be a moment sooner than must be. I have an iron constitution which is proof against everything, but there is no healing to the heart after such a rending asunder.

She continued, noting that the doctor had seen some improvement in Cecco and that "if all goes as at present . . . he will return home cured."[16] It was false optimism. Although Cecco showed promise as a writer he was more a scholar than the popularizer his mother was. He produced some articles on heraldry, hoped to work at the British Museum but was never well enough to take up an appointment there, worked part-time at the Royal Library and collaborated with his mother on *The Victorian Age in English Literature* (although some editions do not even list him on the title page). He died in October 1894, the last of his mother's children.

If one views Oliphant's life from her husband's death in 1859 to her own passing in 1897, some further patterns emerge: she was a great lover of children, was committed to domestic concerns—comfortable at home, as it were—yet, after overcoming some initial awkwardness and shyness, moved easily in society, and was invariably described by friends as a great intellect, though in her *Autobiography* she appears to deprecate her talents. Finally, she was an enthusiastic and regular traveler to the continent. She often took along friends and their children on her holidays. Whatever her financial constraints—almost annually she went either to Paris, Italy, Switzerland, the Holy Land, or elsewhere—she spent more than she should and did much of her writing while "on the road."

She horrified her niece Annie by announcing, at age sixty-nine, that she was going to Siena to collect information for a book that J. M. Dent asked her to write. Although probably already suffering from the colon cancer that would end her life,[17] she went there in the spring, collected information and impressions, but lived only to complete an article. Shortly before she left, she had virtually completed the first two volumes of her commissioned work, *Annals of a Publishing House: William Blackwood and His Sons*, a rich, anecdotal history of the firm down to the mid-1850s.

Soon after her return to England she went into her final decline. She learned in June that she was dying and so would not live to complete the third volume of the *Annals*. Her approaching death, the Colbys note, was "news she received with great serenity." (214) She spent her last weeks receiving final visits from friends, correcting proofs for the history, and arranging her tangled finances. Before her death on the twenty-fifth—three days after the Queen's Jubilee—she wrote William Blackwood. "I am very grateful to get away to 'the rest that remaineth,'" she said, "and very comfortable in my mind reposing on Our Dear Lord. Goodbye—my love to you all" (A&L 242). It is little wonder after her hard, tragedy-filled life that she viewed death as a relief and welcome release.

The image of Oliphant the "gentle subversive" traced in the following essays reflects the changing scholarly view of her. As Elisabeth Jay wrote in her preface to Oliphant's *Autobiography:*

> Throughout her work Oliphant cast a wry eye upon the comparative lots of men and women and the subtleties of the human temperament, which often submits against its own better judgement to the orthodoxies society imposes. For society, as she often remarked, looked after its own, and virtue all too frequently had a way of becoming its own reward in the socially inferior position of the single woman. Such a view of life was not without its consequences for her writing and some of those novels which appear most completely to collude with the moral and stylistic conventions of the day do so only after a subtly subversive examination of many of the age's most treasured assumptions. (*A* xvi–xvii)

Oliphant's starting point, as she liked to insist, was the real, round world that contained all things. Or, to quote Penelope Fitzgerald, Oliphant asks "us to consider, not how things ought to be, but how (in her experience and ours) they are."[18] If future critics will continue to examine her writing critically and sympathetically, there can be little doubt she will emerge as an incisive and gifted writer in several genres, in addition to being, as Merryn Williams has asserted, "one of the great Victorian novelists."[19]

Notes

1. Margaret Oliphant, "Anthony Trollope," *Good Words* 24 (1883) 142–44.
2. A brief bibliography of significant criticism of Oliphant includes the following works: the pioneer biography of Robert and Vineta Colby, *The Equivocal Virtue: Mrs. Oliphant and the Victorian Literary Market Place* (Hamden, CT: Archon, 1966); see also the essays of Q. D. Leavis introducing reprints of the *Autobiography and Letters* (Leicester University Press, 1974) and *Miss Marjoribanks* (London: Zodiak, 1969); John Stock Clarke, "Mrs. Oliphant's Unacknowledged Social Novels," *Notes and Queries* 28 (October 1981) 408–13; "Mrs. Oliphant: A Case for Reconsideration," *English* 27 (1979) 123–33; *Margaret Oliphant (1828–1897): A Bibliography*, Victorian Fiction Research Guides, 11 (St. Lucia, Australia: Univer-

sity of Queensland Department of English, 1986); "The 'Rival Novelist'—Hardy and Mrs. Oliphant," *The Thomas Hardy Journal* 5 (October 1989) 51–61; Margarete [Rubik] Holubetz, "Mrs. Oliphant's Unconventional Heroines," *Wiener Beitraege zur Englischen Philologie* 79 (1982–83) 13–29; "The Return of the Convict in Mrs. Oliphant's *The Son of His Father*," *Wiener Beitraege zur Englischen Philologie* 80 (1985–86) 201–15; J. A. Haythornethwaite, "The Wages of Success: *Miss Marjoribanks,* Margaret Oliphant and the House of Blackwood," *Publishing History* 15 (1984) 91–107; Gaye Tuchman with Nina Fortin, *Edging Women Out: Victorian Novelists, Publishers, and Social Change* (New Haven: Yale University Press 1989); and Merryn Williams, *Margaret Oliphant: A Critical Biography* (New York: St. Martin's, 1986); and Joseph H. O'Mealy, "Mrs. Oliphant, *Miss Marjoribanks,* and the Victorian Canon," *Victorian Newsletter* 82 (Fall 1992) 44–49; D. J. Trela, "Two Margaret Oliphants Review George Eliot," *George Eliot-George Henry Lewes Studies* 22–23 (September 1993) 37–60. The introductions to novel and short story reprints by Williams, Jennifer Uglow, and Penelope Fitzgerald are noted on the page of works frequently cited, as is Elisabeth Jay's "complete" version of the *Autobiography*. Other references to significant articles on or books dealing in part with Oliphant come in the notes to the essays. The most sensitive literary criticism of Oliphant deals with her *Autobiography,* the work that, in some form, has been most continuously in print.

3. *Precipitous City: The Story of Literacy Edinburgh* (Edinburgh: Mainstream; New York: Taplinger, 1980) 153. Royal mistakenly calls Oliphant Edinburgh's "first full-time woman of letters," but she actually spent only a few years of her writing life in that city. While much of her work was published by the Blackwoods, most of her fiction and book-length nonfiction appeared under other imprints.

4. See J. S. Clarke, "The 'Rival Novelist'—Hardy and Mrs Oliphant" *The Thomas Hardy Journal* 5 (October 1989) 50–61; Norman Page, "Hardy, Mrs. Oliphant and *Jude the Obscure*," *Victorian Newsletter* 46 (1974) 22–24; and Margaret Oliphant and Francis Romano Oliphant, *The Victorian Age of English Literature* (London; Percival and Co., 1892) 2:204–205.

5. The lack of credibility in fictional characters was a touchstone for Oliphant and led her into strongly worded criticism of Sissy Jupe in Dickens's *Hard Times* and of Dinah Morris and Romola dei Bardi in Eliot's *Adam Bede* and *Romola*.

6. "Victorian Women Prose-Writers" in *The Victorians,* ed. Arthur Pollard (New York: Peter Bedrick, 1987). In fairness to Shaw, she does note Oliphant's "satisfaction with things as they were arose from something very close to contempt for legislative procedure and a sense of women's certain difference from, and probable superiority to, men" but she is nonetheless mystified by Oliphant's frequent ironic tone and unaware of her later support for women's rights.

7. Huntington Library MSs, HM35050.

8. Williams, 4. In this biographical sketch all material will be drawn from the Williams and Colby biographies, except as noted.

9. *Annals of a Publishing House: William Blackwood and His Sons, Their Magazine and Friends,* 2 vols. (Edinburgh: Blackwood, 1897) 2:429.

10. *A Memoir of the Life of John Tulloch, D.D. LL.D.*, 3d ed., (Edinburgh: Blackwood, 1889) 20.

11. NLS, 23219.

12. *Annals*, 2:415–16.
13. See D. J. Trela, "Negotiating from Weakness? Margaret Oliphant and the House of Blackwood, 1852–1861," unpublished paper delivered at the Midwest MLA conference, November, 1990.
14. *A* 91; *A&L*, 70; cf. *Annals*, 2:487–88.
15. Mrs. Gerald (Mary) Porter, *Annals of a Publishing House: John Blackwood* (Edinburgh: Blackwood, 1898) 3:340. Mary Porter was John Blackwood's daughter. An excellent yet somewhat judgmental account of Oliphant's dealings with the Blackwoods and other publishing houses can be found in chapter 5 of *The Equivocal Virtue*, "Author and Publisher."
16. Huntington Library MSs, Pigott, Box 2; The letter is dated 16 January [1891] from "Davos: Platz" in Switzerland where Oliphant went with Cecco after Cyril's death. Edward Pigott was the licenser of plays at the time.
17. NLS, 21219 contains her death certificate that notes she was the wife of a stained-glass painter but does not mention her own profession of author. It states the cause of death as "malignant disease of the colon," which does suggest, if not confirm, cancer.
18. *Miss Marjoribanks*, xi.
19. *The Doctor's Family*, vii.

Margaret Oliphant:
Critical Essays
on a Gentle Subversive

Part 1
Fiction

The Paradoxes of Oliphant's Reputation

JOHN STOCK CLARKE

MARGARET Oliphant had a talent fit to be compared with all but the greatest Victorian novelists. What is remarkable about her reputation, at least since 1900, is the consistent undervaluing of her work, and the persistent myths with which this reputation has been encrusted. These myths were so often repeated, and yet are so contrary to the truth when objectively examined, that one must call them paradoxes—defining the word as a statement that is blatantly contradicted by the evidence while still retaining its currency.

I

Of all these myths, or paradoxes, the most obsessive, inevitable, and damaging to Oliphant's credit as a distinguished novelist is the conviction that she crippled her talent by overproduction. At times this seemed to be her own belief. Speaking in her autobiography of her incapacity for "the steady monotony of self-denial" when in financial difficulties, she continues: "the still better kind of self-denial which should have made a truer artist than myself pursue the higher objective of art, instead of the mere necessities of living, was wanting too. I pay the penalty in that I shall not leave anything behind me that will live" (*A* 136). Many critics have taken this too literally and in isolation from other comments. Yet she is speaking with the defensive self-abasement that tries to assuage acute doubts by overstating what in fact she does not seriously believe. ("I don't always think such small beer of myself as I say," she writes in the very next paragraph.)

Typical of the commentators who followed Oliphant's lead are a father and daughter, Leslie Stephen and Virginia Woolf. Stephen, in 1899, in an article not devoted to Oliphant, uses her autobiography to illustrate a point:

> Mrs. Oliphant thought (and, as I believe, with some justice) that, if freed from pecuniary pressure, she could have rivalled some more successful authors, and possibly have written a novel fit to stand on the same shelf with *Adam Bede*. She resigned her chance of such fame because she wished to send her sons to Eton. It is, of course, clear enough that, if she had sent them to some humbler school, she might have come nearer to combining the two aims, and have kept her family without sacrificing her talents to over-production. But, granting the force of the dilemma, I confess that I honour rather than blame the choice. I take it to be better for a parent to do his (or her) parental duty than to sacrifice the duty to "art" or the demands of posterity.[1]

The tone of this is surprisingly philistine from one of the most eminent critics of the Victorian age. (In his next sentence Stephen says "I have a low opinion of artistic masterpieces," and one notes the belittling inverted commas that enclose the word "art.") His approval is very much a left-handed compliment, but it derives from an uncritical acceptance of what Oliphant said in her autobiography.

Virginia Woolf repeated the argument in 1938 with feminist bitterness. She invites her reader to examine Oliphant's voluminous work and suggests that such reading must have

> smeared your mind and dejected your imagination and led you to deplore the fact that Mrs. Oliphant sold her brain, her very admirable brain, prostituted her culture and enslaved her intellectual liberty in order that she might earn her living and educate her children.

Woolf goes on "to applaud her choice and admire her courage."[2] But her approval is not much more acceptable than Stephen's, if Oliphant's courage must be set off against the enslavement of her intellectual liberty. Yet objective examination of her career proves that Woolf exaggerates. Oliphant did indeed have a "very admirable brain"; and her intellectual powers were unimpaired to the very end of her life. What damage may have been done to her powers as a novelist it is my purpose to examine.

Critics have tended to take their opinions from other critics; for most of the twentieth century it has been generally felt acceptable to dismiss Oliphant as a writer with a vulnerable talent that was effectively killed off by the writing of two, three, or more books a year. Influenced by these preconceived ideas, commentators were ready enough to see in her work what they expected to see, rather than what a sympathetic reading would reveal.[3]

At this point one aspect of the myth must be challenged. It was not merely to "earn her living and educate her children" that Oliphant was driven by a compulsion to write. This compulsion motivated her at the very beginning of her career, when she started her second novel on the very day that she had finished her first (*A* 30). She worked on two novels concurrently in 1850 (*Caleb Field* and *Merkland*), and went straight on to rewrite a novel (*John Drayton*) that her brother William Wilson had been unable to complete. There was no financial pressure upon her till many years later; and at certain points in her career she was financially secure enough not to have to write for money. Yet from the first the craving to write could not be withstood.

II

We may examine the creation of this orthodoxy in two histories of nineteenth-century literature published in the Edwardian decade: George Saintsbury's *History of Nineteenth-Century Literature* (3d ed., 1901), and Hugh Walker's *Literature of the Victorian Age* (1910). Saintsbury had reviewed many Oliphant novels in *The Academy* and had often been very perceptive. But in his *History* he appoints himself spokesman for posterity and, while speaking of "quite extraordinary promise" and stating that "Some not incompetent judges were disposed to put this promise on a level with George Eliot's own," he nevertheless proceeds:

> But this kind of writing . . . requires the most careful and delicate treatment; it cannot be done hurriedly, and it cannot be done often or in great volume. Mrs. Oliphant never lost the touch to the last; but the wild hurry of her composition—two, three, four, even five books in a year, besides minor things—made it impossible for these touches not to be lost in inferior work. The second volumes of her three-volume novels became a by-word with critics for their intrepid "padding" . . . . (S)ome quite late novels . . . showed . . . that there was no positive irreparable degeneration of her talent. But no human being, not Shakespeare or Scott, could have made the things that she wrote good in the time in which she wrote them.[4]

Saintsbury comments very justly when he says that the later novels showed no degeneration of her talent; but he fails to consider the full implications of this concession.

Hugh Walker nine years later largely dismisses Oliphant as a novelist, and praises only her biographies. Inevitably he refers to her overproductivity, and firmly concludes that her work is "extremely flimsy" and that she "has written nothing that is likely to live" (which, of course, echoes her own words). He continues:

> The criticism made against her over and over again, and with justice, is that her writings are all of a high mediocre level; and the conclusion was drawn that this was just the level of her mind.[5]

To be fair to Walker, he does not unequivocally agree with this deplorable conclusion; nevertheless, if he has any doubts about Oliphant's intellectual powers, he cannot be taken seriously. But this book, carrying the prestige of Cambridge University Press, remained in print until the 1940s, and no doubt encouraged many critics to take a disparaging view of Oliphant.

Yet we are here facing a true paradox: novelists who produce too much work, leaving no time for careful revision, are very likely to produce badly flawed work, slovenly, stereotyped, superficial, inartistic; yet at no time in Oliphant's career did this occur with any consistency. There are slack passages, there is carelessness of detail in many novels; yet she could always—in her next book, perhaps in the very book that at first seemed so blemished—rediscover her true gifts and write with the authentic Oliphant voice. Much the same could be said of many novelists who cannot be described as overproductive.

III

In the 1880s and 1890s it was by no means obvious that Oliphant's reputation would collapse as abruptly as it did. There were many perceptive reviews of her work, which paid tribute to her strengths and analyzed the deficiencies of particular novels with no notion that these were destructive to her talent. Good reviews appeared in *The Athenaeum* and *The Spectator* by Meredith Townsend, James Ashcroft Nobel, and others, and in *The Academy* by various reviewers, including George Saintsbury. Her distinctive qualities were recognized: her ironic, disillusioned view of life, her capacity for the presentation of tragedy in ordinary life without lapsing into melodrama,[6] her skill in achieving a balance of sympathies for most unusual and flawed characters. And interestingly her tendency to a bias against male characters was often shrewdly perceived—for example, by Meredith Townsend in *The Cornhill Magazine* in 1899[7]—though not fully understood, often being considered a mere freak or eccentricity, or a limitation of sympathies, rather than what it was: a protest against the exploitation of women in Victorian society.

A particularly perceptive review in 1889 in *The Spectator* illustrates this theme. It is by James Ashcroft Noble, of *A Poor Gentleman*, a little-known novel, but still with many characteristic Oliphant qualities:

> Mrs. Oliphant's contributions to fiction may be divided into at least three classes, and *A Poor Gentleman* is one of her stories of slow movement and minute observation. They are stories which owe their attractiveness not to the intrinsic interest of their incidents, or even of their characters, but entirely to the skill with which incidents in themselves trivial, and characters in themselves commonplace, are made so intensely real by a concentrated imaginative effort as to bring them within the range of that living sympathy which always follows upon any vivid realization even of the simplest human experiences.

Noble goes on to praise Oliphant's insight into the morbid and neurotic hero Edward Penton; we are put "into his place, and feel with him the apparent reasonableness of the emotion which from the outside looks so utterly and so irritatingly unreasonable." To create a full understanding of such a man, says Noble, reveals

> that higher and finer effectiveness which is always present when imagination employs itself in the task of quickening our sympathy by enlarging the area of our apprehension.[8]

Here is praise that estimates Oliphant by the highest standards, and pays her the compliment of using adequate critical terminology—as she deserves. It is a paradox that such insights should coexist with the inability of other critics to recognize Oliphant's true gifts.

That peculiarly ambiguous and transitional decade, the 1890s, was a sensitive period for Oliphant's reputation. The transformed literary climate, the climax of developments that went back to the 1860s, seemed unpropitious to a balanced verdict. New artistic ideals were making the poets and novelists of an earlier generation seem unsophisticated—naively anecdotal or ponderously didactic, tediously voluminous or gushingly sentimental. The nineties favored concentration and concision, elegance of language instead of didacticism, ambiguity instead of finality. The main preoccupations of the decade—the pursuit of the exquisite in sensation and experience, the cult of extreme, doctrinaire realism, the insistence on a perfection of artistic form—encouraged critics to dismiss Oliphant. Oscar Wilde mocked her by saying "Mrs. Oliphant prattles pleasantly about curates, lawn-tennis parties, domesticity, and other wearisome things."[9] The *Pall Mall Gazette* complained that she "never troubles to bring [her characters] into relation with the detailed facts of life."[10] Henry James called her the great *improvisatrice* (and thus a female equivalent of Trollope) and regretted what he saw as her lack of artistry.[11]

It was nevertheless possible, even in the 1890s, to reach a balanced verdict on Oliphant. Many obituarists in 1897 and reviewers of the *Autobiography and Letters* in 1899 made perceptive comments. Howard Overing Sturgis, aesthete, dandy, and author of the fine novel *Belchamber* (1904), contributed a sympathetic portrait to *Temple Bar* in October 1899. He was not misled by her overproductiveness:

> Her best work was of a very high order of merit . . . . But if she lowered her position as a writer, by accepting hack work, which an author richer in this world's gear might have thought unworthy of her genius, she never pandered to the public by consciously bad work, in exchange for popularity or wealth. She never wrote a word she did not believe to be true in the best sense, nor gave her readers anything but honest work for their money, and as good of its kind as she could spare the time to make it.[12]

Perhaps the implications of "hack work" and "as good of its kind as she could spare the time to make it" are unreasonably harsh. Even so, it is much to be regretted that few critics followed Sturgis's lead.[13]

Another commentary of 1899 is worth quoting. It is a review of the *Autobiography and Letters* in the *Pall Mall Gazette*, signed by "GSS," who is George Slythe Street, a highly characteristic voice of the nineties, author of *Autobiography of a Boy* (1894), a gentle satire on the affectations of the decade. Although in his review Street assesses Oliphant with the characteristic literary values of the decade, he does not dismiss her work. Indeed he defends her against her own self-judgment:

> She herself seems to have had sometimes a wistful regret that in art she had never time to do herself justice. Perhaps she exaggerated the difference. In the house of art are many mansions, and they are not all for those who polish and polish and correct and correct. It may be true that her books would have gained in most instances by compression, selection and a previously pondered plan. But her distinguishing intellectual quality and her keen and sane perception of the life within her ken are obvious enough, through all the hurry, to those who have eyes to see.[14]

Oliphant was no Flaubert, and we can, if we look, find carelessness of detail and stylistic lapses in her books; but these do far less harm to the final value of her work than critics have asserted. The virtues that Street praises consistently reveal themselves in novel after novel.

Perhaps the shrewdest answer to the accusation of overproduction came from another fellow novelist, though a more conventional one than Sturgis or Street. This novelist, James Payn, was prolific and best known for *Lost Sir Massingberd* (1864); he had been editor of *The Cornhill Magazine* in succession to Leslie Stephen. A fortnight after Oliphant's death he contributed a short note to *The Illustrated London News,* as part of his regular column "Our Note Book." He regrets that the obituaries have not done Oliphant justice, and believes that she deserves a higher reputation than she has yet had. He highly praises one of her latest stories, *Mr. Sandford.*

> No living writer—far less in her seventieth year—could have written it. It is a curious proof that the constant exercise of the mind does not weaken it, though, indeed, there is less of imagination in the narrative than of the experience of life. It was that in which she excelled.[15]

This is an effective response to the views of Stephen, Woolf, Saintsbury, and Walker. Oliphant was constantly practicing her art and developing her powers. If we concede that she did write too much, her overproductivity did not destroy her talents; it enhanced them. The constant exercise of the mind does not necessarily weaken it.

IV

We have examined the central paradox of Oliphant's reputation. Other paradoxes—or misinterpretations of the provable facts—need not be considered in such detail. If we make a careful examination of the gap between the achievement and the myths, we will identify four paradoxes. She was considered to be unskilled in the handling of the three-volume novel, whereas in her mature work she displayed considerable expertise in this area. Her more misguided admirers described her as safe, comfortable, and—a favorite epithet—"wholesome," whereas she was often disturbing and unconventional and even at times more than a little shocking. Her detractors considered her characters to be largely stereotypes, whereas she was deeply suspicious of all literary stereotypes, and set out to undermine them in her finest novels. Finally, she was supposed to be out of sympathy with the women's movement, whereas in her later life—and in the implications of many of her novels from *The Chronicles of Carlingford* onward—she identified herself with most of the views of her more radical female contemporaries.

The three-volume novel was increasingly unpopular throughout the Victorian age, both with younger novelists and with critics. With the support of the circulating libraries it survived until the 1890s, when, almost overnight, it was abandoned, overwhelmed by the demand for brevity and concision. The three-decker now seemed as archaic as the heroic couplet. Saintsbury's comment, quoted earlier, that Oliphant's novels "became a by-word with critics for their intrepid 'padding,'" is typical of the critical orthodoxies of the nineties and of the Edwardians. But Oliphant needed the spaciousness of the three-decker to develop her gifts. Her weaker books are usually her shorter ones—in particular *Oliver's Bride* (1886) and *The Mystery of Mrs. Blencarrow* (1889)—since there is no scope for her to develop the strange situations and characters that interest her, by means of the "concentrated imaginative effort" of which Noble spoke in his review of *A Poor Gentleman*. The longer novels substantiate her themes with circumstantial detail and deep studies of motivation. The truth is that she handled the three-volume novel very skillfully. She interweaves theme, plot, and character expertly, using subplots and subsidiary characters to echo the main characters, directly or ironically, antithetically or symmetrically. She frequently treats the three volumes in thematically different ways, and elaborates the difficult second volume, where the denouement must be delayed, with enrichments and ironies and subplots—which must not be called "padding." Many examples could be cited from *Miss Marjoribanks* and *Agnes* (two very different books, but both of 1866) to *Sir Robert's Fortune*. *The Wizard's Son* (1884), her most elaborately and self-consciously structured novel (though not entirely successful), interweaves theme, symbol, and parallelism of character with great sophistication. *Hester* (1883) is one of the most thematically unified and structurally integrated of Victorian novels, built round themes of money and love, into which all the characters (largely members of one family) interlock, while all chapters serve to promote, ironically delay, or enrich by choreic commentary, the development of the plot. One may sample Oliphant's career at virtually two-yearly intervals from 1870 onward and find a consistent, and developing, expertise in handling the three-decker.

Of course it is no defense against an accusation of verbosity and padding to point out that Oliphant had a natural feeling for structure, although it does suggest that Street's regret for her lack of "a previously pondered plan" is largely unjustified. Yet it is another irony that these accusations were being made in the 1890s when Oliphant, sensitive as always to changing aesthetic climates, was tightening her style and aiming at greater brevity. She was not always successful with her shorter works; yet through the eighties and nineties she was practicing the art of the short story and produced some fine examples of the form, showing admirable economy and concentration, and proving, again, that constant work had enriched her talent rather than damaged it. Examples are "Dr. Barrere," "Queen Eleanor and Fair Rosamond," "Mademoiselle," "A Girl of the Period," "A Story of a Wedding Tour," and its sequel "John," "Isabel Dysart," "A Widow's Tale," and three of her *Stories of the Seen and Unseen*, "Old Lady Mary," "The Portrait," and the superb "The Library Window." And a very interesting novella *Two Strangers* (1895) is an ironic, understated, inconclusive story with a limited cast and a sparsely concentrated handling of theme, very characteristic of its decade.

One of the most regrettable labels tied to Oliphant by reviewers is that her tone is healthy, sane, "wholesome," "charming," and entirely uncontroversial. James Payn helps to promote this myth. His obituary note, quoted before, continues:

> She drew from the living model, but never from the nude. She scorned the modern method of recommending that philosophy which, missing its mark, becomes "Procuress to the Lords of Hell." She "wrote of nothing base." If her lines did not always lie (as, indeed, they did not) in pleasant places, she had little knowledge of the dark side of life.[16]

Payn's version of the wholesomeness myth is not as cloying as it sometimes was, and we may excuse him, since on a superficial view Oliphant does not seem to challenge orthodox ideas too alarmingly. She did not write overtly about sexual matters, and she offered few challenges to the family, for which she felt a high respect. But she did know something "of the dark side of life," and was interested in exploring the stranger, more perverse sides of human nature. She proves by no means cozy, safe, and reassuring; her novels are full of disturbed, unbalanced people driven into strange, irrational, and even grotesque behavior. She was fascinated by neurotics, obsessives, people with dislocated moral values; and she returns again to unusual states of mind: self-deception, monomania, melancholia. Between the self-tormenting heroine of *The Days of my Life* (1857) and the clergyman of *The Unjust Steward* (1896), painfully obsessed with a minor crisis of conscience, there are many fascinating examples. One may select six: Winfred Ochterlony in *Madonna Mary* (1866), an adolescent possessed by a sullen, bitter egotism that blinds him to all considerations but self-interest, even if it means disgracing his mother; Mrs. Burton in *At His Gates* (1872), an emotionally anesthetized woman, incapable of affection and observing tragic events with cynical indifference; Edgar Earnshaw in *For Love and Life* (1874), a remarkable study of loneliness, disorientation and inability to adjust to an alien environment; Miss Susan in *Whiteladies* (1875), a respectable and honorable woman driven by obsessive feelings to commit a mean and dishonorable act against a resented enemy; Edward Vernon in *Hester* (1883), motivated by an irrational hatred of his foster mother Catherine, which transforms itself into a sort of financial death wish and compulsive speculations on money that are bound to produce disaster; Gervase Burton in *Sons and*

Daughters (1890), whose overscrupulous conscience about money is so fanatical that it threatens his own financial security and drives his wife to desperation. It is evidently to this aspect of Oliphant that Lucy Stebbins is referring when she says:

> [Oliphant] had early begun to introduce into each novel a bizarre incident, a fantastic character, a situation beyond the reach of the domestic. On the surface this appears due to a feeling that the public must have a sop of melodrama, but where the eccentricity appears in upwards of a hundred novels, we suspect that it is the visible sign of her own hunger for excitement.[17]

Stebbins here both exaggerates and misinterprets. The "eccentricity" does not appear as frequently as she says; and, even if Oliphant did hunger for excitement, she transformed that hunger into an imaginative exploration of the stranger directions of the human mind; and only when her imagination failed her did she lapse into melodrama, sensationalism, or conventional villains. Usually when she creates villains their modes of thought and the compulsions that lead them to behave as they do are observed with remarkable insight. Notable examples are Mr. Burton in *At His Gates,* Edward in *Hester,* and Ronald Lumsden in *Sir Robert's Fortune*—to whom I shall later return.

It is fascinating to note that at times Oliphant, so far from seeming "wholesome," was capable of shocking some reviewers. *The Times* found the treatment of euthanasia in *Carita* (serialized in 1876) "revolting"; Julia Wedgwood was obliged to "protest against allusions to vice" in *A Country Gentleman and his Family* (1886); and C. L. Graves considered the disenchanted view of marriage shown in "Queen Eleanor and Fair Rosamond" and "A Story of a Wedding Tour" (posthumously published in 1898) "intrinsically ugly or even repulsive."[18]

If Oliphant took pains to rehabilitate the melodramatic villain, and treated marriage with disillusion and quiet detachment, then the accusation that her characters are stereotypes proves untenable. But the accusation was made, by contemporaries and by twentieth-century critics as late as Valentine Cunningham in 1975.[19]

Ardent heroes and tenderhearted heroines, elderly ladies both forthright and gentle, overbearing fathers, affectionate mothers, loyal servants, weak and reckless young men—such characters appear in novel after novel. But usually they are presented with characteristic Oliphant irony; the lovable, self-effacing heroine, for example, may very well be shown to be weak and foolish and lacking the courage to assert herself. Or else she will eventually develop a strength and self-reliance that at first are not suggested, often as a result of disillusion with the man she at first naively loves. Close examination of the thought processes of a supposed stereotype will give an extra dimension, and will create ambiguity or ambivalence. Conventional situations—courtship, grief, parental anxiety—are viewed from an unexpected perspective that demythologizes them. Character types—especially women—whom other novelists might view with straightforward disapproval, are seen from their own point of view, so that the reader is obliged to respond with sympathy. The adventuress (Lucy Crofton in the novel of that name, Bice in *Sir Tom*, Laura Lance in *The Sorceress*) is shown to be an intelligent, clear-sighted woman, finding a legitimate route to financial security in a world that exploits women. But there is no need to go into further detail on this theme since Margarete Rubik carefully covers the same themes in her article.

In many of Oliphant's novels there is a note of raw, bitter protest—in particular protest against the injustices inflicted upon women by men. Yet the myth—or paradox—has been that she was consistently out of sympathy with the women's movement. Though initially scornful of women's rights, she became more and more radical as the years passed.[20] And in 1884 in a letter to *The Spectator* she responded to an antisuffragist article by coming out very firmly in favor of the franchise for women householders—who have no available man to represent their political views. She concludes her letter:

> And pray tell me in what respect it would be better for me to borrow a share in a man for political purposes than to have a vote of my own?[21]

Five years later in a review of the anonymous novel *Ideala* (in fact by Sarah Grand) she committed herself to full sympathy with "the singular and scarcely recognized revolution which has taken place in the position and aspirations of women during the last generation."[22]

To continue with this theme would be to duplicate Merryn Williams's article. Accordingly, it will be enough now to illustrate the radicalisms of Oliphant's views on the relationship of the sexes by briefly examining her treatment of marriage in novels from *Agnes* (1866) to *Sir Robert's Fortune* (1894). In between appeared *At His Gates* (1872), *The Ladies Lindores* (1883), and its sequel *Lady Car* (1889), *A Country Gentleman and his Family* (1885), and its sequel *A House Divided Against Itself* (1886), and *The Marriage of Elinor* (1892). These novels chart the progress of their heroines toward disillusion, sometimes moderate, sometimes bitter, as their husbands prove to be exploitative, or weakly egotistical, or brutally authoritarian, and always unable to allow a woman her right to independent powers of thought. The heroines discover their individuality as women; they learn to act and think for themselves and to recognize the methods used by men to exploit women. The last of the series, *Sir Robert's Fortune*, is as severe an analysis of marriage (though not from the sexual point of view) as *Jude the Obscure*, which she notoriously attacked two years later.[23] This novel might be described as rewriting of the medieval tale of Patient Griselda. Like Walter in that story Ronald Lumsden inflicts a series of humiliations upon his wife Lily, assuming without the slightest reference to her feelings that everything he does will be to their eventual benefit. (He is carrying out a sustained deception of Lily's uncle and guardian Sir Robert, to secure his fortune.) He exploits and manipulates her and consistently overwhelms her protests by tender lovemaking, which takes for granted that she need not think for herself. Lily, unlike Griselda, is driven to bitter disillusion; and she ends with uncompromising rejection of Ronald—and also with full acknowledgement of herself as "her own woman."[24] Ronald, it should be noted, is never treated as a villain, merely as a perversely well-meaning man with a disastrously limited imagination, who invariably adopts the patriarchal view that a woman must necessarily subordinate herself to a man.

V

How was it possible that such a distinguished and individual novelist, celebrated by so many of her contemporaries for her remarkable contribution to English literature, should subsequently be dismissed and ignored, misinterpreted and misjudged, as surely no other important English writer has been? Some contemporaries ventured to compare her with Jane Austen, Scott, and George Eliot. Writing in *The Scottish Review* in 1897, William

Wallace acknowledged that George Eliot achieved much that was beyond Oliphant's powers, and yet insisted that the comparison is sometimes in the latter's favor: "Mrs. Oliphant grasped the realities of Carlingford as George Eliot never grasped the realities of Middlemarch." He praises Oliphant highly, but in the end uses the overproduction myth to deny her major status.[25] The comparison with Eliot persisted into the present century, usually (until very lately) to Oliphant's serious disadvantage.

A series of misfortunes seems to have haunted Oliphant's reputation in the last years of her life and in the Edwardian decade. The persistent delusion that she was old-fashioned and conventional (partly the aftereffect of her attack upon *Jude the Obscure*); her popularity with the circulating libraries, including Mudie's, considered to be the haven for the mediocre;[26] her inability to achieve a consistent perfection of style, although in this she was fairly typical of her generation; her determination, from a deep distaste for publicity, to isolate herself from the literary world—all these disadvantages made it less likely that unobservant critics would look at her work objectively. The overproduction myth, promoted as it was by respected critics like Saintsbury, could be relied on to reinforce a condescending view of Oliphant. And as her books went rapidly out of print in this century it became more certain that nobody, without the serious intention of making a reassessment of her work, would venture to investigate so voluminous a writer. Her rediscovery started slowly in the 1940s (mainly with Lucy Stebbins's *Victorian Album*), but was not seriously boosted until Colby's *The Equivocal Virtue* of 1966 and Q. D. Leavis's introductions to the reprints of *Miss Marjoribanks* (1969) and the *Autobiography and Letters* (1974). But as the twentieth century draws to its close we may now hope that the paradoxes of Oliphant's reputation will be resolved.

Notes

1. "Studies of a Biographer—Southey's Letters," *National Review* 33 (July 1899) 741.

2. *Three Guineas* (London: Hogarth Press, 1938) 166.

3. A regrettable example is a review of Colby in *Blackwood's* 303 (March 1968) 287–88. The reviewer, Robert H. Hill, refuses to accept that Oliphant has much talent. It is a pity that such an opinion should appear in a periodical to which Oliphant contributed so much during her career.

4. George Saintsbury, *History of Nineteenth Century Literature*, 3d ed. (London: Macmillan, 1901) 347–48. The first edition (1896) did not include Oliphant.

5. Hugh Walker, *Literature of the Victorian Era* (Cambridge University Press, 1910; ed. used dated 1940) 738, 749–50.

6. This pattern in her fiction is similar to her own standard for judging the fiction of other authors that Dale Kramer has analyzed and called by the term *domestic tragedy* in his essay in this volume.

7. Meredith Townsend, "Mrs. Oliphant," *Cornhill Magazine* 79 (June 1899) 773–79. Townsend states that Oliphant in a letter to him had said "she knew little of men who were at once good and strong." Unreasonably he concludes that "her men, therefore, are either lay figures . . . or they are weak, ineffectual men" (778).

8. (James Ashcroft Noble), *Spectator*, 27 July 1889, 114–15.

9. Oscar Wilde, "The Decay of Lying" in *Intentions* (London: Osgood, McIlvaine and Co, 1891) 11.

10. "Of the Old School," review of *The Prodigals and Their Inheritance, Pall Mall Gazette*, 21 June 1894, 4.

11. Henry James, *Notes on Novelists* (London: Dent, 1914) 347–60. This includes an unenthusiastic analysis of *Kirsteen*. A more severe analysis of *Kirsteen* was spoken by James to A. C. Benson in 1900, see Benson's *Diary*, ed. Percy Lubbock, (London: Hutchinson, 1926) 47, entry for 17 January 1900.

12. Howard Overing Sturgis, "A Sketch from Memory," *Temple Bar* 118 (October 1899) 233–34.

13. Q. D. Leavis quoted the passage in her introduction to the Leicester University Press ed. of *A&L* [26].

14. G. S. S., *Pall Mall Gazette*, 4 May 1899, 4.

15. James Payn, "Our Note Book," *Illustrated London News*, 10 July 1897, 36. Payn gives Oliphant pride of place. *Mr. Sandford* was not written in 1897, as Payn seems to suppose, although it was included that year in *The Ways of Life*, about a month before her death. It was originally serialized in *The Cornhill Magazine* in 1888, as Payn ought to have remembered, since he was editor at the time.

16. Payn, 36.

17. Lucy Poate Stebbins, *A Victorian Album* (London: Secker and Warburg, 1946) 179.

18. *The Times*, 18 August 1876, 4; Julia Wedgwood, *Contemporary Review* 50, 299–300; (C. L. Graves), review of *A Widow's Tale and Other Stories, Spectator*, 23 July 1898, 121. *The Times* reviewer was so indignant that he published his comment before the serial of *Carità* was complete.

19. See for example J. Y. Eccles, *Academy*, 4 July 1896, 9–10; *Saturday Review*, 20 May 1899, 627–28; Ernest Albert Baker, *The History of the English Novel* (London: H. F. & G. Witherby, 1939) 10: 200–204; Valentine Cunningham, *Everywhere Spoken Against; Dissent in the Victorian Novel* (Oxford University Press, 1978), 232, 255, etc.

20. "The Laws Concerning Women," *Blackwood's* 79 (April 1856) 379–87; "The Condition of Women," *Blackwood's* 83 (February 1858) 139–54; "The Great Unrepresented," *Blackwood's* 100 (September 1866) 367–79; review of *The Subjection of Women* by John Stuart Mill and *Women's Work and Women's Culture, a Series of Essays*, ed. Josephine Butler, *Edinburgh Review* 130 (October 1869) 572–602;

"The Grievances of Women," *Fraser's Magazine* 101 (May 1880) 698–710. In this last article Oliphant identifies herself unequivocally with the views of the women's movement, and writes with considerable bitterness against male prejudice.

21. *Spectator*, 1 November 1884, 1437. The letter is signed merely "M," but Oliphant's authorship is proved by a manuscript book of contributors held by *The Spectator*.

22. *Blackwood's* 146 (August 1889) 257.

23. "The Anti-Marriage League," *Blackwood's* 159 (January 1896) 135–49.

24. *Sir Robert's Fortune* (London: Methuen, 1895) 182. It was serialized in *Atalanta* during 1894.

25. "Mrs. Oliphant and her Rivals," *Scottish Review* 30 (October 1897) 282–300. The author is named simply as "An Old Personal Friend."

26. See, for example, Alan F. Walbank, *Queens of the Circulating Library, Selections from Victorian Lady Novelists 1850–1900* (London: Evans Brothers, 1950). Oliphant occupies pp. 83–120, with extracts from *Salem Chapel, Carita, The Primrose Path*, and *Within the Precincts*. To be fair to Walbank, one must recognize that he clearly admires Oliphant. For example, he describes *Salem Chapel* as "superior to George Eliot's *Felix Holt*" (87). Continuing research since the writing of this article has proved that many reviewers in the later years of Oliphant's career were not deceived by the overproduction myth.

The Subversion of Literary Clichés in Oliphant's Fiction

MARGARETE RUBIK

WHERE in Victorian literature would you find a heroine who arrogantly cuts men down to their "proper level" yet is presented as thoroughly likable and competent? Where would a girl who marries a rich boor solely because managing his political career seems an attractive intellectual challenge to her have the full sympathy of the author and every hope of happiness and success? Where would an orphan girl be presented not as lonely and unprotected, but as unpleasant and deceitful, yet instead of coming to grief be rewarded for her duplicity with a millionaire husband? Which author would dare to describe a widow openly rejoicing at the demise of her husband or to comment upon the death of a mother in the following sarcastic manner?

> And it was at this moment of all others, just at the same time as Mrs. Marjoribanks finished her pale career, that poor Mrs. Lake thought fit to die, to the injury of her daughter's prospects and the destruction of her hopes. Naturally Barbara had never quite forgiven that injury.[1]

One would normally expect in a nineteenth-century novel to find a submissive heroine or at least one who, like Charlotte Bronte's Shirley, for all her talk of emancipation in fact dreams of a man who will be her "master" and "break [her] in."[2] Mercenary marriages are generally denounced as immoral in Victorian fiction and lead to unhappiness and lifelong remorse. The mention of an orphan was sure to conjure up pathetic images of helpless children at the mercy of unfeeling relatives. Poetic justice demanded "good" and "bad" characters to be rewarded at the end of a novel according to their deserts. Whatever the character qualities of a person in life, decorum required after his death that the widow show proper signs of grief and affliction; any display of satisfaction and relief would have been considered highly improper, even scandalous, since a woman was expected to learn to love even a seemingly repulsive husband.

Most Victorian authors comply with such rules. In the novels of Margaret Oliphant, however, clichés are often turned upside down. Although until recently dismissed as little more than a conventional writer of trite love stories, Oliphant is, in fact, a much more vigorous and unconventional novelist than most critics allow. Her treatment of the traditional themes of the domestic novel is often highly unusual and quite "un-Victorian." Much more uncompromisingly than many famous authors of the time she disappoints stereotyped expectations, ridicules maudlin Victorian values and denounces the false pathos and sentimentality of her contemporaries.

To be sure, many of her stories seem, on the surface, to be constructed according to stereotypes, but John Stock Clarke has pointed out that, while "she accepts the conventions in one part of the book, ... the pattern or plot development of the book will suggest a very different view."[3] Indeed, the challenging of traditional attitudes and beliefs is one of the characteristics of Oliphant's writing. In her novels she questions and reassesses many Victorian precepts and clichés—the role of women and the relationship of the sexes, the convention of the happy ending and the concept of poetic justice, the treatment of death, and, quite generally, the Victorian moral code of behavior.

Her remarkable originality of tone and attitude can be illustrated by a comparison of some of her novels with various famous literary works that she obviously uses as foils; for she sometimes takes as a starting point for her novels well-known motifs and literary models, but views them from unconventional angles and develops solutions diametrically opposed to precedent. The effect of her new version is almost always to counterpoint a heroic view of life with a prosaic one and to oppose a realistic assessment to an idealized conception.

A telling example of this method is *Phoebe Junior, A Last Chronicle of Carlingford,* which in its subtitle pays conscious tribute to Trollope's Barchester series and indeed uses some of Trollope's plot elements, in particular the incident of the check that the Reverend Crawley, in *The Last Chronicle of Barset,* is accused of stealing. In Trollope's novel the ladies in Barchester know all along "that an ordained clergyman could not become a thief," and at the end of the book Crawley is vindicated as the victim of a misunderstanding.[4] In Oliphant's version, however, the clergyman May actually does forge a bill. In her more disturbing view, class is no guarantee for impeccable behavior; for all his refined veneer a gentleman can be as irresponsible and unscrupulous as any common criminal—an idea she also develops in *A Son of His Father*, a novel that will be treated more extensively later.

Considering the conspicuousness of many of these inversions it is surprising how thoroughly both her contemporaries and many later critics managed to overlook the subversive aspects of her writing. Her novels were rendered harmless and recommended as "wholesome" reading for women and children, even though it is quite obvious that many of her characters, evaluations, and views do not conform to Victorian ideals. Some contemporary reviewers, indeed, were confused at what they considered to be an unnatural and untrue reversal of gender roles in her novels, as, for example, when one clearly exasperated critic in the *Spectator* complained: "We cannot recall among all her books one picture of a thoroughly competent man who is also good, or one ... whom a male reader thoroughly likes."[5]

Oliphant consistently describes women as the stronger, cleverer, and more active sex, whereas men are painted as incompetent weaklings—an inversion of conventional assumptions that has generally been attributed to her personal experience with the men of her family. Her portrayal of women, in particular, is one of the most subversive aspects of her writing. To draw as positive heroines—and not as viragos!—women who are much more intelligent than their male partners and who, instead of looking up to their lovers as mentors, actually manipulate and instruct them, turns upside down the approved Victorian code of female behavior. Such a character constellation in fact deliberately undercuts the principal premises of romantic fiction, where the female must always be weaker than the male, or, as Jenni Calder notes, the "essential ambience of romantic love would be lost."[6]

Energetic, unsentimental, independent figures, such as Lucilla Marjoribanks, Phoebe Junior, or Patty Hewitt in *The Cuckoo in the Nest* are unlike most other character types in Victorian fiction and have many qualities traditionally deemed masculine. While even most women novelists considered it "unthinkable, unrealistic and unhealthy to give to their female characters such traditionally masculine power as the power of control," to use the words of

Judith Lowder Newton, Oliphant's heroines excel in the male domains of bank management, estate management, and politics and are often more interested in a career and in intellectual challenge than in love.[7]

At a time when marriage was considered the chief desideratum for a girl, Oliphant sympathizes with women who choose to remain unmarried and thus independent and who laugh at the common opinion that a husband is "the one thing needful for a woman," like the heroines of *Diana Trelawny* (8) and *Kirsteen* or Rosamond in *The Railwayman and His Children*. Such an approval of the wish for freedom and self-determination is obviously contrary to the conventions of her time, when, as Patricia Thomson has noted, women who preferred a profession to domesticity and dependence on others were considered "new alarming phenomena that deserved no sympathy."[8] Oliphant is aware of the threat such female autonomy and competence poses to entrenched beliefs and sarcastically shows in her novels the aggressive reaction of many men, like Sir Alexander in *Kirsteen*, who insists he would prefer a girl to marry any "chimney sweep" rather than support herself by independent work (341). In *The Curate in Charge* the heroine, determined to make a living as a schoolmistress, is sternly reproved by one of the rich villagers:

> An independent woman, Cicely, is an anomaly; men detest the very name of it. (194)

Of course Oliphant knew that a life of self-determination and independence was a rare option in a repressive society in which the role of a woman was primarily that of a wife and mother in which a girl, as Jenni Calder observes, normally "exchanged her father's authority and identity for her husband's."[9] Many of her heroines do indeed marry, though they often choose men they can instruct and guide and thus, in fact, retain their power of disposition and achieve a vicarious career within a socially acceptable frame. Oliphant is convinced that love, supposed to be "a woman's all," is not enough to satisfy a woman. Accordingly she does not believe that a woman should necessarily invest all her feelings into her husband. In "Queen Elinor and Fair Rosamond," one of her most cooly ironic and uncompromising stories, she shows that a married woman may well retain her independence of mind and heart

According to popular legend, Fair Rosamond, the mistress of Henry II, was poisoned by the jealous queen. Oliphant's version of the well-known story deals with a bigamous businessman, who divides his time between a legitimate wife in Liverpool and an unsuspecting second wife in London. In her tale, however, the betrayed first wife does not react with fierce jealousy, as the queen Elinor in the legend, nor does she break her heart, as a soft-hearted Victorian matron might have done, but coolly enforces a separation. Contrary to precedent, Elinor's sympathies belong to the cheated second wife, and she feels only contempt for her cowardly husband—a notion that subverts the traditional motif of female rivalry. There is no tragedy, no pathos, no sentimental remorse to edify the romantic reader, only a calm pity when she sees him again years later:

> To see him elderly, stout, and (but perhaps this was one effect of some refinement of jealous and wounded feeling on the part of Mrs Lycett-Landon) oh so commonplace! and fallen from his natural level, shuffling his feet, reddening, smiling that confused and foolish smile, conciliating the children, gave his wife almost the keenest pangs she had yet suffered.... Tragedy is terrible, but when it drops into tragicomedy, tragi-farce in the end, that is the most terrible of all. (*A Widow's Tale*, 113)

Oliphant's view of marriage is obviously not idealized, but down to earth and unsentimental. On occasion, she can paint savagely disillusioning pictures of married life, as, for instance, the sketch of the frustrated wife who makes her husband roar with laughter at her witticisms, yet "all the time ... would have liked to throw him down and trample on him, or put pins into him, or scratch his beaming, jovial countenance" (*Miss Marjoribanks*, 244). As a rule, however, she concentrates on average marriages with their daily frictions and trivial irritations. Indolent and self-indulgent, the men in her novels, under various pretenses, withdraw from all domestic responsibilities and leave their wives to solve the problems of daily life.

> That she was careful and troubled about many things was the Rector's favourite joke. "My careful wife—my anxious wife," he called her, and, poor soul, not without cause. For it stands to reason that when a man must not be disturbed about bills, for example, his wife must be, and doubly; and when a clergyman dislikes poverty, and unlovely cottages,

and poor rooms, which are less sweet than the lawn and the roses, why his wife must, and make up for his fastidiousness. (10)

This description closely resembles the state of affairs that Shaw's Candida, more than twenty years later, sarcastically outlines.

> Ask the tradesmen who want to worry James and spoil his beautiful sermons who it is that puts them off. When there is money to give, he gives it: when there is money to refuse, I refuse it. I build a castle of comfort and indulgence and love for him, and stand sentinel always to keep little vulgar cares out.[10]

This is entirely different from the admiring support Victorian husbands felt entitled to expect from their wives, for, like Shaw, Oliphant knew that such pampering in reality involved secret contempt and a realization that a man cannot be encumbered with the responsibilities and cares a woman is willing to shoulder.

And yet, loss of respect is, in Oliphant's view, by no means incompatible with love, as many novelists with a more romantic and idealistic attitude seem to think. In her writing she is always doubtful of sentimental ideals and what she regards as utopian expectations of human perfection. In *Shirley* Charlotte Bronte claims that "meanness" kills love and that true affection is impossible without respect.[11] To Oliphant, however, disillusionment is an inevitable process in the course of life, and to believe, like Charlotte Bronte or George Eliot, that a woman disappointed in a man necessarily falls out of love with him seems to Oliphant too simplistic a solution. In "A Widow's Tale" she writes that

> in a great many histories of human experience it is taken for granted—and indeed, perhaps, before the reign of analysis began it was almost always taken for granted—that when man and woman of the nobler kind found that a lover was unworthy, their love died along with respect. This has simplified matters in many a story. It is such a good way out of it, and saves so much trouble! The last instance I can remember is that of the noble Romola and Tito her husband, whom, though he gives her endless trouble, she is able to drop out of her stronghold of love as soon as she knows how little worthy of it is the fascinating, delightful, false Greek. My own experience is all the other way. Life, I think, is not so easy as that comes to. (*A Widow's Tale*, 49)

The passing shot at her famous rival is characteristic of Oliphant, who prides herself on a view of life more realistic than that of many contemporaries. In her novels characters unable to accept human faults and vainly striving for unattainable ideals are bound to fail in an imperfect world. The title character of *Lady Car*, for instance, makes herself perfectly miserable in a love marriage because she will not forgive her husband for falling off from the one-time ideal. On the other hand, the cold-blooded match in *The Railwayman and His Children* of two characters who have no illusion whatsoever about each other turns out to be quite successful:

> "I will always maintain," said Eddy, "that there never were two people so fit to go together as you and I. We haven't any wild admiration of each other; we know each other's deficiencies exactly; we don't go in for perfection, do we? But we suit, my little May, we suit down to the ground. You would know what you had to expect in me, and I could keep you in order." (391)

This is not the rhetoric one would expect in a Victorian marriage proposal. When Oliphant describes love scenes, she does not trick the reader into identifying with the lovers, but views their affectations from an ironic distance. She enjoys presenting absurd love scenes involving elderly, awkward suitors who feel ill at ease in their romantic roles, such as the prudish Reverend Proctor in *The Perpetual Curate*, who angers his bride by a reference to her advanced age and a reluctance to kiss her, or the otherworldly protagonist in *Curate in Charge*, who quite by "accident" stumbles into a second marriage simply because he does not have the heart to dismiss the old governess. Upon hearing that she will have to apply to a charity, he tells her in "a troubled voice" that he has "no objection" to taking her for a wife. The funereal tone and wording are grotesquely at odds with the romantic cliché and poor Miss Brown's conviction "that he must have been a victim of despairing love for her all this time" (32–33).

Not content with debunking the romantic ideal, she actually shows in her novels that the romantic love her contemporaries extol is really of very secondary importance and that a marriage of convenience can be much happier than a love-match. Women who desperately try to "catch" a husband because this is their only chance to escape from a dreary home are treated with pity and understanding. "Mercenary" characters like the heroines of *The Sorceress* or *Phoebe Junior*, who marry for money, nevertheless make their husbands excellent wives, whereas the poor girl in *For Love and Life* who heroically rejects a rich suitor to wait for her sweetheart finds herself jilted in the end. Now obviously a great many Victorian writers regard romantic infatuation as an insufficient basis for marriage, but husband-hunting girls and "adventuresses" are generally presented with ridicule or moral indignation in most novels of the period, and "mercenary" marriages are almost universally condemned. Even Thackeray, who in *The Newcomes* assumes a worldly pose and ridicules daydreams a la Philemon and Baucis in fact considers Ethel Newcome as unfit for a heroine as long as she adheres to her materialistic values.[12] Oliphant, on the other hand, does not censure characters such as Bice in *Sir Tom* for their materialism, though the girl makes no pretense at loving the marquis she marries. Ironically, despite her cold-bloodedness, she will make life more agreeable and amusing to him than a more sentimental bride:

> According to her code no professions of attachment or pretence of feeling were necessary. She had indeed no theories in her mind about being a good wife; but she would not be a bad one. She would keep her part of the compact; there should be nothing to complain of, nothing to object to. She would do her best to amuse the man she had to live with and make his life agreeable to him, which is a thing not always taken into consideration in marriage contracts much more ideal in character.[13] (344)

Oliphant has a highly unusual ability to accept self-seeking and egotism as natural human qualities and to condone mixed, or even selfish motives. It is typical that in her novel *A House Divided Against Itself,* which in its character grouping invites comparison with Gaskell's *Wives and Daughters,* she prefers the worldly mother to the misanthropic father—while Gaskell criticizes Mrs. Gibson's shallowness and idealizes her naive husband—and regards the behavior of the flirtatious sister as amusing rather than morally reprehensible. She never demands of her heroines the exemplary behavior many Victorian novelists seem to expect of high-minded girls.

She sides with figures such as Phoebe Junior or Patty Hewitt, who show a lusty egotism in fighting for their happiness and rejects the ideal of female self-denial as neurotic.[14] It is interesting, in this context, to compare her novel *Joyce* with Eliot's *Mill on the Floss,* both of which deal with a similar situation: the heroine is made to agree to an engagement with a man she does not love and later falls in love with another man already bound to another girl. Like Eliot's Maggy Tulliver the idealistic Joyce opts for self-renunciation, gives up the man, and flees to a remote island because she thinks she has no right to break her word or destroy the happiness of the innocent girl doting on her lover. Unlike Eliot, however, who sees self-gratification as a temptation and approves of Maggy's selflessness, Oliphant regards the doctrine of self-sacrifice as destructive. She would have endorsed the argument, which Eliot indignantly rejects as selfish, that it is a "perverted notion of right" that leads a girl to give up mutual hopes of happiness "for the sake of a mere idea, and not any substantial good."[15] Joyce is simply too much of a coward to risk harming another in the struggle of life. Oliphant, however, makes clear that the hope to protect somebody forever from disappointment and pain is naive and childish. Ironically, Joyce's heroic renunciation turns out to be entirely useless: the man she loves returns to India as a misanthrope; his bride, entirely unworthy of the sacrifice, soon consoles herself with another suitor, and Joyce's own vulgar fiance—like Trollope's Mr. Slope—in righteous indignation at her behavior marries a rich widow.

Considering her ironic, unsentimental view of life, it is hardly surprising that Oliphant frequently expresses her weariness with popular love stories. To be sure, she catered to the taste of her readers often enough by ending her novels with the customary wedding bells. But she also draws attention to the arbitrariness of any conclusion and ridicules the cliché of a happy ending as a naive artifice, "a contemptible expedient," as she says in *The Curate in Charge* (193), which waters down into sweet domesticity the courageous resolve of the heroine to work for her living.

Since she regards marriage as a mixed blessing, she can, on occasion, be very cynical about the convention. Popular prejudice, she scoffs in *A Son of the Soil*, requires "a distinct conclusion of one kind or another" for the end of a novel:

> Until a man is dead, it is impossible to say what he has done, or to make any real estimate of his work; and Colin, so far from being dead, is only as yet at the commencement of his career.... There is only one other ending in life, which is equally satisfactory, and, at least on the face of it, more cheerful than dying; and that, we need not say, is marriage. (2:221)

Marriage is here compared with dying, and, indeed, the protagonist through his marriage buries all hope of a brilliant career. No providential interposition, Oliphant sardonically remarks, conveniently rescues him from the uncongenial bride:

> If this had been anything but a true history, it would have been now the time for Alice Meredith to overhear a chance conversation, or find a dropped letter, which would betray to her Colin's secret; but this is not an accident with which the present historian can give interest to his closing chapter. (2:285)

As in the case of Joyce, however, Oliphant is careful not to sentimentalize Colin's fate or turn him into a tragic hero. Fulfillment in love, she assures us, is not an indispensable ingredient for a comfortable life.

Oliphant's disparagement of the convention of the happy ending with wedding bells also becomes obvious in novels such as *Hester* and *Old Mr. Tredgold,* where she argues with ironic logic that if, according to the traditional view, one suitor makes a happy ending, two suitors must needs mean unconditional bliss.

> Now, the good ending of a novel means generally that the hero and heroine should be married and sent off with blessings upon their wedding tour. What am I to say? I can but leave this question to time and the insight of the reader. If it is a fine thing for a young lady to be married, it must be a finer thing still that she should have, as people say, two strings to her bow. . . . If Katherine marries the doctor, James Standford . . . no doubt in India will marry yet another wife and be more or less happy. If she should marry Standford, Dr. Burnet will feel it, but it will not break his heart. And then the two who make up their minds to this step will live happy—more or less—ever after. What more is there to be said?[16] (450)

In reality, however, the heroines' choice signifies their dilemma. In a restrictive social structure few creditable possibilities for making a living are available to them other than marrying men they do not care for. The time-honored belief that marriage is the true fulfillment of a woman's life is questioned here, although, on the surface, the requirements for a traditional happy ending are conscientiously fulfilled.

Just as Oliphant is contemptuous of the facile happy ending with which fictional troubles are generally solved, she is also skeptical of the concept of poetic justice that, as Thomas Vargish has shown, many Victorian authors adhere to. The belief in such a cozy scheme of timely punishments and rewards seems to her childish and naive—a skepticism hardly surprising, as Elisabeth Jay suggests, considering the many domestic tragedies in her life.[17] Oliphant frequently refuses to punish those of her characters who offend against the approved code of behavior, and in *The Second Son* and *Old Mr. Tredgold* she turns the concept of poetic justice upside down by letting the undutiful characters triumph over the good ones—an ending that was regarded as unusual and daring by her contemporaries. As Gertrude Slater observed in the *Westminster Review:* "And who, except Mrs. Oliphant, would have ventured on such a conclusion to this story, a conclusion so entirely at variance with the requirements of poetic justice?"[18]

Even when, to satisfy her readers, she does use the convention, Oliphant manages to ridicule it at the same time. She herself, she smilingly confesses in *The Perpetual Curate,* has no great faith in such divine intervention on behalf of a deserving hero; but after his acquittal and advancement to the post of Rector of Carlingford the gratified protagonist of course sees himself as vindicated by poetic justice.

> [He] went upon his way, pleasing himself with those maxims about the ultimate prevalence of justice and truth, which make it apparent that goodness is always victorious, and wickedness punished, in the end. Somehow even a popular fallacy has an aspect of truth when it suits one's own case. (440)

Oliphant cleverly anticipates the reader's objections to such a convenient solution by making the ever-critical aunt Leonora in the novel shake her head at her nephew's good luck:

> "I suppose this is what fools call poetical justice," said Miss Leonora, "which is just of a piece with everything else that is poetical—weak folly and nonsense that no sensible man would have anything to say to. How a young man like you, who know how to conduct yourself in some things, and have, I don't deny, many good qualities, can give in to come to an ending like a trashy novel, is more than I can understand. You are fit to be put in a book of the Good-child series, Frank, as an illustration of the reward of virtue," said the strong-minded

woman, with a little snort of scorn; "and, of course, you are going to marry, and live happy ever after, like a fairy tale." (535–36)

Next to an author's treatment of love and marriage, the description of death is, perhaps, most indicative of her general attitude. As was suggested briefly at the beginning, Oliphant's treatment of death is quite unusual for her time. Most nineteenth-century novelists turn deathbed scenes into lachrymose farewells, in which the sick person sweetly bids his relatives adieu and departs peacefully, consoled by visions of angels or dead relatives come to fetch him into heaven. Oliphant, on the other hand, confronts death without idealizing it and refuses to de-mystify it by such maudlin assurances of eternal reward. On the contrary, her characters often raise disturbing questions about the unknown they will soon enter. For example, the clergyman Mr. Damerel in *A Rose in June* asks on his deathbed:

> "Happy, am I? I don't know—why should I be happy? I know what I am leaving, but I don't know what I am going to. I don't know anything about it. Something is going to happen to me of which I have not the least conception what it is." . . . He was departing . . . curious and solitary, not knowing where he was going. To God's presence; ah, yes! but what did that mean? (96)[19]

Oliphant's descriptions of death are often unheroic. Her dying characters are not ennobled by the approach of death but retain all their trivial weaknesses and often have no solemn words of farewell for their relatives and friends. Indeed, in *The Laird of Norlaw* she explicitly ridicules one of the famous deathbed scenes of Victorian fiction and, by a shift of perspective, renders absurd Colonel Newcome's "heart-rending" cry for his long-lost love, with which Thackeray obviously means to touch the reader's heart. In Oliphant's novel, too, the sick man with his last breath sighs for the sweetheart of his youth—only he has a wife standing by, who naturally has little sympathy for such romantic faithfulness:

> A very pretty picture, with love, and nothing else, for its theme. Yet, unfortunately, these pretty stories have a dark enough aspect often on the other side; and the Mistress, mortified, silent, indignant, cheated in her own perfect confidence and honest tenderness, when you saw her behind the scenes of the other pretty picture, took a great

deal of the beauty out of that first-love and romantic constancy of Norlaw. (51)

To substitute an ironically detached view for a view charged with emotion is a trademark of Oliphant's style. Instead of wallowing in sentimentality, she not only tones down the pathos of these scenes but sometimes even approaches death with a degree of entirely un-Victorian black humor.

A selfish young dandy, forced to interrupt the love-intrigue he has in hand, is "ready to upbraid his father with dying at such an inconvenient moment. Yesterday it would not have mattered, or tomorrow—but today!" (Carita 298). A tyrannical father absurdly reproaches his son for tumbling to death down the stairs after he has disinherited him: "'Well, well' the Squire said to himself, with a sigh, 'that this was how children treated one, after all the trouble they were to bring up: went against you; contradicted you; died if they could not have their own way otherwise, and thought that was the thing that would annoy you most'" (*The Second Son*, 3:36).

The description of a funeral is turned to a farce in *The Cuckoo in the Nest* when the very woman who most disliked the deceased plays the role of the bereaved daughter-in-law to perfection:

> Patty had a deep crape veil, behind which was visible a white handkerchief often pressed to her eyes, and in the other hand a large wreath. Gervase stood beside her, in black clothes to be sure, and with a deep hatband covering his hat, but with no such monumental aspect of woe. . . . Sometimes Patty almost bent him down on the side on which she leant, by a new access of grief. Her shoulders heaved, her sobs were audible . . . The village crowding round watched with bated breath. It was difficult for these spectators to refuse a murmur of applause. How beautifully she did it. What a mourner she made, far better than any one else there! As for that Mrs. Osborne, her veil was only gauze, and through it you could see that she was not crying at all! She walked by Colonel Piercey's side, but she did not lean upon him as if she required support. There was no heaving in her shoulders. The mind of the village approved the demeanour of Patty with enthusiasm. (195)[20]

Oliphant is amused rather than outraged at this travesty of the excessive grief evinced by many fictional characters. She idealizes the mourners just as little as she does the dying, and she never demands of her figures emotions that cannot be expected in the circumstances, as is also obvious in the case of Lady Car mentioned earlier, who after her husband's death exults at her newly won freedom.

Not only when dealing with death does Oliphant refrain from moralizing; she is essentially undidactic in most of her writing and, as a rule, does not try to teach a moral lesson in her novels. While Victorian literature, as John Reed notes, teems with moralizing tales fashioned on Biblical parables,[21] Oliphant has the courage to show iconoclastically that the Bible can be as much an excuse as a guide. The overtly pious man in *The Curate in Charge*, who puts his trust in God's help for the righteous is, in reality, an indolent egotist who tries to saddle God with the responsibility for his children. After his death nobody lifts a finger to help his destitute family, and his daughters have to accept social descent to find work. Even more radically, biblical injunctions are questioned in *The Son of His Father*, where the commandment to honor your parents is seen as socially ruinous when the father in question is not a venerable patriarch but an incorrigible criminal.

As I have pointed out elsewhere,[22] *The Son of His Father* is also a conscious inversion of the development Dickens makes Pip undergo in *Great Expectations*. Unlike Dickens, Oliphant leads her hero not from horror of the convict to pity and love, but from noncommittal benevolence to an appalled rejection of the criminal who turns out to be his own father. Her version of the return of the convict is much less romantic. She does not sentimentalize the criminal as a victim of an unjust social order; and although she recognizes the cruelty of severing all contact with him, it is also made clear that a man so irresponsible and selfish is a terrible liability to his respectable son. No wonder the hero secretly wishes his father were dead—a tabooed sentiment few Victorian heroes would be allowed to harbor—but there seems to be little chance of such a convenient removal as is the wont in novels.

> His father was not old as fathers ought to be. . . . He was not like an old father of seventy and eighty, the conventional father whom fiction allots to heroes and heroines, and who is likely to die satisfactorily at the end, at least, of a few years' tenderness. No. May would live, it might be, as long as his son. This was an element of despair which it was impossible to strive against, and equally impossible to confess; even to his own heart John could not confess it. It lay heavily in the depth of his heart, a profound burden, like a stone at the bottom of a well. (3:210–11)

John and his family finally bribe the unwanted father to emigrate. Their cold-hearted conduct is very different from the noble self-sacrifice generally evinced by Victorian heroes, but it is approved as legitimate self-preservation by the author.

Margaret Oliphant's answers to moral questions often subvert the high-flown Victorian code of behavior, which she regards as unrealistic, overexacting or even hypocritical. It is typical of Oliphant to debunk grandiose poses and lofty pretenses and to view characters from a prosaic, unidealized angle. Her radically unheroic view of human beings has confused some of her critics, who blamed her "cynical disbelief" in the heroic[23] for her alleged failure as a novelist. Yet it is exactly her distrust of many sacrosanct Victorian beliefs and modes of feeling that makes her such a fascinating and interesting author today.

Editions of Out-of-Print Novels Used

Carita. Leipzig: Tauchnitz, 1885.
The Cuckoo in the Nest. London: Hutchinson, n.d.
Diana Trelawney. Leipzig: Tauchnitz, 1893.
Joyce. London: Macmillan, 1891.
The Laird of Norlaw. London: Hurst and Blackett, n.d.
Old Tredgold. London: Longmans, 1896.
"Queen Eleanor and Fair Rosamond," in *A Widow's Tale and Other Stories* Edinburgh: Blackwood, 1898.
The Railwayman and His Children. London: Macmillan, 1892.
A Rose in June. Leipzig: Tauchnitz, 1874.
The Second Son. London: Macmillan, 1894.
Sir Tom. London: Macmillan, 1893.
The Son of His Father. London: Hurst and Blackett, 1887.
A Son of the Soil. London, Macmillan, 1866.

Notes

1. See *Pheobe, Junior, Lucy Crofton* (London: Hurst and Blackett, 1859), *The Ladies Lindores* (Edinburgh: Blackwood, 1883) and *Miss Marjoribanks* 57–58, 257.

2. *Shirley,* Herbert Rosengarten and Margaret Smith, eds., (Oxford: Clarendon, 1979) 626 and 708. On Victorian attitudes toward mercenary marriages and orphans see John R. Reed, *Victorian Conventions* (Athens: Ohio University Press, 1975) 108f, 252f. On proper mourning cf. John Morley, *Death, Heaven and*

the Victorians (London: Studio Vista, 1971) 17: "A show of exaggerated grief became a mark of would-be gentility."

3. John Stock Clarke, "Mrs. Oliphant: A Case for Reconsideration," *English* 27 (1979) 125.

4. *The Last Chronicle of Barset* (Harmondsworth: Penguin, 1967) 69. It is interesting that the same argument was used by the critic in the *Saturday Review,* 22 July 1876, 112–13 against *Phoebe, Junior*: May was unconvincing since a gentleman would never forge a check. In *Phoebe, Junior* Oliphant also contrasts the world of Charlotte Yonge's *Daisy Chain* with her bleaker version of the family life of another May family, which is governed by strife, jealousy, and self-seeking.

5. *Spectator* 56 (1883) 1661; cf. *Saturday Review,* 5 February 1876, 179–80 and *Spectator* 57 (1884) 713–14.

6. *Women and Marriage in Victorian Fiction* (New York: Oxford University Press, 1976) 114. See also my essay, published under my previous name, Margarete Holubetz, "Mrs. Oliphant's Unconventional Heroines," *Wiener Beitraege zur Englischen Philologie* 79 (1982–83) 13–29.

7. *Women, Power and Subversion: Social Strategies in British Fiction, 1778–1860* (Athens: University of Georgia Press, 1981) 6. The examples of Catherine Vernon as banker, Lucilla Marjoribanks as political campaign manager, and Phoebe, Junior as speech writer for her husband are discussed in Linda Peterson's essay and in unpublished essays by Deborah Morse and Malcolm Woodfield. Diana Trelawney in the novel of that title and Catherine in *Merkland* (London: Colburn, 1850) both manage estates. The critic of the *Spectator* 56 (1883) 1661, noted this propensity when writing "Mrs. Oliphant loves that kind of strong, half-masculine clear-sighted woman, blind to nothing, not even her own foibles, and loves, too, to place her in the position of a man, and show how much better she can control both circumstances and people than a man."

8. *The Victorian Heroine: A Changing Ideal* (Oxford University Press, 1956) 68.

9. Calder 65.

10. *Plays Pleasant* (Harmondsworth: Penguin, 1984) 158.

11. *Shirley* 189.

12. See Everyman ed. (London: Dent, 1910) 1:325, where Lord Kew sarcastically comments on such "billing and cooing in an arbour."

13. Clarke, "Reconsideration" 128 has noted this remarkable passage.

14. Again, her criticism of Eliot by implication illustrates in her less heroic attitude. Thus in *Blackwood's* (July 1874) 76ff., she rejects Romola's childish moral absolutism and accuses Eliot of glorifying an inhuman character ideal and of being unable to accept human weakness. In *Blackwood's* (September 1880) 381, Mary Garth's refusal in *Middlemarch* to help Featherstone destroy his unjust will seems to her stupid and perverse: "Now, to hinder a man from doing what he wishes, the thing being rather right than wrong, when he has only a few minutes to do anything in, because it is to your own advantage, is almost as revolting to good sense and natural justice as to force him in the same circumstances to do something for your advantage—and extremely silly in its superiority to boot. This is putting the vanity of fanciful disinterestedness above both justice and charity."

15. *Mill on the Floss,* World's Classics (Oxford University Press 1981) 513.

16. Cf. *Hester* 495: "What can a young woman desire more than to have such a possibility of choice?" Linda Peterson discusses this passage in her essay.

17. See Vargish, *The Providential Aesthetic in Victorian Fiction* (Charlottesville; University Press of Virginia, 1985) and Jay, *The Religion of the Heart: Anglican Evangelicalism and the Nineteenth Century Novel* (Oxford: Clarendon, 1979) 102.

18. "Mrs. Oliphant as Realist," *Westminster Review* 148 (1897) 683.

19. For an analysis of Victorian deathbed scenes see Margarete Holubetz "Death-Bed Scenes in Victorian Fiction," *English Studies* 67 (1986) 14–34. Williams 66 says apropos the unheroic death of a zealous Evangelical in *A Son of the Soil*, "It is difficult to imagine any other English novelist of the time writing about death in this way."

20. Oliphant may have learned this approach from her Scots predecessors, in particular John Galt, who in *The Entail* has the mourners stumble into the open grave and shows how quickly the tears of the relatives dry at the reading of the will. The scene also bears some similarity to the phony mourning in *Martin Chuzzlewit* although in Dickens the hypocritical mourners are obvious villains. Besides, Dickens focuses mainly on the behavior of those people not really afflicted, specifically the undertaker and Mrs. Gamp.

21. Reed 21ff.

22. Margarete Rubik, "The Return of the Convict in Mrs. Oliphant's *The Son of His Father*," *Wiener Beitraege zur Englischen Philologie* 80 (1986) 201–16.

23. Lucy Poate Stebbins, *A Victorian Album: Some Lady Novelists of the Period.* (New York: Columbia University Press, 1946) 190. As early as the 1850s her publisher Blackwood was shocked at her disillusioning portrait of Bonnie Prince Charlie in *Katie Stewart* (Edinburgh: Blackwood, 1853).

The Female *Bildungsroman:* Tradition and Revision in Oliphant's Fiction

LINDA PETERSON

MODERN critical discussions of Victorian *bildungsroman* distinguish sharply between male and female versions of the form. The male version, so standard distinctions suggest, uses a vocational crisis as its central dilemma, tracing the development of its hero as he seeks to find his place in the world, whether that be through accommodation, rebellion, or withdrawal; the female *bildungsroman,* in contrast, traces "a voyage in," substituting an intense self-consciousness or the psychological development of its heroine for the more active engagement with society of her male counterpart.[1] The male *bildungsroman* locates its action in the public realm; the female, in the domestic—often with marriage as the source of the heroine's dilemma.[2] As Susan J. Rosowski sums it up, the male *bildungsroman* focuses on "apprenticeship," the female on "awakening."[3]

No definition of a genre can encompass all examples—and, inevitably, dichotomies as sharp as Rosowski's leave themselves open to quibbles and exceptions. Indeed, if we follow Franco Moretti's suggestion that the *bildungsroman* as the "symbolic form of modernity" embodies cultural tensions between individuality and socialization, autonomy and normality, interiority and objectification,[4] then we might conclude that sharp gender dichotomies oversimplify an extremely complex form; traditionally, the *bildungsroman* has had to contend with both halves of the dilemma, the professional and the domestic, the social and the psychological, the public and the interior. Perhaps, if our current understanding of the Victorian female *bildungsroman* errs, if we have narrowed its focus and concerns more than is necessary, it is because we have based our criticism on too few novels—usually on Charlotte Bronte's *Jane Eyre* and *Villette,* sometimes on George

Eliot's *Mill on the Floss, Middlemarch,* and *Romola,* novels that reinscribe Victorian ideologies of gender and domesticity even as they protest against them.

As a corrective, then, and as an act of literary recovery, I examine in this essay the practice of Margaret Oliphant who, as a novelist and reviewer, produced and analyzed forms of the *bildungsroman* and whose work provides an alternative view of Victorian versions of this form (as well as some of the best examples from the period). Oliphant was a master of the genre's conventions. Because her mind was essentially critical, because she questioned conventional assumptions about "masculine" and "feminine," "male" plots and "female" plots, her novels are an important antidote to too narrow accounts of this female literary tradition.[5] I thus explore Oliphant's approach to the *bildungsroman,* focusing on four examples that span the latter half of the nineteenth century. In the novels of the Carlingford series (1861–76), I argue, Oliphant employs conventional plots of the *bildungsroman,* counterpointing male and female versions of the form; her intention is not to accept or valorize these plots but instead to subvert the conventions, often through parodying the male and ironizing the female versions. Later, in such novels as *Hester* (1883) and *Kirsteen* (1890), Oliphant becomes more critical of distinctions between "masculine" and "feminine" narratives, and she experiments with conventions of the *bildungsroman,* her female heroines often carrying out actions associated with masculine behavior. These later novels test whether the male novel of "apprenticeship" is a gender-restricted genre and what is lost (or gained) when women adopt patterns traditionally associated with men. More fundamentally, the later novels test whether marriage, the traditional site of female development, can remain at the center of a fictional form that is about *bildung,* development, growth, self-formation.

I. *Miss Marjoribanks:* (Re)Writing the Female *Bildungsroman*

All the novels of Oliphant's Carlingford series are, in one sense or another, versions of the *bildungsroman. The Rector* (1861) deals with the suitability of the vocation its hero, Mr. Proctor, has chosen. *Salem Chapel* (1863) follows the career of Arthur Vincent, a zealous Nonconformist clergyman who, with high ideals, confronts the reality of ministering to a lower-middle-class congregation. *The Perpetual Curate* (1864) traces the progress of a high Anglican clergyman, Frank Wentworth, as he learns to minister successfully to the poor of Carlingford and, less easily, finds economic security without compromising his religious convictions. The latter two novels include subplots common for the genre, *The Perpetual Curate* in the conversion of Frank's brother Gerald to Roman Catholicism, *Salem Chapel* in the romantic adventures that tempt Arthur Vincent and force him to reevaluate his social and religious assumptions.

It is in *Miss Marjoribanks* (1865–66), however, that Oliphant takes up the question of the female *bildungsroman*—and the implications of its conventions. From the first chapter Oliphant makes it clear that her heroine will fulfill the socially accepted patterns of feminine development, which she has learned from ladies' guidebooks and novels. When Lucilla Marjoribanks hears that her invalid mother has died, she resolves to leave school and do her duty by "poor papa":

> All the way home she revolved the situation in her mind, which was considerably enlightened by novels and popular philosophy.... She made up her mind on her journey to a great many virtuous resolutions; for, in such a case as hers, it was evidently the duty of an only child to devote herself to her father's comfort, and become the sunshine of his life, as so many young persons of her age have been known to become in literature. (25–26)

As the allusion to literary influence hints, this novel abounds in the motifs and sentiments of Victorian domestic fiction and conduct manuals, including the best-selling *Friends in Council;* according to their dictates, Lucilla acts.[6] The plot Lucilla follows is unabashedly conventional: she remains in school to study domestic management and political economy; then she returns home to "be a comfort to dear papa"; she fulfills her responsibility to Carlingford society with great success; she is wooed by several suitors, one her dull, if devoted cousin Tom, another the more polished, if also more dangerous Mr. Cavendish; she is deserted by Cavendish (and at least two other beaux) and so must face society according to the best principles of her feminine "philosophy"; in the end, after considerable trials, Lucilla marries the appropriate man and finds her place in the world. Structurally,

Oliphant even divides Lucilla's progress into two phases characteristic of the *bildungsroman* plot, the first one of "youthful confidence and undaunted trust in her own resources," the second marked by "that sense of failure which is inevitable to every high intelligence after a little intercourse with the world" (338).

Yet if the structure and episodic details of *Miss Marjoribanks* are conventional, Oliphant's treatment is not. Everything is shot through with irony, from the little *bon mots* Lucilla utters to the major episodes of female development she must undergo. The irony makes the reader suspect the motives of Lucilla, whom some critics have called a "female egoist" hiding beneath conventional sentiments,[7] but it should also make us suspect the conventions of the female *bildungsroman* itself, which Lucilla seems so intent on fulfilling. Oliphant's publisher John Blackwood noticed a certain "hardness of tone" in the novel as if he somehow intuited that the irony was not meant simply as a display of wit. Blackwood was a shrewd reader. In *Miss Marjoribanks* the irony directs itself repeatedly against the assumptions of the fictional genre Oliphant ostensibly imitates.

As a means of locating that irony and its effects, we might focus on a crucial, if conventional episode in Lucilla's progress and the language Oliphant chooses to present it. The episode is the one in which Mr. Cavendish begins to propose marriage but, inadvertently interrupted, deserts Lucilla for Barbara Lake. This desertion parodies the "trial" that the heroine of the *bildungsroman* must invariably face—as Jane Eyre is tested by Rochester's apparent engagement to Blanche Ingram; Caroline Helstone laid low by Robert Moore's proposal to Shirley Keeldar; or, later in the century, Dorothea Brooke shocked by her discovery of Will Ladislaw and Rosamund Vincy tete-a-tete. Lucilla faces the trial but without the usual reaction. When Mr. Cavendish fails to complete his proposal, she does not weep or bemoan her state, but writes a note to Mrs. Chilley, thereby feeling "her mind relieved." "Not that it had been much distressed before," the narrator comments.

> But when she had put it in black and white, and concluded upon it, her satisfaction was more complete; and no such troublous thoughts as those which disturbed the hero of this day's transactions—no such tears as poured forth from the eyes of Barbara Lake—interfered with the maidenly composure of Lucilla's meditations. Notwithstanding all that people say to the contrary, there is a power in virtue which makes

itself felt in such an emergency. Miss Marjoribanks could turn from Mr. Cavendish, who had thus failed to fulfill the demands of his position, to the serene idea of the Archdeacon, with that delightful consciousness of having nothing to reproach herself with, which is balm to a well-regulated mind. She had done her duty, whatever happened. (201)

The commentary directs itself overtly against Barbara Lake, the poor, artistic young woman who—like Jane Eyre, Lucy Snowe, and heroines of their ilk—falls in love above her station and gives way to her emotions. Barbara has, as her sister Rose laments, "no proper pride." On this level Oliphant's treatment ironizes the female *bildungsroman* in which the central crisis is invariably an intense romantic involvement, and self-development emerges from the emotional and moral testing that accompany it. The irony also directs itself, however, against Lucilla Marjoribanks who, according to philosophical "principles," has not engaged her affections. The product of Victorian guides to self-conduct, Lucilla is a little too well-regulated, a little too delighted with her behavior to serve as a counterexample to Barbara.

The effect of this complex irony is to undercut both the central assumption of the traditional female *bildungsroman* (that moral growth results from romantic or emotional trials) and the philosophy of the heroine whom Oliphant offers in contrast (that young women do best avoiding such trials). One senses that Oliphant, like her contemporary Harriet Martineau, found the female *bildungsroman* too obsessively focused on love, as if that were the only important aspect of a woman's existence. In a *Blackwood's* article published just after *Miss Marjoribanks,* Oliphant criticized modern fiction that offered as heroines "women driven wild with love for the man who leads them on to desperation . . . ; women who pray their lovers to carry them off from husbands and homes they hate; women, at the very least of it, who give and receive frantic embraces, and live in a voluptuous dream, either waiting for or brooding over the inevitable lover."[8] Yet Oliphant seems uneasy about offering an alternative to romance and marriage. Lucilla's commitment to duty—"I have always been brought up to believe that duty was happiness" (93)—threatens to empty her life of adequate shape or depth (a threat evidenced in Victorian domestic memoirs, which depended on plots external to the self). Years after her admirable behavior in the face of Cavendish's desertion, she realizes that she has found no proper sphere, "that her capabilities were greater than her work" (395). Her only real option is to accept a proposal of marriage.

That proposals of marriage determine the shape of a woman's life, and thus the shape of the female *bildungsroman,* the novel ruefully accedes. Summing up the first, not-quite-successful phase of Lucilla's development, the narrator admits "there can be little doubt that the chief way in which society is supposed to signify its approval and admiration and enthusiasm for a lady, is by making dozens of proposals to her, as may be ascertained from all the best-informed sources" (339). The narrator's irony, enveloped in the certainty of the "best-informed sources," hides a lament that this should be so. But the novel, like society, finally signifies its approval of Lucilla by granting her two proposals, both from honorable men—thus anticipating (or reinforcing) the modern critical view that "the feminine *bildungs* takes place in or on the periphery of marriage."[9] The only female character who imagines a pattern of self-development independent of marriage proposals—Rose Lake—faces a far worse fate: the loss of her artistic career. For all its irony, for all its probing and satirizing of conventions, then, *Miss Marjoribanks* attempts no alternative structure for the female *bildungsroman.*

The limitation of Oliphant's irony reveals itself also in the language that both heroine and narrator use: in the "principles" that motivate Lucilla's actions and the mock heroic with which Oliphant describes them. Lucilla's principles are either conventional Victorian sentiments or, paradoxically, little *bon mots* that seem to defy convention. On the one hand, Lucilla justifies her behavior by repeating conventional wisdom: "I have always been brought up to believe that duty is happiness" or "It is one of my principles never to laugh about anything that has to do with religion." On the other, Lucilla amuses her listeners by uttering what seem to be shocking sentiments: "It is one of my principles always to flirt in the middle of company" (119) or, to Mr. Cavendish, "I have always reckoned upon you as such a valuable assistant. It is always an advantage to have a man who flirts" (105) or, to her father, "I am not going to swindle you, after you have had the drawing room done up, and everything" (202).

The power of the "principles" is that they allow Lucilla independence of action under the cover of conventional behavior (after all, she worries very little about the *real* comfort of her father, who often escapes to his library during her "evenings"). Further, the *bon mots* give her social control under the cover of innocent wit (in fact, Lucilla knows quite well that flirtatious men add the sexual excitement necessary for a successful social gathering). But neither conventional sentiments nor ironic witticisms have power enough to alter Lucilla's predicament. Whether conventional or anticonventional, they never allow Lucilla to escape the framework of convention. Her language lacks the power to create new patterns of action. Irony allows her only to negate, not to construct.

And the same holds true for the figurative language Oliphant uses to describe Lucilla's actions. Like Thackeray's *Vanity Fair*, *Miss Marjoribanks* uses the mock heroic as a major linguistic and structural device. Lucilla's social plans are described as a "campaign"; "like other conquerors," she is "destined to build her victory upon sacrifice" (109); her enemies, "like the Tuscan chivalry in the ballad," can "scarce forbear a cheer at the sight of their opponent's prowess (121–22); when she scores a victory over Barbara Lake, her "formerly triumphant rival," the narrator comments that "she drove her chariot over Barbara" (175); and so on throughout the novel. As a complement to such military language, the language of social politics is also employed. When Mr. Cavendish wishes to praise Lucilla's social "statesmanship," for instance, he says: "I think you ought to be Prime Minister" (111).

Margarete Rubik-Holubetz has argued that "the mock heroic tone lends" a "certain heroic grandeur" to Lucilla's actions—and, indeed, Lucilla *is* larger than life.[10] Despite the apparent praise of Lucilla's abilities, the mock-heroic language tends ultimately, I believe, to diminish feminine action in the social sphere. Lucilla is a superb strategist, with brains and poise enough to earn a place in Parliament. But the mock-heroic continually reminds us how serious real warfare is deemed in the world outside the novel and how trivial Lucilla's skirmishes seem by comparison. We have not escaped the social framework of *The Rape of the Lock,* where young girls may play at epic heroism—but only until it is time for them to assume the responsibilities of marriage and motherhood in the "real" world.

In the end Lucilla puts her play aside and assumes those "real" responsibilities. The novel thus acquiesces in the convention that marriage and family will be the means by which a woman finds her place in, and leaves her mark on, the world. But even as *Miss Marjoribanks* acquiesces, there is a hint of what lies ahead in other

Oliphant novels. For, if Lucilla's actions take the form of mock heroic, so too do the actions of the male characters in the novel. Mr. Cavendish, after disgracing himself by flirting with Barbara Lake, must face something worse than "the Balaclava charge itself" (150); later, in preparing for his confrontation with Archdeacon Beverly, he dresses "like Nelson going into gala uniform for a battle" (289). So, too, General Travers, mistaking Rose Lake for Lucilla, begins "in the most cruel and uncomfortable way his campaign in Carlingford" (258). Even Tom and Mr. Ashburton are made into social warriors, called "rivals" in the same "field" (477). These descriptions of male behavior as mock heroic have the effect of diminishing, too, the "careers" of men in the "real" world. And such diminishment of male patterns will be a strategy Oliphant develops in the last *bildungsroman* of the Carlingford series.

II. *Phoebe, Junior:* Counterpointing Male and Female Forms

Like its predecessors in the Carlingford series, *Phoebe, Junior* traces the development—moral, psychological, intellectual, vocational—of young persons of both sexes, in this case counterpointing assumptions of the male and female *bildungsroman*. Phoebe Beecham, the heroine of this second-generation novel, must find her way in the well-to-do society of London Dissenters, where finding one's way means, for her as for Miss Marjoribanks, finding the right husband through whom she can work her will on the world. A girl with brains, style, and wit, Phoebe begins by doing her duty—not to her father, as Miss Marjoribanks had, but to her sickly grandmother, the now old, still buttery Mrs. Tozer. Doing her duty leads Phoebe from London to Carlingford and, once there, into encounters with two suitors. As in conventional domestic fiction, Phoebe must choose between the two men: between the sensitive, refined (and Anglican) Reginald May and the rougher, duller, richer (and Dissenting) Clarence Copperhead. Phoebe finally chooses Clarence, but not until she has been led to examine her moral positions on love, money, religion, social status, and the family.

The novel focuses, in other words, on Phoebe's self-development, and the major details of her plot reenact common features of the female *bildungsroman:* a domestic duty initiating the action, two lovers representing different sets of values, the "right" marital choice epitomizing the heroine's moral progress.[11] Many of the assumptions about female development are conventional, too: that domestic (not religious or intellectual) crises provide the testing grounds for women's development; that this development occurs inwardly, as women sort through their feelings about love and marriage; and, most Victorian of all, that women affect society not directly but through male agents, their husbands, brothers, or sons.

For all its traces of conventionality, however, *Phoebe, Junior* has a highly unconventional effect and moves beyond Oliphant's ironic vision in *Miss Marjoribanks*. Here Oliphant plays off plots and counterplots to challenge assumptions about the differences between male and female development. Within the experiences of Phoebe, Oliphant juxtaposes a romantic feminine plot against a more hardheaded feminist one to undermine the former. Further, she sets off her heroine's complex development against the more superficial plot of Clarence, Phoebe's lover, to challenge the presumed superiority of the masculine *bildung*.

Within the heroine's experience, for instance, the romantic plot associated with Reginald May is allowed to give Phoebe an erotic thrill, those "warmer" and "more delightful" feelings (268) that other Victorian novelists reveled in.[12] Oliphant's Phoebe has the sense to see where this plot will lead: to a domestic situation, not unlike the household of the elder Mr. May, where women are adored but subservient, where women feel but do not think, where women decorate but do not shape or lead. The novel hints early on that Reginald is a chip off the old block: "how like Reginald is to papa!" his sister declares when father and son battle over the sinecure. Phoebe comprehends the danger when Reginald talks about this sister's romance with Northcote; he speaks of it as something that "would never do," as if he, the masculine authority, has the power to decide female fates.

Knowing this, and knowing also the difficulties of marrying into an Anglican family, Phoebe relegates the romantic plot to the world of fantasy (which is where Oliphant suggests such plots belong). Sometimes Phoebe retreats there to enjoy it, "to expend a little tender regret and gratitude upon poor Reginald" (268). But she does not allow foolish romance to obstruct her progress in the real world. Rather, Phoebe chooses to marry Clarence—

not because of his money (though she admits it is no small advantage), but because with him she will have the power to teach and to lead, intellectually and socially. Oliphant reverses, in other words, what Elaine Baruch has identified as a common pattern in the nineteenth-century *bildungsroman:* that of a woman's education through marriage to an older, wiser man.[13] As Phoebe reasons it, "He was not very wise, nor a man to be enthusiastic about, but he would be a career.... She did not think of it humbly like this, but with a big capital—a Career" (234). That Oliphant imagines Phoebe's marital choice as a Career—and the term recurs throughout the novel—suggests her intention to revise and recreate the novel of female vocation, with the exploration of marriage as its focus.

It suggests, too, that Oliphant means to ironize male and female versions of the form through her treatment of the hero's and heroine's plots. In Oliphant, there are few cases in which women are not smarter or wiser than men. No Emmas recognizing the superior virtues of Mr. Knightleys, not even an Elizabeth Bennet balancing the qualities of Mr. Darcy—in Oliphant's fiction, women hold most of the (intellectual) cards. Even beyond this reversal of conventional male and female abilities, *Phoebe, Junior* undermines the assumptions of the masculine *bildungsroman,* for Clarence Copperhead's "career" is a parody of that form.

In this novel all of the young characters are seeking their place in the world, and Clarence *should* undergo at least some of the conventional episodes of a novel of development. He should, in response to some repressive or hostile force, "attempt to learn the nature of the world, discover its meaning and pattern, and acquire a philosophy of life and 'the art of living.'"[14] But Clarence does nothing of the sort. He gets sent down from Oxford, then sent away to Carlingford to study with a tutor. There, in recurring scenes that emblematize his relation to Phoebe and the world around him, he spends his evenings fiddling, while Phoebe "accompanies" him:

> He was serenely happy, caressing his fiddle between his cheek and his shoulder, and raising his pale eyes to the ceiling in an ecstasy. The music, and the audience, and the accompanist all together were delightful to him. He could have gone on, he felt, [*sic*] not only till midnight, but till morning, and so on to midnight again. (221)

Though these scenes are "the crown of Clarence Copperhead's content and conscious success" and though the formal arrangement of player and accompanist seems to put Clarence in control, Oliphant makes it clear that Phoebe directs the action. Phoebe helps Clarence through the difficult music, keeping "time with her head, and with her hand when she could take it from the piano, until she had triumphantly tided him over the bad passage, or they had come to the point of shipwreck again" (221–22). This reversal of masculine and feminine roles, with Phoebe directing and Clarence following her lead, holds in their lives as in their music. In the finale, the narrator reports the success of Phoebe's career, telling of the latest speech that she has composed for Clarence to read in Parliament (339).

Such role reversal might be dismissed as merely humorous, the satiric play of a female novelist who thought herself more competent than the men around her. But the novel repeats, more seriously, the counterpointing of male and female plots in the lives of Ursula and Reginald May. When Ursula and Reginald first appear, they seem to fit the stereotypes of a serious young clergyman facing a vocational crisis and a silly younger sister dreaming of romance. We find Ursula thinking of "the pretty dress" she wore to the Copperhead ball, while Reginald is described as "very clever," a young man "making his own way at the university by means of scholarships . . . and to hear him talk with his father about Greek poetry and philosophy was a very fine thing indeed" (30). Yet when Ursula and Reginald reappear at home, Oliphant redefines what a "serious" vocation might mean. Reginald, in a quandary about the chaplaincy he has been offered, sits "with a candle all to himself, at writing-table in the corner" (105). Ursula works at the center-table, darning the stockings that have piled up during her holiday in London. Masculine brain work seems more significant than mindless domestic drudgery. Yet, in the narrator's commentary, the relative value of the work is challenged:

> What Reginald was doing at the writing-table was probably a great deal less useful; but the girls respected his occupation as not one ever thought of respecting theirs, and carried on their conversation under their breath, not to interrupt him. (105)

The public valuing of masculine work, and undervaluing of feminine, is one of the novel's central concerns—not only in such explicit commentary, but also in the construction of this subplot.

The plots of *Phoebe, Junior* suggest that neither masculine nor feminine patterns of self-development are intrinsically "better." Though the two Mays's lives seem to take such different courses—with Reginald devoting himself to a serious vocation and Ursula merely marrying and becoming a footnote to Northcote's career—in fact the plot emphasizes similar causes and patterns of growth in both male and female characters. Both Mays are initially obstructed (or prodded) by their father, Reginald about the chaplaincy, Ursula about domestic management; both their lives change course dramatically when Northcote appears, Reginald's after Northcote's speech against sinecures, Ursula's after Northcote's kindness at dinner; and both find their vocations simply by doing the duty near at hand, Reginald as college chaplain, Ursula as housewife. It is true that, despite the parallels, Reginald's *bildung* receives greater recognition than Ursula's. In the finale, those characters with public careers, like Reginald and Northcote, get a full paragraph of wrap-up, while Ursula becomes only a detail in the story of Northcote's self-development.

But Phoebe gets full treatment in the finale, too, with her husband Clarence functioning only as a detail. By constructing the last chapter to focus on Reginald, Northcote, *and* Phoebe, Oliphant challenges the assumption that only the male *bildungsroman* can trace a pattern of achievement and growth. Phoebe's "Career" gets the equal treatment it deserves.

Oliphant is shrewd enough to realize, however, that in the world outside the one she constructs, Phoebe's experiences may not be recognized as a pattern of self-development and public achievement. After Phoebe announces her engagement to Clarence, and just as she wages moral battle with her grandfather over Mr. May's debt, the men begin to tell their version of Phoebe's story. "She's a good girl," Tozer tells Clarence, "you'll never regret it, sir.... She'll do you credit, however grand you may make her" (314). And Clarence, relishing the homage, talks about her as "a clever one," in approximately the same language he uses to describe his new mare that "the governor gave a cool hundred and fifty for" (316). Phoebe, the narrator reminds us, "had more brains than both of her interlocutors put together," but despite her superiority, she is "put down and silenced by the talk" (316). Whether or not a story is perceived as a *bildungsroman* depends, this passage suggests, on the narrator and the audience. A male narrator and male audience are unlikely to tell a woman's story as one of growth or achievement. The most Oliphant can do, in 1876, is construct her heroine's tale as if it did belong within that literary tradition. Beyond that, she can only show, through irony and parody, that our assumptions about male and female development (or lack thereof) depend on the narrative conventions that novelists choose.

III. *Hester:* Testing the Masculine Heroine

After working out the limitations of the female *bildungsroman* in the Carlingford series, Oliphant later experimented with what might be called a "masculine heroine"—the female protagonist who adopts masculine patterns of action. Thus in *Hester* (1883) Oliphant turns away from a *bildungsroman* that locates a woman's career within the domestic sphere and toward a masculine narrative that propels the heroine into the public realm. Hester, the heroine, never quite makes it into that realm. Like Lucilla Marjoribanks and Phoebe Beecham before her, she must remain a lady and "consent," as the narrator puts it, "to be bound by other people's rules, and to put her hand to nothing that was unbecoming" (77). The frustration that ensues from such consenting—especially if a girl has, like Hester, a capacity for business—preoccupies Oliphant for much of the novel. Yet despite her attack on social conventions that restrict women's actions, Oliphant seems unable (or unwilling) to devise a literary solution that would break with the traditional focus of the female *bildungsroman* and move her heroine into the world of work.

The novel begins as if it intends to create a new kind of heroine, Oliphant's version of the New Woman of the 1880s.[15] As background to the primary plot, chapters 1–6 contrast Hester's mother, a delicate, "unpractical" figure out of an early Victorian drawing room (6), with Hester's Aunt Catherine, a strong woman who inherits the paternal "genius for business" (20) and, in a financial panic, saves the Vernon bank. This contrast seems to establish Catherine Vernon as the role model for Hester. Early scenes show Hester helping schoolboys with their lessons, figuring out their sums, and wishing "Why was not she a man?" (82). More explicitly, various characters point out the parallels between her and her competent Aunt Catherine.

Despite the parallels, Hester does not take Catherine Vernon as her model but instead sets herself against her aunt. Oliphant makes the rationale for this opposition—and the motivation for much of the plot—the natural antipathy of two strong, like-minded women, both "very sure that her own way was the right one" (89).[16] The novel betrays, however, Oliphant's deep ambivalence about the strong female character she had created and her hesitation to make Catherine a role model for the female *bildungsroman*. Her hesitation hinges on Catherine's assumption of "masculine" patterns and the loss of "feminine" values that results.

Catherine Vernon's life represents a pattern of male success. Although she initially takes over the bank to prevent a crisis and later tells Hester that women should intervene only "to save the family" (76), in fact Catherine lives out the plot of a masculine *bildungsroman*. Deserted (or neglected) by the man she loves, she moves into the male world of work, then into a male version of public philanthropy, putting her name on streets, squares, almshouses, and other public buildings. That this is "masculine" achievement the narrator makes explicit: "The people spoke of her, as they sometimes do of a very popular man, by her Christian name" (20).

Catherine's achievement is masculine in a more subtle sense, moreover. It deals with power, power that originates in money and extends its grasp over the lives of other characters. That the male *bildungsroman* deals in money and power is no new insight—as Dickens registered in *Great Expectations*. What Oliphant seems to fear is the introduction of these terms into the female *bildungsroman*. Catherine is philanthropic, generous, even benevolent, but her knowledge of power seems to result in a loss of feminine virtues. Characters critical of her public achievements voice their criticism in terms of this loss. Mrs. Merridew notes that Catherine's business engagements have given her "an unfeminine turn of mind" (313). Hester interprets Catherine's manipulation of Edward as an unfortunate example of what happens when woman attains power: "Oh, how true it must be after all," she thinks, "the picture of the tyrannical, narrow despot, exacting, remorseless, descending to the lowest details, which a woman, when endued with irresponsible power, was understood to make" (303–304). Captain Morgan, a gentler and more subtle judge, discusses Catherine's loss in terms of "innocence."

In a speech to Hester about the importance of "soft, innocent creatures" like his wife and Mrs. John, the Captain articulates what I take to be Oliphant's fear:

> You are tempted to despise [them], you clever ones, but it is a great mistake. . . . It is such souls as these that keep the world steady. We should all tumble to pieces if the race was made up of people like Catherine Vernon and you. (93)

The danger of the masculine heroine, this passage implies, is that she threatens the extinction of the race—not simply because she remains single and produces no children, but because she fails to reproduce the values associated with the feminine: kindness, faithfulness, patience, forgiveness. A modern psychologist like Nancy Chodorow would call this "the reproduction of mothering." In *Hester* it is Mrs. Morgan who expresses these feminine values most concretely when she argues for a continuing relationship with her children and grandchildren, even though it means the end of "peace and quiet"; "I like to see the children come and go—one here, one there. One in need of your sympathy, another of your help, another . . . of your pardon" (169). Hers are selfless values, rooted in the woman's "relational" understanding of her place in the community.[17]

By presenting Catherine's plot as a possible model and then preventing Hester from following it fully, Oliphant is able to experiment with a mixture of masculine and feminine values. Catherine's values are predominately masculine: public achievement, family (paternal) name, self-respect. But, exposed to masculine knowledge, she loses feminine innocence and becomes "cynical," laughing at human foibles that a woman might better weep over or try to reform (184). This cynicism has devastating effects on Edward's life and, almost, on Hester's. Oliphant intends, I think, for Hester to witness the defects of Catherine's life but avoid its extremes, to balance masculine and feminine. And the novel succeeds in that it shows Hester gaining a masculine knowledge of the self and others, while maintaining certain feminine values associated with the family. (Hester can reason out, for example, the psychological motivations of male characters like Roland and Edward, but she is appalled when Captain Morgan uses reason to argue for breaking ties with his adult children.)

Despite this success, the narrative structure of *Hester* shows the strains of trying to coordinate elements of both the male and female *bildungsroman*. From the female *bildungsroman* Oliphant takes the main plot, the story of courtship and romance that puts forward Harry first, then Roland, then Edward as possible suitors. From the male *bildungsroman* Oliphant takes the subplot in which Hester searches for her paternal heritage; this quest for knowledge leads Hester to fall from innocence, just as "the guilty pair in Paradise, in the morning of the world, must have woke out of their sleep, and felt . . . the sense of ill" (462). Both plots come skillfully together as Hester discovers her father's perfidy and Edward's at the same moment. But neither plot nor subplot takes Hester very far toward resolving the dilemma of her life: what to do with herself. The romance plot seems repetitive and inconclusive, first with its multiple chapters (10–16) giving various characters' speculations on Harry's proposal, then with similar treatments of Roland and Edward. In the subplot, Edward is quite right (in this, if in nothing else) to ridicule Hester for not knowing her father's history; surely chapter 39 is too late for an intelligent heroine to discover what everyone else has known all along.

Beyond difficulties with plot and subplot, however, the novel never resolves whether Hester—or her real-world counterparts—should follow a masculine or feminine pattern in the future. In the final chapter, having discovered the faithlessness of man, Hester insists, "I will never marry" (493) and asks Catherine to train her in the business. This decision seems sensible, given Hester's experiences and abilities. Yet Catherine insists that Hester should marry and thus forget Edward, and the novel concludes by noting "that there are two men whom she may choose between, and marry either if she pleases. . . . What can a young woman desire more than to have such a possibility of choice?" (495). What more indeed! A great deal more, the novel has implied. But Oliphant seems to have abandoned these implications, unable to imagine closure without marriage. Perhaps she felt neither satisfied with the traditional feminine plot of marriage and motherhood, nor comfortable with the masculine pattern of quest and self-fulfillment, and so ended in the only way possible—with a question.

IV. *Kirsteen:* Appropriating the Male *Bildungsroman*

In *Kirsteen*, Oliphant explores less ambivalently the implications of a female heroine following male life patterns—almost as if, in the decade of the 1880s, she had imagined a way to reconcile the masculine and feminine opposition that had stymied her in *Hester*. The primary plot of *Kirsteen* is, with slight variations, the plot of a male *bildungsroman*. A spirited young Scotswoman, Kirsteen leaves her Highland home to escape a marriage and future life she dreads; she flees to London to make her name and fortune. Once in the metropolis she learns the dressmaker's trade; raises the business she has entered to a flourishing, fashionable establishment; and returns to her family as its "standby" and, in economic terms, its most successful member. The novel reenacts, in other words, a classic Victorian tale of self-help: of country to city, rags to riches, obscurity to fame, insignificance to public importance (though with a variation on the heroine's status, which is aristocratic—Kirsteen is the daughter of a Highland laird—rather than middle or working class).

That Oliphant means to invoke masculine patterns of self-development and social achievement is evident from Kirsteen's articulate statement of her plans for life in London. When she explains that she has come "not to see the world, but to make my fortune," her mentor Miss Jean expresses dismay:

> That's all very well in a lad,—and there's just quantities of them goes into the city without a penny and comes out like nabobs in their carriages—but not women, my dear, let along young lassies like you. (157)

Kirsteen proves that anything lads can do lassies can do better. She not only makes her fortune but also rebuilds the family estate that her forefathers lost and her brothers have failed to buy back. This plot of female competence versus male impotence continues Oliphant's strategy of depicting strong women and thus countering fictional conventions. As with *Hester*, it may also represent Oliphant's response to the "New Woman" novel of the '80s and '90s, which featured highly competent women with (in Oliphant's view) highly undesirable sexual conduct. Oliphant creates a heroine who is competent but utterly pure.

While making Kirsteen a masculine heroine, Oliphant exposes the limitations of the conventional feminine *bildungsroman* to an extent unparalleled in *Hester*. The opening chapter of *Kirsteen* presents two images of Victorian womanhood: Mrs. Douglas, Kirsteen's mother, a powerless feminine figure reduced to silence and tears; and Marg'ret, the old servant, powerful but single and virtually sexless. (We were never ones "that had much to do with the men" (157), Miss Jean says of herself and her sister Marg'ret.) These older women represent the limited possibilities for Kirsteen: marriage or spinsterhood, social position with the burdens of being a wife or personal freedom without the benefits of being a mother. Both are more extreme than the contrasting women in *Hester*. Neither appeals fully to the reader, who sees Kirsteen falling in love and, perhaps, into the trap of romance that leads to the bonds of marriage.

Subsequently, the novel develops even more images of womanhood that become warnings to Kirsteen of how effectively feminine life patterns can subdue a strong woman. Kirsteen's elder sister Anne, initially a rebel against her father's will, reappears happy in Glasgow with her husband and bairns; in an emergency, however, Anne cannot rouse herself to face the darkness of a Highland night or the danger of her father's wrath. Another sister Mary hopes, as her name hints, to marry the elderly suitor Kirsteen has refused, primarily for the wealth and social position he offers. As in Jane Austen's novels, such minor female figures represent paths the heroine must avoid. Kirsteen shows contempt for both. When Mary weds Glendochart, Kirsteen mentally echoes her father's contempt for a girl who would take her sister's "leavings." When Anne trembles, Kirsteen thinks:

> Was this the effect of marrying and being happy as people say? The little plump mother with her rosy face no longer capable of responding to any call outside her own circle of existence, the babies delving with their spoons into the porridge, covering their faces and pinafores, or holding up little gaping mouths to be fed. It had been a delightful picture which she had come in upon before at an earlier stage ... but now it was sweet no longer. The prosaic interior, the bondage of all these little necessities, the loosening of all other bonds of older date or wider reach, was this what happiness meant? (254)

The criticism of marriage and motherhood is more probing here than in earlier Oliphant novels—and it is particularly startling given Oliphant's lifelong criticism of books that depicted motherhood as anything less than "sacred."

In 1863 Oliphant had criticized Anne Thackeray Ritchie's novel, *The Story of Elizabeth*, for its depiction of a mother-daughter rivalry in romance, a subject she considered wholly unsuitable for fiction.[18] In 1877 she had chastised Harriet Martineau for publishing an "unfavorable estimate" of her mother in the *Autobiography:* "When it [autobiography] leads to the desecration of the home, and the holding up of the chief figure in it to deliberate blame and insult, what can anyone say?"[19] Yet the dual depiction of Ann—first as a happy mother surrounded by cherubic faces, then as a quailing female afraid to leave the safety of hearth and home—shows that Oliphant could recognize the hellish bondage that even a "sacred" role might impose. If Kirsteen remains respectful of her mother, even more so than Hester does of Mrs. John, the novel's representation of marriage and motherhood make it impossible that *Kirsteen* should end with Hester's choice of "two good men."

The burden of *Kirsteen*, however, is not simply to prove that marriage constrains women (a point many a Victorian novel had made before), but more radically that marriage limits self-development—that it is essentially alien to the concept of *bildung.* That the female *bildungsroman* must abandon its obsession with marriage as the focus of its plot—whether marriage as a reward for the heroine's development or marriage as the site of the heroine's growth—is the insight that Oliphant reaches in this late work. *Kirsteen* thus challenges the tradition of Bronte, Gaskell, and Eliot in which Jane Eyre wins Rochester, Margaret Hale wins Thornton, and Dorothea Brooke wins Will Ladislaw—all after suitable bouts with the "wrong" man. Expecting the heroine to discover the "right" man and grow in the process is, to mix metaphors, barking up the wrong tree. In *Kirsteen* growth is dissociated from marriage, self-development occurs in the public realm, not in the domestic.

Despite this challenge to the dominant tradition of the female *bildungsroman,* Oliphant finds it difficult to give up the romantic plot. The novel begins as a romantic tale, when Ronald Drummond asks Kirsteen, "Will ye wait for me till I come back?" and she answers, "That I will" (17). It is true that Oliphant quickly sets this plot aside as she sends Ronald off to India and Kirsteen to London—just as, in *Great Expectations,* Dickens sends Estella off to France so that Pip can proceed with his intellectual and moral development in London. It is also true that Kirsteen must face the limitations of the romantic plot she initiates—just as Pip, in *Great Expectations,* must learn the limitations of the fairy tales he projects for himself. Yet the romantic plot retains a centrality in *Kirsteen* that it lacks in *Great Expectations* or other male *bildungsromane*.

This centrality is emblematized by the testament and the bloodstained handkerchief that Kirsteen enshrines in "a little silver casket" as "her sacred things." We are told that "the silver casket stood in Kirsteen's room during her whole life within reach of her hand" (241). The testament and handkerchief—in effect, a book and an art object containing the record of romantic love—represent the feminine tale that can no longer be told. We might assume that Oliphant here recognizes the death of the traditional heroine's life-pattern. Yet these romantic emblems are also the basis of—perhaps even the source of—the masculine plot that Kirsteen assumes. With them succouring her in private, she can go forth into the public realm. With "no one to object any more than to praise," she is "independent" (241), free to pursue her career as an "artist"—which she does with a passion.

"Thus life was over for Kirsteen; and life began," Oliphant writes (241), as if to suggest that the two plots—the "old" feminine plot of romance, the "new" masculine plot of public achievement—are intertwined. By linking the two plots, she is, I suggest, both indulging in personal sentiment and anticipating a development in modern psychology. Personally, Oliphant had a predilection for secret romances kept well hidden from public view. In an 1870 review essay, "Miss Austen and Miss Mitford," she wondered at the absence of romance in the lives of these two prominent authors:

> Had they been married women whose romance ended naturally in the commonplace way, the omission would have been less noteworthy; but there is a charm in the love which has never come to anything— the tender, pathetic, sweet recollection laid up in a virgin life, amid the faded rose-leaves and fallen flowers of youth—which is infinitely sweet and touching,—more touching than the successful and prosperous can ever be."[20]

Oliphant sentimentally gives Kirsteen that "tender, pathetic, sweet recollection" as the inspiration for her "career." The reader thus sees her as romantic heroine and New Woman both. After Ronald's death, Kirsteen "t[akes] up her work with fresh vigour" (241) and creates genuinely artistic fashions.

Psychologically, Kirsteen's approach to her 'career' anticipates the analyses of modern theorists like Chodorow, who note that women define their identity "relationally" (i.e., in relation to other people, especially family members) rather than "positionally" as men do (i.e., according to the status they have achieved in the world).[21] Kirsteen's initial motive for working in London emphasizes family contribution; she imagines providing for her mother, making Jeanie an heiress, "'Oh, that I may make my fortune and help them all,' was the real petition of her heart" (158–59). After Ronald's death, this sense of contribution is even stronger, as her mother calls on her to be the "standby" of the family and her father asks that she buy back a portion of their ancient estate.

Oliphant's insight into female development is more than psychological. It is also narrative. It shapes the plot of *Kirsteen*, as it was unable to do in *Hester*. Technically, Kirsteen's *bildung* ends with chapter 33, with the death of Ronald Drummond, her success in the professional realm, and her acceptance of a life different from the one she had planned. Yet the novel continues for another thirteen chapters, narrating the death of Mrs. Douglas and the romance of Kirsteen's younger sister Jeanie. These addenda are significant because they show Kirsteen's personal growth spreading its influence in communal service—a modification of the traditional closure in the female *bildungsroman*, where marriage signifies the heroine's successful (re)integration into the community. Here, family service signals that (re)integration.

Nonetheless, the reintroduction of Jeanie and the romance plot, the traditional site of female self-development, has seemed to many readers regressive, given what Oliphant has already accomplished within Kirsteen's.[22] The reintroduction of the romance plot occurs, perhaps, because Oliphant remained ambivalent about women's appropriation of masculine life-patterns. On the one hand, we see the personal and familial gain that results from Kirsteen's "masculine" career; on the other, we sense the emotional loss, and through Jeanie's plot, the unsuitability of Kirsteen's actions for all women. Thus *Kirsteen* ends with the same ambivalence we found in *Hester*, though with a more positive view of the "masculine heroine."

That an individual woman can—and has the right to—model her life on the male *bildungsroman*, the novel asserts without apology. That her version of her life-story will be comprehended, let alone accepted by others, the novel ruefully disclaims. The final chapter makes it clear that Kirsteen's story will not be read by all as a successful *bildungsroman*. Her eldest brother, who has profited by her fortune, expresses his shock at having "a London mantua-maker" for a sister, "sewing for her bread." Other characters simply interpret her experiences as a failed feminine plot, "deplor[ing] the miserable way of life she had chosen, and that she had no man" (341).

With *Kirsteen* Oliphant completes the exploration of a genre that occupied her attention from the 1860s through 1890s. Though she is often considered conservative on social issues involving women, in her fiction she was genuinely revisionary. Her Carlingford novels parody the traditions of male and female *bildungsromane* alike, thus challenging values sacred to the Victorian ideology of separate spheres and testing the limits of the feminine. In *Hester* and *Kirsteen* she is more directly subversive. Not only does she abandon a feminine tradition that makes marriage the crux of women's self-development, but she also appropriates male forms of action for her heroines and, simultaneously, anticipates a fictional tradition that will define the female self relationally, as part of a community of women rather than as an entity separate and distinct from the world.[23] If her *bildungsromane* were not canonized, as were novels like *Jane Eyre* and *The Mill on the Floss*, it may not be just that Oliphant wrote too many, too quickly. It may also be that she refused to do the cultural work of Victorian patriarchy by keeping love and marriage at the center of fictions of female development.

Notes

1. Elizabeth Abel, Marianne Hirsch, and Elizabeth Langland summarize these critical discussions in their introduction to *The Voyage In: Fictions of Female Development* (Hanover, New Hampshire: University Press of New England, 1983) 3–14, though they take issue with overly sharp distinctions between male and female forms of the *bildungsroman*. They argue—correctly, I believe—that women writers have also developed an "apprenticeship" tradition that intersects in many significant ways with the male tradition, and their argument is implicitly supported by Rita Felski's discussion of national differences in "The Novel of Self-Discovery: A Necessary Fiction?" *Southern Review* 19 (1986) 131–48, and Annis Pratt's *Archetypal Patterns in Women's Fiction* (Bloomington: Indiana University Press, 1981). The standard history of the English *bildungsroman*, on which many subsequent discussions have been based, is Jerome Hamilton Buckley's *Season of Youth: The Bildungsroman from Dickens to Golding* (Cambridge: Harvard

University Press, 1974); Buckley defines the form simply as a "novel of youth or apprenticeship" and, except in his treatment of *The Mill on the Floss,* does not concern himself with gender.

2. See Elaine Hoffman Baruch's discussion of this feature in "The Feminine *Bildungsroman:* Education through Marriage," *Massachusetts Review* 22 (1981) 335–37, which treats late-eighteenth through early twentieth-century English and European novels.

3. "The Novel of Awakening," in Abel, Hirsch, and Landland, eds., p. 49; originally published in *Genre* 12 (1979) 313–32. For a similar view of the European female *bildungsroman,* which emphasizes "awakening" and "autonomy" rather than "social integration," see Elaine Martin, "Theoretical Soundings: The Female Archetypal Quest in Contemporary French and German Women's Fiction," *Perspectives on Contemporary Literature* 8 (1983) 48–57.

4. "The Comfort of Civilization," *Representations* 12 (1985) 115–16; this essay became the introduction to *The Way of the World: The Bildungsroman in European Culture* (London: Verso, 1987).

5. Throughout I use "male" and "female" to refer to the sex of the author or protagonist, "masculine" and "feminine" to refer to attributes or attitudes culturally associated with men and women. Although these distinctions are modern ones, I believe Oliphant's fiction and literary criticism show her to be sensitive to the associations of certain genres or modes with women and the 'feminine,' and thus to anticipate modern discussions of gender and genre.

6. The Colbys, 65–66, point out that much of Lucilla's behavior derives from *Friends in Council,* which the headmistriss of Lucilla's school gives as a prize to superior students.

7. Colby, 65.

8. "Novels," *Blackwood's Edinburgh Magazine* 102 (1867) 259.

9. Felski, p. 335.

10. "The Triumph of the Gifted Woman: The Comic Manipulation of Cliche in Mrs. Oliphant's *Miss Majoribanks* [sic]," *Zesszyty Naukowe Uniwersytetu Jagiellonskirco* 51 (1981) 45.

11. Merryn Williams, 85–86, criticizes *Phoebe, Junior* for its lack of a "central theme." Though the notion of "theme" can be misleading, I believe the novel does in fact pursue the theme of moral and vocational development quite consistently.

12. Oliphant's dislike of heroines who, like Bronte's Shirley, passionately bewail their plight or novelists who, like Mary Elizabeth Braddon, revel in the erotic adventures of their heroines is evident from her literary reviews. See, for example, "Novels," 257–80.

13. Baruch, 335–39.

14. C. Hugh Holman, *A Handbook to Literature,* 3d. ed. (New York: Odyssey Press, 1972) s.v. bildungsroman. One might argue that Clarence does learn "the nature of the world" and acquire "a philosophy of life" in that he discovers his limitations and learns that he is better off with Phoebe directing his life for him. But this self-knowledge only parodies what is expected in the male *bildungsroman.*

15. Discussion of the "New Woman" novels of the 1880s and 1890s tends to stress Oliphant's antagonism, especially her attack on Hardy's *Tess of the d'Urbervilles* and *Jude the Obscure* in reviews for *Blackwood's* (see Gail Cunningham, *The*

New Woman and the Victorian Novel [London: Macmillan, 1978] 45–50, 115–117, and Lloyd Fernando, *"New Women" in the Late Victorian Novel* [University Park: Pennsylvania State University Press, 1977] 141–46). Despite her dislike of the New Woman's sexual attitudes, Oliphant was sympathetic—as Uglow points out in her edition of *Hester*, xiii–xiv—to the New Woman's desire for "real work" and for an end to being "undervalued by men."

16. Some critics believe that, when this antipathy is overcome in the final scenes, Oliphant signals her approval of Catherine as "the embodiment of strength for the future"; according to Uglow, Catherine points the way to a "new breed of 'odd women,' the solitary heroines of the 1890s" (xxi). While Catherine does anticipate certain features of the New Woman, Oliphant remained ambivalent, I believe, about the combination of strengths *and* weaknesses that this new heroine embodied. Hester is rather the inheritor of two female traditions, the female represented by Mrs. John and the feminist embodied in Catherine.

17. See Nancy Chodorow, *The Reproduction of Mothering: Psychoanalysis and the Sociology of Gender* (Berkeley: University of California Press, 1978) 126–27, 179, passim.

18. See "Novels," *Blackwood's Edinburgh Magazine* 94 (1863) 173–74. The novel was published anonymously; hence Oliphant may not have known the identity of its author when she wrote the review.

19. See "Harriet Martineau," *Blackwood's Edinburgh Magazine* 121 (1877) 476.

20. "Miss Austen and Miss Mitford," *Blackwood's Edinburgh Magazine* 107 (1870) 298.

21. Chodorow, 126–27, 169 ff.

22. I base this statement about readers' response on the comments of participants in an NEH Institute, "The Victorian Age," held at Yale University, July 1988. I wish to thank various participants in this and the 1991 NEH Institute for their assistance with my work on *Miss Marjoribanks* and *Kirsteen*.

23. For a discussion of this tradition, see Nina Auerbach's *Communities of Women: An Idea in Fiction* (Cambridge: Harvard University Press, 1978) that, unfortunately, excludes Oliphant.

The Haunted Interpreter in Oliphant's Supernatural Fiction

ESTHER H. SCHOR

I

IN 1880, with the publication of "Earthbound," Margaret Oliphant invented the rubric under which she published most of her twelve stories and three novels that treat supernatural themes. Since then, Oliphant's rubric, "A Story [or Stories] of the Seen and the Unseen," has licensed readers to consign these fictions to "the supernatural," a minor Victorian subgenre supposedly dedicated to reviving domestic and Christian pieties. John R. Reed, for instance, compares Oliphant's supernatural writings unfavorably to Bulwer-Lytton's novels of the occult, *Zanoni* (1842) and *A Strange Story* (1862), calling them "less intellectual and less adept."[1] Margaret K. Gray finds Oliphant offering a homespun "theology of her own, a simple faith in which God's existence was affirmed. . . . [as] a God of Love, an ever-forgiving, consoling deity."[2] While Reed considers Oliphant's supernatural fictions "a form of social protest" against materialism and aestheticism and Gray reads them as personal consolations, both critics condescend to Oliphant as a pious domesticator of the supernatural.

Readers of Oliphant's supernatural fiction can be grateful to feminist critics such as Ellen Moers and Ann Douglas, who have replaced monolithic accounts of a minor genre with varied testimonies as to how supernatural fictions and their predominantly female readership have accommodated a wide range of literary experimentation.[3] Upon closer inspection, Oliphant's chosen rubric, "Stories of the Seen and the Unseen," suggests the flexibility and subtlety with which she, too, experimented with the supernatural mode. "Earthbound," for example, is concerned with eruptions of the Unseen in the seen, mundane world; the "Little

Pilgrim" series and "The Land of Darkness" reveal events and characters occurring in unseen realms, both heavenly and hellish; and "Old Lady Mary," shifts the setting from the Seen to the Unseen and back. In several stories, even the difference between the Seen and the Unseen proves critical, not essential. Oliphant's placement of such diverse writings under a single rubric is easily attributed to her reliable, if not unfailing, instincts for the market. She at times published mediocre sequels to her more popular works, and the supernatural fictions of the early 1880s were nothing if not popular. *A Beleaguered City* (1880), for example, was reprinted four times by 1897; in 1882, Macmillan printed over twenty thousand copies of the hugely successful *Little Pilgrim in the Unseen*.[4] It would only have been reasonable for Oliphant, who never held a salaried position, to wish her readers to identify her later supernatural fictions with these early successes.

In this essay, I will consider two of Oliphant's supernatural fictions from the late 1870s as highly experimental narratives about interpretation. In both "Earthbound" and *A Beleaguered City*, the encroachment of the Unseen on the Seen causes an interpretive crisis. While Oliphant's haunted interpreters enact our task as readers by confronting an uninterpreted "text," they also interrogate Oliphant's own authority as an interpreter of literature. As John Blackwood's "general utility woman" (her own phrase),[5] Oliphant had published nearly ninety critical essays on literature, art, and history by the late 1870s. Merryn Williams's bibliography reveals that in the 1870s Oliphant published essays on an extraordinarily varied group of English and Continental writers, in addition to seventeen books of fiction.[6] By the end of this decade, Oliphant was writing fictions in which the meanings of signs and figures are radically indeterminate. Creating apparitions that stubbornly resist definitive interpretation, Oliphant foregrounds the interpretive strategies of the haunted. In "Earthbound," a hermeneutic romance worthy of late Borges, she demonstrates a congruence between interpretive and sexual mastery. In *A Beleaguered City*, Oliphant presents a public crisis of interpretation, considering how both gender and class are implicated in authorizing interpretations. Allegorizing the interpretation of texts as an affair between persons, Oliphant deftly conflates the discourses of interpretation and social relations. For Oliphant's haunted interpreters, confronting the unexplained figure often leads to an uncanny exchange of roles: as the ghostly figure assumes authority, the interpreters take on the aura of the irrational. By means of such transfigurations, these fictions reconfigure—surprisingly, and even subversively—familiar relations between interpreters and texts, interpreters and other interpreters, and interpreters and themselves.

II

From the start of "Earthbound," Oliphant estranges her reader from the set-piece of a Victorian Christmas:

> There was but a small party for Christmas at Daintrey. The family were in mourning, which meant more than it usually means, and the whole life of the place was subdued. . . . Christmas was coming; and though there could be no Christmas festivities in the ordinary sense of the word, one or two old friends and connections were invited. (30)

Commonly understood terms and conventions are first rendered uncertain, then shown to have multiple meanings. Mourning, as it happens, "usually" means something quite different to men, to women, and to children. Lady Beresford's "heart was still bleeding," though she seldom takes a moment away from her family to mourn her son; Sir Robert, however, becomes "morose with his grief," (31) while the children appear to be less encumbered by grief than either parent. Accordingly, the young and the old celebrate "Christmas festivities" rather differently:

> The commonplace ghost-stories which are among the ordinary foolishnesses of Christmas did not suit with the more serious tone in which their thoughts flowed; but there was some talk among the older people about those sensations and presentiments that seem sometimes to convey a kind of prophecy, only understood after the event, of sorrow on the way; and the young ones amused themselves after a sort with discussions of those new-fangled fancies which have replaced that old favourite lore. They talked about what is called spiritualism, and of many things, both in that fantastic faith and in the older ghostly traditions, which we are all half glad to think cannot be explained. (32–33)

As the spiritualism of the young supplants their elders' ghostlier lore, Oliphant identifies a common satisfaction in things inexplicable. Like the inscrutable loss of Willie Beresford, which initiates the family's mourning, the talk of ghosts and spirits motivates a social discourse in which the generations meet. Though the unexplained may generate a variety of responses, Oliphant places it within the public domain.

At the Beresford estate, Edmund Coventry is something of an outsider. Beyond his ties to Sir Robert, his former guardian, Edmund has a shadowy past with "no relations to speak of" (32).

> He was a young man of excellent character and very fair fortune; and, if the truth must be told, the heads of the house at Daintrey had concluded that he would be a very convenient match for Maud, who was the second girl. Perhaps it would be better to say that one of the heads of the house had already perceived and accepted this view. (31)

While Lady Beresford observes that Edmund and Maud "were like brother and sister," she maintains that "there was always a possibility of something more" (34). Still, the "self-indulgent" Sir Robert, evidently made uncomfortable by the prospect of Edmund's visit, is reluctant to "perceive and accept" the anticipated marriage. Indeed, the "possibility of something more" points ironically toward an incestuous link between Sir Robert's daughter, Maud, and the suggestively named Edmund. Oliphant's tacit questioning of Edmund's paternity may seem tentative compared to Emily Bronte's devious insinuations about Heathcliff's paternity; unlike Catherine and Heathcliff, Maud Beresford and Edmund do eventually marry. But the relationship between Edmund and Maud Beresford is secondary to that between Edmund and a mysterious woman in white, who cryptically reveals that "I was Maud." Insofar as Edmund's desire for this woman prevents his desire for Maud Beresford, it displaces and absorbs the transgressive alliance for which Lady Beresford hopes.

In "Earthbound," the polysemous word "Maud"—a single name that refers to two very different women—mocks the desirous Edmund's attempt to learn the identity of the woman in white. Only by identifying her can he marry her and legally consummate his implicitly transgressive desire. Unwilling to accept her resistance, Edmund attempts to bring his ethereal visitant into the mundane, natural world. Her mobility itself is a threat, albeit an alluring one, which he counters by trying to arrest her and affix her to him. At Maud Beresford's suggestion, he seeks her in the keeper's cottage, as though wanting to transfer this "kept" woman to his own safekeeping. The more elusive she is, the more he delights in "the little mystery"—an ambiguous term referring both to her identity and, deprecatingly, her person. Perplexed by her willfulness, Edmund reassures himself that "she did not look at all like one of those women who assert a right to walk alone, and to do whatever pleases them" (44).

Edmund's behavior is, at best, paradoxical: he seeks to legitimate the apparition only so that he may then cancel her autonomy through sexual mastery. Thus, to legitimate the woman in white—to confer upon her the status of legal person—would be to determine and constrain her significance by an act of will.[7] Oliphant, by linking interpretive will with sexual mastery, dramatizes the consequences of taking the inexplicable out of the public domain and into the realm of the private. Edmund's will to possess the mysterious woman produces a mode of reading that Oliphant finds too close for moral comfort.

Even a brief account of Edmund's confrontations with the female figure will suggest how masterfully Oliphant sustains her discursive *double entendre*. For Edmund, the tantalizing female "figure" is simultaneously a woman to be possessed and a text to be interpreted. His initial impulse, for example, is to decide what genre of female she is: woman? or lady?

> But when he had crossed that bridge of light he was still more surprised to see in front of him, at the end of the avenue, a woman, a lady, walking along with the most composed and gentle tread. The road was not exactly a private road—all the people from the village ... used it. ... The dress, too, struck him with great surprise. It was a white dress, with a black mantle round the shoulders, and a large hat: not unlike the costume which people in aesthetic circles begin to affect, but far more real and natural, it seemed to him. (36)

Her social class is not so easily read. As Maud Beresford points out, even a dressmaker "may walk like a lady and dress like a lady" (40). Clad in black and white, the illegible figure is unwittingly associated by Edmund with the artistry of "aesthetic circles." Though he realizes how unnatural white garb is for winter, Edmund resists interpreting her costume as a sign of artfulness. She always *seems* to be "far more real and natural"; as Edmund tells Maud Beresford, "she did not look like art-needlework—she looked quite natural" (39). He pursues her "composed and gentle tread" down well-worn paths like a reader making the public space of a text his own private property.

What Edmund neglects—and what Oliphant insists upon—is the mysterious figure's own authority to signify. While enjoying Edmund's company, the female figure thwarts his attempts to identify her, showing her face reluctantly. His persistence drives her to respond to his gaze by gazing—and speaking—back: "So you see me! was, in tones of gentle pleasure, what she said" (46). In the allusive lime-tree grove, she permits him to walk beside her for the first time. Earthbound yet liminal, the female figure recalls the lamed Coleridge wandering imaginatively between his embowered "prison" and the sublime hilltops:

> [Edmund] walked on beside her confused, trembling, afraid, yet full of a strange happiness; and the moon, which had been rising all the time, came shining upon them through the lofty, slender lime branches. It seemed to him, in his bewildered condition, that it was like some poem he had read, or some dream he had dreamt, to walk thus in this measured soft cadence, with the moon upon their heads all broken and chequered by the anatomy of the great trees, like dark lines traced upon the sky. (47)

For once, Edmund keeps pace with the "measured soft cadence" of the figure—here, creative and luminous—as they pass together through the "dark lines" (47). The idyll occurs under the aegis of the moon, associated earlier with both female creativity and liminality: "an early pale-eyed young moon, with a certain eagerness about her, as though full of impatience to see what was going on in the earth, had got up hastily in a bit of blue. She touched the mists, and made them poetical" (41). Momentarily, Edmund seems to join the figure in her own context, sensing that "it was like some poem he had read." But this romance of reading merely leaves Edmund lusting to read still more closely:

> "Give me your hand. Won't you give me your hand?" . . .
> She shook her head gently, standing so near him, her hands crossed, clasping each other. He had only to put out his arms and take her into them, but he could not. She was close, close to him, and yet—what was it that stood between? (54)

The female figure, refusing her marital hand, clasps not his hand, but her own instead. Unable to consummate his love, Edmund begins virtually to impersonate her. He "haunts" the lime-tree grove in her absence. While entertaining the possibility that she is a madwoman (for, like Maud Beresford, he has evidently read his Wilkie Collins), Edmund comes perilously close to losing his own reason. He becomes incapable "of cool judgment or criticism" (45), and is thought mad by young Fred.

Sir Robert shows Edmund an eighteenth-century portrait of a woman and explains that Edmund, having seen the portrait in the family gallery, is now simply deluded. Edmund resists Sir Robert's historicism, and with good reason: the framed and dated portrait parodies his own desire to contain a ghost within the structure of marriage. He even misreads the portrait's date, "1777": "'Seven, seven, seven,' he said to himself; 'seven is one of the numbers of perfection'" (57). But perhaps it is more than Sir Robert's historicism that disturbs Edmund. For Sir Robert's revelation simultaneously legitimates the apparition as a Beresford ancestress, and implicitly initiates Edmund into the family circle as the illegitimate son of Sir Robert. Whereas Edmund proves illegitimate, the figure proves legitimate; since they are *both* Beresfords, his desire for her proves patently incestuous. Knowing himself powerless to possess her, Edmund pleads with her to possess him—to transform *him* into *her* text:

> "Touch me—mark me, that I may be yours always. If not in life, yet in death. Say we shall meet when I die."
>
> Once more she shook her head. "How can I tell? I do not know you in the soul. . . . Good-bye, brother—good bye!"
>
> "I will not let you go!" he cried; "I will not let you go!" and seized her in his arms.
>
> Then in Edmund's head was a roaring of echoes, a clanging of noises, a blast as of great trumpets and music; and he knew no more. (61)

This sisterly farewell—"goodbye, brother"—makes literal the transgressive closeness of Edmund's embrace. As though Edmund's readerly grasp were not sufficiently dubious, Oliphant shows that this violent mode of reading is tantamount to rape— the rape, in Edmund's case, of his own consciousness.

Inscribed in the denouement of "Earthbound" is a pathetic desublimation of another, more famous, literary embrace. In Canto XXI of the *Purgatorio* (which Oliphant quotes in a footnote), Dante reveals to the poet Statius that his interlocutor has been none other than Virgil himself. When Statius attempts to embrace his beloved precursor, Virgil prevents him, saying, "Frate, non far, che tu se'ombra e ombra vedi" (Brother, there's no need— you are a shade, a shade is what you see.") Statius replies:

> Ed ei surgendo: "Or puoi la quantitate comprender de l'amor ch'a te mi scalda, quand'io dismento nostra vanitate, trattando l'ombre come cosa salda."
> And, rising, he: "Now you can understand how much love burns in me for you, when I forget our insubstantiality, treating the shades as one treats solid things.")[8]

Embracing Virgil, the loving Statius feels them both to be more substantial than the shades—or texts—they are; but Edmund's possessive embrace routs his beloved figure, leaving Edmund himself a senseless body on the attic floor. Statius's sublime love of Virgil is grotesquely deflated in what one might call, after Susan Sontag, Edmund's "erotics of reading."[9] Edmund's close reading dismantles the dialectic between reader and text enacted by Dante and Virgil, a dialectic that, as Oliphant suggests in the lime-tree grove idyll, constitutes the loving act of reading well. Moreover, Edmund's attempt to displace the inexplicable figure from the public to the private realm only reveals harshly his own tenuous linkage to the social order. Both as a reader and as a lover, Edmund Coventry fails.[10]

III

A Beleaguered City, written in 1878, concerns the possession not of an individual, but of the Burgundian city of Semur.[11] In this novella, the strange reversal of roles that is so gradual in "Earthbound" is abrupt and peremptory. One evening, a mysterious sign on the cathedral door declares Semur's residents to be dwelling there illegitimately; soon the populace is silently and summarily expelled. The town's mayor, Martin Dupin, reflects that "It was rather now as if the world had become a grave in which we, though living, were held fast" (47;22). Ironically, the possession of Semur *dis*possesses its inhabitants, most of whom weather the three-day ordeal outside the city walls. For the predominant portion of Semur's populace, the city's besiegers remain entirely inaccessible, unseen, unheard, and distant; throughout the episode, Semur remains shrouded in clouds. Unlike "Earthbound," which dwells chiefly on the tantalizing proximity between the haunted interpreter and the unexplained, *A Beleaguered City* subordinates confrontations with the unseen to the public drama of interpretive debate.

Whereas in "Earthbound," gender and class articulate relations between the interpreter and his "text," in *A Beleaguered City* differing interpretations articulate the town's complex and often occult relations of class and gender. The novella comprises Dupin's official compilation of discrete documents by himself and four other narrators, a procedure designed "to present one coherent and trustworthy chronicle to the world" (20;10). But even Dupin acknowledges that the account becomes less coherent as it becomes more complete:

> The narratives which I have collected from the different eye-witnesses during the time of my own absence, will show how everything passed while I, with M. le Curé, was recovering possession of our city.... [I]n their accounts there are naturally discrepancies, owing to their different points of view and different ways of regarding the subject. (241;103)

Readers who attempt to "decode" Oliphant's moral message in *A Beleaguered City* attribute to her the same interpretive absoluteness that she labors here to undermine. In this novella Oliphant broods on the ways in which public and private authority are mutually implicated in the social matrix.

In what Dupin calls "the first important incident in this narrative" (51;24), Oliphant foregrounds interpretation. Dupin beholds a mysterious sign on the facade of the cathedral:

> It was as I have seen an illumination of lamps in a stormy night; one moment the whole seems black as the wind sweeps over it, the next it springs into life again; and thus you go on, by turns losing and discovering the device formed by the lights. Thus from moment to moment there appeared before us, in letters that seemed to blaze and flicker, something that looked like a great official placard. "*Sommation*"—this was how it was headed. I read a few words at a time, as it came and went.... It was a summons to the people of Semur by name—myself at the head as Maire (and I heard afterwards that every man who saw it saw his own name, though the whole *facade* of the

Cathedral would not have held a full list of all the people of Semur)—to yield their places, which they had not filled aright, to those who knew the meaning of life, being dead. NOUS AUTRES MORTS—these were the words which blazed out oftenest of all, so that every one saw them. And "Go!" this terrible placard said—"Go! leave this place to us who know the true signification of life." These words I remember, but not the rest; and even at this moment it struck me that there was no explanation, nothing but this *vraie signification de la vie*. (53–55;25)

While in "Earthbound" the female figure is difficult to read, she is at least a figure in black and white; here, the luminous text is even less integral, not inscribed, but variously blazing and flickering. Insofar as each witness reads his own name on the sign (and Dupin is vexed to find his own name so prominent), the text's instability becomes politically ominous.[12] Dupin, at the center of political authority, trusts that the terrible phrase, "NOUS AUTRES MORTS," will ensure an interpretive consensus, even as it polarizes the human and the supernatural realms. Oliphant imbues our own reading with some of the strangeness of Dupin's by using "gigantic" uppercase letters and, more important, by including the French version of the sign. The sign's indeterminacy is signified by its reduction to "nothing but" the inexplicable and untranslated phrase, "*vraie signification de la vie.*" Paradoxically, the sign's meaning is only intelligible to one who knows the meaning of life; but the monition only exists because Semur's residents do not. The enigmatic "meaning" of the sign, in other words, is that none of its readers are able to interpret it.

To resist the imposing apparition, the people of Semur do the one thing in their power: transform themselves from objects into subjects by reading the sign. In the resulting welter of interpretation, the community's central political tensions are expressed. Dupin, ever conscious that he is "at once the representative of the popular opinion and its guide" (42;20), refuses to "yield credence to a miracle." Sending for the scientist, M. Clairon, Dupin pledges his own allegiance to materialism; in the preceding chapter, he comforts himself with the knowledge that "all sensations of the body must have their origin in the body" (44;21). By his own account, Dupin is "a man of my century," unwilling to close ranks with the clerical party, though tolerant of "conscientious faith" (18–19;10). While awaiting the arrival of Clairon, he reveals his prejudices against the Curé by accusing him of an imposture: "M.

le Curé,' I said, 'this is a strange ornament that you have placed on the front of your church.'" The Curé, for his part, surprises Dupin by casting suspicions on the nuns of the Hospital of St. Jean: "'It is never well to offend women, M. le Maire,' he said." (56–8;26–7) Dupin realizes for the first time that the Curé and the *religieuses* are not aligned, as he had previously supposed. On the contrary, the women of the hospital (angered by complaints that their masses are disturbing patients) are suspected by the clerical and secular authorities alike. It is hardly coincidental that Dupin's initial response to the strange sign—"What is this? is it some witchcraft?"—points in the same direction as the Curé's. Dupin's own interests, as he relates in chapter 1, lie in the preservation of the patriarchal order; though a bourgeois, he is heir to "the position held by the Dupins from father to son." He abominates that "class" of women "who profess the same freedom of thought as is generally accorded to men" (13;8), and maintains that it is incumbent upon women to compensate with piety for their lesser "weight" in the world. Semur's nuns unsettle Dupin's *idee fixe* about women expressly because they enlist religious faith in the service of secular power. Fearing an alliance between Semur's women and the unseen powers, Dupin retorts to his wife, "'You love these dead tyrants. . . . you love them best'" (107;47).

As for the nuns, they find a curious source of support in the money-worshipping underclass that Dupin disdains: "The men would all sell their souls for a *grosse pièce* of fifty sous" (15;9). As the refractory *vaurien* Jacques Richard declares, "*L'argent c'est le bon Dieu*" (6;5). Unlike Semur's more affluent, educated, and enfranchised bourgeoisie, these men prove to have a "religious" culture; just as they had made a cult of silver, they now make a cult of the nuns. While Dupin excoriates their profane materialism (unwilling to acknowledge his own loftier scientific materialism), they are readier than many of Semur's women to credit the nuns' claims that the dead have risen angrily on the nuns' behalf. Finally, the "enlightened" Clairon arrives to offer the least persuasive interpretation of all:

> [M]any of us thought that when science thus came forward capable of finding out everything, the miracle would disappear. But instead of this it seemed to glow brighter than ever. That great word "*Sommation*" blazed out, so that we saw his figure waver against the light as if giving

way before the flames that scorched him. He was so near that his outline was marked out dark against the glare they gave. (58–59;27)

Dupin, hoping to support and be supported by a definitive interpretation, finds Clairon transformed into a figure of darkness—yet another figure whose meaning is uncertain.

While the incident of the sign provides a colorful mapping of the city's class, religious, and gender relations, it is nonetheless a map drawn by Dupin, who insists on preserving the normative shape of authority in Semur throughout the crisis. By contrast, the import of interpretive difference in Dupin's compilation is both to undermine his authorial control of the document, and to question the adequacy of his centrist, tolerant notion of government. Chapters 5 through 9, which treat the period of Dupin's return to the occupied town with the Cure, are framed by the Mayor's narration. Dupin also narrates chapter 6, but here his account stands beside that of the four other narrators whom he recruits for assistance: Paul Lecamus; M. de Bois-Sombre; Dupin's wife, Agnes Dupin; and his mother, Madame Veuve Dupin.[13] Dupin regards Lecamus as "something of a visionary, though his conduct is irreproachable, and his life honourable and industrious" (24–25;13). Dupin's tentative tolerance for Lecamus reflects his ambivalence about his own "faculty of imagination"; just as Dupin assures himself that Lecamus is "quite free from revolutionary sentiments," he assures his reader that, in writing his account, Dupin himself has kept his imagination firmly in check. Still, in an earlier chapter, it is Lecamus who ventures outside the city walls with Dupin, where both men uncannily sense the presence of an unseen crowd. Dupin's response is duplicitous: in public, he announces staunchly that he has seen nothing; then shakily asks Lecamus in private, "how do you explain—" (40;19). That Dupin requests Lecamus to write an official account of his sojourn among the Unseen suggests that Dupin expects the visionary to say what he as Mayor cannot. Lecamus does exactly that, narrating his ravishment by the soul of his departed wife—a sublimer embrace, perhaps, than that of Edmund Coventry, but ultimately an *amour fatale*. Of Dupin's other surrogate, Bois-Sombre, he remarks that he "is an excellent fellow; but he smells a little of the *mousquetaire*" (257;110). The aristocratic Bois-Sombre, his family holdings having been drastically reduced during the Revolution, resents having to forfeit his sole residence "probably to the licence of a mob—for one can never tell at what moment Republican institutions may break down and sink back into the chaos from which they arose" (177;76). An essentialist in matters of class, Bois-Sombre dismisses Dupin's foolish attempt to transfer his scarf of office to him; blood, after all, will tell. Whereas Lecamus enacts Dupin's imaginative impulses, Bois-Sombre enacts Dupin's defense of the official authority against the leftist threat posed by the self-authorized "hare-brained enthusiast" Lecamus (174;75).

In its first published version, *A Beleaguered City* includes only the additional narrative of Agnes Dupin; Oliphant added the narrative of Madame Veuve Dupin while revising the novella for publication as a book. The revision (and Oliphant made but a handful of extensive revisions during her prolific career) is crucial: taken together, chapters 8 and 9 undermine powerfully Dupin's complacent relegation of women to "the devout sex." The object of Oliphant's criticism is not Dupin as husband, son, father, Mayor, or even Dupin as self-proclaimed "man of my century," but Dupin as a man of the future—as *historian*. Dupin expresses an ideology that, according to the historian Peter Brown, has pervaded British historiography since the Enlightenment. In *The Cult of the Saints*, Brown describes the persistent "two-tiered model" used by Hume, Gibbon, the early Newman, and numerous twentieth-century historians, to interpret the history of religious cultures.

> The views of the potentially enlightened few are thought of as being subject to continuous upward pressure from habitual ways of thinking current among "the vulgar."[14]

Brown argues that this model expresses the biases of Protestant ideologues, who exploited it to stress affinities between benighted, pagan forms of worship and Roman Catholicism.

> Rather than present the rise of the cult of the saints in terms of a dialogue between two parties, the few and the many, let us attempt to see it as part of a greater whole—the lurching forward of an increasing proportion of late-antique society toward radically new forms of reverence . . . deriving its momentum from the need to play out the common preoccupation of all, the few and the "vulgar" alike, with new forms of the exercise of power, new bonds of human dependence, new, intimate, hopes for protection and justice in a changing world. (22)

Perhaps Oliphant's extended sojourn in Italy and her study of the French monastic revival left her impatient with this historiographical bias against Catholicism. But in *A Beleaguered City*, Oliphant shrewdly intuits the bias against *women* implied by the "two-tiered model," which, in Dupin's hands, relegates females to a superstitious underclass. *A Beleaguered City* articulates a rich spectrum of difference among Semur's women, most of whom would probably describe themselves as "devout." While Agnes Dupin claims to have witnessed the spirits, her testament differs from that of Mère Julie.

> In the night the Mère Julie had roused us, saying she had seen a procession of angels coming to restore us to the city. Ah! to those who have no knowledge it is easy to speak of processions of angels. But to those who have seen what an angel is—how they flock upon us unawares in the darkness, so that one is confused, and scarce can tell if it is reality or a dream; to those who have heard a little voice soft as the dew coming out of heaven! I said to them—for all were in a great tumult—that the angels do not come in processions, they steal upon us unaware, they reveal themselves in the soul. (193;83)

Agnes Dupin's intimation challenges her to accept an unfamiliar mode of consciousness neither fully wakeful nor fully dreamlike. Whereas Mère Julie's vision is derived heavily from scripture, Agnes's more idiosyncratic vision involves a paradoxical exertion of faith in the self. Her mother-in-law, who cannot perceive the angels, strives toward a faith expressed in good works:[15]

> God, He knows what it is we can do and what we cannot. I could not tell even to Him all the terror and the misery and the darkness there was in me; but I put my faith in Him. . . . We are not made alike, neither in the body nor in the soul. (223;96)

Whereas Agnes Dupin's account concentrates on spiritual issues, Madame Veuve Dupin's explains in detail the administration of a large, diverse community of women and children. Crucially, Madame Veuve Dupin supplies the social context for the women's various responses to the crisis. Her portrait of Sister Mariette, who smiles resignedly throughout, is implicitly critical: "She had no son, no husband among the watchers" (227;97), observes Madame Dupin curtly. Even Mère Julie's prophecy is compromised by her having knowingly sold inferior pears to the Dupins.

Though proud of her son, Madame Veuve Dupin is openly critical of him for opposing the nuns of the Hospital. Oliphant, by revising, substitutes for a pious version of the female voice, a pluralistic array of female voices.

Dupin's document reveals a greater ambivalence toward pluralism by simultaneously authorizing and repressing other voices. For even as his four surrogates suggest Dupin's pluralistic tolerance of several interpretive positions in the social spectrum, they also suggest that any single interpretation advanced by Dupin entails the subordination of others *within his own consciousness*.[16] Dupin's two male surrogates suggest his need to repress both his imagination and his love of control; while both qualities remain obscured to him he inscribes them in his document through the narratives of others. Dupin fails as well to acknowledge his own femininity, as we learn during his climactic journey into the possessed town. On entering the library "where my father and grandfather conducted their affairs," he finds a change:

> The old bureau which my grandfather had used, at which I remember standing by his knee, had been drawn from the corner where I had placed it out of the way . . . and replaced, as in old times, in the middle of the room. . . . Some of the old drawers were open, full of old papers. I glanced over them in my agitation, to see if there might be any writing, any message addressed to me; but there was nothing, nothing but this silent sign of those who had been here. (162–63;70)

Finding no patriarchal message addressed to him, Dupin is placed in much the same position as his mother, who locates herself at the margins of written language.[17] Dispossessed in the library of his male predecessors, Dupin finds himself possessed by "an inspiration from above" (167;72). He hears the strange Latin words "*Laetatus sum*" spring from his tongue—"no thought of mine." Impulsively and silently, he and the Curè serve mass:

> The days of my childhood seemed to come back to me. All trouble, and care, and mystery, and pain, seemed left behind. All I could see was the glimmer on the altar of the great candle-sticks, the sacred pyx in its shrine, the chalice, and the book. I was again an *enfant de choeur* robed in white, like the angels, no doubt, no disquiet in my soul—and my father kneeling behind among the faithful, bowing his head, with a sweetness which I too knew, being a father, because it was his

child that tinkled the bell and swung the censer.... My heart grew soft within me as the heart of a little child. (168;72–73)

Weeping at the altar, Dupin finds his habitual demeanor softened and made "childlike." While he never speaks of himself as effeminized, he describes in unaccustomed terms his paternal role as one of "sweetness," a role related not to patriarchal inheritance, but to parenting and the giving of nourishment.

Narrating the aftermath in chapter 10, Dupin thoroughly denies this experience of masculinity. Describing a visit to the cathedral after the ordeal, Dupin recurs to his accustomed construction of gender:

> The great Cathedral walls seemed to throb with the sound that rolled upward *mâle* and deep, as no song has ever risen from Semur in the memory of man.... Such a submission of our intellects, as I felt in determining to make it, must have been pleasing to heaven. The women, they are always praying; but when we thus presented ourselves to give thanks, it meant something, a real homage; and with a feeling of solemnity we separated, aware that we had contented both earth and heaven. (252–53;108)

Earlier, Dupin supposes charitably that "The *bon Dieu*—if, indeed, that great Being is as represented to us by the Church—must naturally care as much for one-half of His creatures as for the other" (13;8). Here, presuming to please both the city of God and the city of man, Dupin constructs the former on the model of the latter. The distance traveled between Dupin's two remarks suggests his clearer awareness *after* the ordeal that the Church represents God with its own masculinist bias. Semur's nuns have already realized that the Hospital would be more hospitable to them than the Church; even there, male patients attempt to circumscribe their freedom to worship. *A Beleaguered City* suggests that the enfranchisement of religious women is not simply a matter of where one stakes a claim. According to Madame Veuve Dupin, the religious life of Semur's female encampment revolves around a God different from the Curé's:

> One cry seemed to rise round us as we went, each infant moving the others to sympathy, till it rose like one breath, a wail of "Maman! Maman!" a cry that had no meaning, through having so much meaning.... The Holy Mother could not but hear it. (213–14;92)

Indeed, Semur's women seem to address themselves to a female God. Oliphant is at her shrewdest in having this cry originate in the lungs of infants. For while "Maman" is perhaps a far cry from mariolatry, it suggests that belief in the *Bon Dieu,* the *fils de Dieu,* and even the *Saint-Pere* is only learned later—at the behest of the Church.

When Madame Veuve Dupin asks her son, "Why is it that you look so unfavorably upon everything that comes from the community of St. Jean?" he replies resonantly, "What have I to do with the community?" (262;112). It may be true that Martin Dupin survives as Semur's public authority only by refusing to answer this question. But he survives as an author only by including the answer within the leaves of his file. Dupin's multivocal document, by enfranchising a wider spectrum of the community than Dupin does as mayor, deconstructs his own interpretive authority. The document of Semur's ordeal bespeaks a far more radical conception of both political and interpretive authority than Dupin's centrist, tolerant, but patriarchal rhetoric can sustain. More important, it suggests that such rhetoric can only legitimate itself as part of a varied and differentiated social discourse. In the gap between Dupin's rhetorical stance and those others voiced in his document, Oliphant exposes the conceptual threads that link psychological repression to social oppression. Oliphant's *Beleaguered City* is not a hotbed of political unrest, but a place in which the fuller enfranchisement of the social body depends on fuller and more complex recognitions of the self. What the inexplicable makes impossible is a mechanistic, rationalized view of the social body. The populace of Semur see themselves inscribed in the mysterious sign because they, too, cannot be interpreted by a univocal, authorized rhetoric, however benign or humane.

IV

In her introduction to the *Autobiography and Letters,* Q. D. Leavis describes Oliphant's supernatural fiction as "over-rated":

Though Mrs Oliphant valued them highly herself and some have Dantean overtones, they represent a self-indulgence, the complement of her hard-headed professional self which required some non-dogmatic vaguely religious sustenance.[18]

Clearly, Leavis gets it wrong: as both "Earthbound" and *A Beleaguered City* demonstrate, fiction can be nondogmatic, yet hardheaded; "vaguely religious," but not self-indulgent. And yet, Leavis also gets it right by observing that Oliphant's supernatural fictions are the "complement of her hard-headed professional self." Having lived so much of her life as a reader on the public pages of *Blackwood's* and other literary journals, Oliphant was keenly aware of her own authority as an arbiter of literary fates and fortunes. A published writer of fiction since her twenties, Oliphant had realized early that such critical pronouncements as she was paid to deliver had consequences for writers and their books. But by the late 1870s, she had come to reckon with her own power as a critic to shape the tastes and expectations of a nation's readers. In the mode of supernatural fiction, Oliphant explored her ambivalence about her own critical professionalism. What does it mean, these fictions ask, to use a rhetoric of distinctions, decisions, and determinations to account for a literary text? to assimilate one's mixed and perhaps irreconcilable responses to a single, morally viable and socially responsible position? to authorize and canonize the reading of a single reader? In "Earthbound" and *A Beleaguered City*, Oliphant provisionally views the burden of interpreting literary texts—those linguistic apparitions that resist explanation—as a shared burden. In "Earthbound," Edmund's close reading—an attempt to possess meaning by transforming a text into private property—renders illegitimate his claims as reader. In *A Beleaguered City*, on the other hand, Dupin's political authority is legitimated only because his interpretive authority is dialectical. If, as these fictions suggest, the way we love and the way we govern are crucially linked to the way we read, we can see why Oliphant found the task of being a critic formidable.

Finally, the "vaguely religious" quality of Oliphant's supernaturalism, as Leavis would have it, deserves a clarifying comment. Oliphant's supernatural fictions are indeed "religious" insofar as they provide a phenomenology of faith in that which cannot be fully grasped. But I would argue that these fictions are not, except idiomatically, Christian. Her last supernatural tale, "The Library Window" (1896), finds Oliphant veering away from faith in a Christian God, toward an entirely secular faith in what we might call (in an age in which authors are wanted more dead than alive) the "afterlife" of the author. The narrator, a dreamy, bookish girl visiting her elderly aunt, sees an old man writing ceaselessly in a window across the street, only to discover that the window is a *trompe l'oiel.* Though the panes of the window prove fictitious, the girl clings to her faith in the real pains of the writerly apparition. Late in the story, the aunt "explains" the apparition by spinning a gothic tale replete with a thwarted mistress, vengeful brothers, and a magic ring, but the girl prefers her own naturalized faith in what she cannot explain. Of the magic ring, which she inherits but will not wear, the narrator remarks, "If any one would steal it, it would be a relief to my mind" (248;331). With cunning and wit, Oliphant saves the inexplicable from being reduced to a supernatural mode or subgenre—that is, to yet another authorized interpretive instrument. Bidding farewell to the supernatural, she dispenses with both gothicism and Christian piety as so many magic rings. Oliphant's supernatural fictions, far from being the "vaguely religious sustenance" of a self-indulgent journalist, are incisive essays in the cultural practice of interpretation.

Notes

Reprinted from *Women's Studies: An Interdisciplinary Journal,* 22:3 (1993) 371–88.

1. *Victorian Conventions* (Athens: Ohio University Press, 1975) 465. Additional treatments of the supernatural as a subgenre can be found in Jack Sullivan, *Elegant Nightmares* (Athens: Ohio University Press, 1978), Julia Briggs, *Night Visitors* (London: Faber, 1977). An extensive bibliography can be found in E. F. Bleiler, *The Guide to Supernatural Fiction* (Kent: Kent State University Press, 1983).

2. "Introduction" to Oliphant, *Selected Short Stories of The Supernatural* (Edinburgh: Scottish Academic Press, 1985) xi. Similarly, Reed, 464, maintains that "Underlying all of Mrs. Oliphant's stories of the seen and the unseen was the desire to affirm the existence of a transcendental, Christian creator and the immortality of the soul against the increasing materialism and estheticism of her time." Gray, 250, notes that Oliphant did not use this rubric for "The Land of Darkness" and "On the Dark Mountains." Excerpts are drawn from Gray's and Williams's editions.

3. Moers's "Female Gothic," with its graphic, violent allegorizations of sexuality, entails what Alfred Bendixen has called "covert investigations of psychosexual themes," encoded speakings of the unspeakable. Alternatively, Douglas reads Elizabeth Stuart Phelps's *The Gates Ajar,* a utopian novel set in heaven, as an incipiently feminist critique of the patriarchal and capitalist values of Jacksonian America. (Vineta and Robert Colby, 89, note that Oliphant reviewed Phelps's book.) While Moers deals primarily with British writers and Douglas with American ones, their differing accounts evoke not national styles but rather diverse and complementary strains that are too often homogenized in treatments of a supernatural subgenre. See Moers, *Literary Women* (New York: Oxford

University Press, 1976; reprint 1985); Ann Douglas, *The Feminization of American Culture* (New York: Knopf, 1977); Alfred Bendixen, ed., *Haunted Women* (New York: Ungar, 1985). For other feminist perspectives on women writers and supernaturalism, see Sandra M. Gilbert and Susan Gubar, *The Madwoman in the Attic* (New Haven: Yale University Press, 1979); Nina Auerbach, *Woman and the Demon* (Cambridge: Harvard University Press, 1982); and Elaine Showalter, *A Literature of Their Own* (Princeton: Princeton University Press, 1977). I am indebted to Elaine Showalter for several bibliographical suggestions.

4. Colby 105. For an account of the composition and revision of *A Beleaguered City*, see Colby 256, n.14.

5. Quoted in Williams 23.

6. These writers included Dickens, Scott, Wordsworth, Cowper, Coleridge, Burns, Voltaire, Shelley, Byron, Goethe, Dumas, Schiller, Thackeray, Macaulay, de Musset, Martineau, DeQuincey, Daudet, Shakespeare, Turgenev, Dante, and Moliere (Williams 208–9). For the best available bibliography of Oliphant's works, see Clarke, *Bibliography*.

7. Throughout the second half of the century, the "coverture" of married women by their husbands was gradually eroded by the passage of acts regarding divorce, child custody, the right to sue, and the ownership of property. (A bill for women's suffrage, having been defeated in 1866, was not passed until 1918.) Between the defeat of the Married Women's Property Act in 1856 and its passage in 1882, Oliphant became increasingly sympathetic to the women's rights movement. As Williams has shown, Oliphant's novels of the 1860s typically show women working outside the home (106–12). In "Earthbound," the elusive woman's resistance to Edmund's marital overtures (despite her pleasure in his company) suggests Oliphant's sensitivity to the issue of legal autonomy for women. Williams's bibliography reveals dramatically Oliphant's dependence on the Blackwoods and other male publishers, lending credence to Williams's observation that Oliphant prudently remained silent when she differed from the conservative editorial position of *Blackwood's*. One notes that neither "Earthbound" nor *A Beleaguered City* was published in the "Maga," though Oliphant's letters indicate that the latter sat at *Blackwood's* for months before appearing in the *New Quarterly Magazine*.

8. *Purgatorio*, Allen Mandelbaum, trans. (New York: Bantam, 1982) 188–89.

9. It is startling to realize that what Sontag calls for in her 1964 essay, "Against Interpretation"—"an Erotics of Art"—was described and rejected by Oliphant nearly ninety years earlier. See Susan Sontag, *Against Interpretation* (New York: Dell, 1966) 14.

10. The conclusion of "Earthbound" is worth a moment's consideration. Discovered on the attic floor, Edmund is "pale as a ghost," his candle "burnt out to the socket." Oliphant's allusion to Book I of Wordsworth's *The Excursion*—"they whose hearts are dry as summer dust / Burn to the socket" (a passage misquoted by Shelley in the Preface to *Alastor*)—suggests that Edmund has his heart, if not his life, snuffed out by the episode. One year later he renews his acquaintance with the Beresfords and pleases Lady Beresford (if not Sir Robert, Maud, and himself) by marrying her daughter. The ghost's fate, appropriately, is undetermined. That she never again accosts anyone may indeed mean that "she is earth-

bound no more." But it may also mean that her Purgatorial penance has become even lonelier as a result of her misalliance with Edmund.

11. Excerpts from *A Beleaguered City* are drawn from the Greenwood Press reprint of the Macmillan edition of 1900 (Westport, Connecticut: Greenwood Press, 1970). Citations refer to both the Greenwood and 1988 Oxford editions respectively. Oliphant and her son Cecco visited Semur in 1871; for Cecco's letter describing the physical features of Semur, see *A&L* 233–34.

12. Later in the novella, Dupin describes a trumpet blast, noting that "there was not one of us that did not feel that this was addressed to himself" (119;52).

13. For a thoughtful discussion of possible sources and influences for *A Beleaguered City*, see Robert and Vineta Colby, "*A Beleaguered City*: A Fable for the Victorian Age," *Nineteenth-Century Fiction* 16:4 (1962) 283–302. The Colbys mention the varied testimonies in Collins's *The Moonstone* and Browning's *The Ring and the Book* as influential, particularly the latter. The suggestion is interesting for revealing that, like these earlier fictions, *A Beleaguered City* also revolves around a trial: the trial of Dupin's authority. For a general discussion of Oliphant's supernatural fiction, see Colby, 75–108.

14. *The Cult of the Saints* (Chicago: University of Chicago Press, 1981) 17.

15. Madame Dupin's troubled faith is reminiscent of Oliphant's while mourning for her daughter, Maggie. Here Oliphant recalls what her friend, John (Principal) Tulloch, had said of Tennyson's *In Memoriam:* "The Principal calls 'In Memoriam' an embodiment of the spirit of this age, which he says does not know what to think, yet thinks and wonders and stops itself, and thinks again; which believes and does not believe, and perhaps, I think, carries the human yearning and longing farther than it was ever carried before. Perhaps my own thoughts are much of the same kind. I try to realize heaven to myself, and I cannot do it" (*A* 6). Like Lady Beresford and Agnes Dupin, many of Oliphant's female characters have had their faith and strength tested by the loss of a child.

16. The Colbys read *A Beleaguered City* as a "parable of the human faculties," suggesting the allegorical quality of figures such as Lecamus, Clairon and even Dupin (93). This reading, however, tends to underestimate the manner in which such allegorical characters complicate our understanding of Dupin. *A Beleaguered City* is both a psychomachia of Dupin and a politics of interpretation in Semur; Oliphant exploits this duplicity to meditate on how the public and private spheres are linked in the phenomenon of "official" representation.

17. "I have not the aptitude of expressing myself in writing, and it may well be that the phrases I employ may fail in the correctness which good French requires" (204;88).

18. "Introduction." *A&L* 22.

Part 2
Nonfiction

The Making of a Novelist: Oliphant and John Blackwood at Work on *The Perpetual Curate*

JOANNE SHATTOCK

IN the winter of 1860 Margaret Oliphant was thirty-one, a widow, and mother of three young children, and the modestly successful author of several novels and of numerous articles in *Blackwood's*. Her husband had died the previous year while they were on a visit to Rome, leaving her homeless, in debt, and seven months pregnant. Her publishers had been sympathetic. Henry Blackett, of Hurst and Blackett, had offered to come to Rome to assist in bringing her home. John Blackwood had telegraphed at once, inviting her to draw on him for as much money as she needed. Once the new baby had arrived, she returned home, settled in Edinburgh and wrote a stream of articles for *Blackwood's* in the hope that they would help clear her debt and further her career.

The articles were politely refused by John Blackwood, and his brother, but the offers of financial assistance were renewed. In a fit of despair, after yet another embarrassing session in which her latest offerings had been rejected, she sat up most of the night and wrote at one stretch a story that was to trigger the Carlingford series.

"The Executor" was published in *Blackwood's* in May 1861, and as Oliphant recollected in her *Autobiography*, "my fortune, comparatively speaking, was made" (*A* 91). It was a tale of an unexpected inheritance and a belated but accommodating marriage, and although technically the first of the series, it was not reprinted until 1986[1]. Its main characters, the lawyer John Brown, and the surgeon Edward Rider, were to reappear in later stories in minor roles. Carlingford was sketchily introduced as "a prosperous town where successive colonies were settling," with a poor district, and a principal thoroughfare, Grove Street.

In September 1861 *Blackwood's* published "The Rector," a story in one part that contained the kernel of the entire series. Carlingford was developed more fully this time, and had a Cranford-like atmosphere:

> It is a considerable town, it is true, nowadays, but then there are no alien activities to disturb the place—no manufactures, and not much trade. And there is a very respectable amount of very good society at Carlingford. To begin with, it is a pretty place—mild, sheltered, not far from town; and naturally its very reputation for good society increases the amount of that much prized article. The advantages of the town in this respect have already put five per cent upon the house-rents; but this, of course, only refers to the real town, where you can go through an entire street of high garden-walls, with houses inside full of the retired exclusive comforts, the dainty economical refinement peculiar to such places; and where the good people consider their own society as a warrant to gentility less splendid, but not less assured, than the favour of Majesty itself. (Chapter 1)

"The Rector" introduced several major characters of the Carlingford series: the Reverend Cecil Wentworth, the Perpetual Curate of the Chapel of St. Roque, "young, handsome, and fervid . . . on the very topmost pinnacle of Anglicanism"; the irascible Mr. Wodehouse, a pillar of the community; and his two daughters, the timid and somewhat faded Miss Wodehouse, and the blue-eyed and dimpled Lucy Wodehouse. The geographical divisions of the town were sketched out: the "best quarter," on the north side of the town, not yet called Grange Lane, the "horrid new suburb," to which young Dr. Rider was devoting himself, and Wharfside, the area by the canal with its bargemen who were Mr. Wentworth's parishioners.

The religious divisions of Carlingford were also marked out. The Evangelical Rector, Mr. Bury, under whose guidance Carlingford church had been "lost in the deepest abysses of Evangelicalism," has been succeeded by the timorous and reluctant Mr. Proctor, until recently a Fellow of All Souls. The former's determination to preach to everyone had half emptied Salem Chapel but had also more than half filled the High Church Chapel of St. Roque's. The lines of the plot were thus already drawn for *The*

Perpetual Curate, which did not begin publication until nearly two years later.

Oliphant chose first to pick up the thread of the young surgeon, Edward Rider, in her next story, "The Doctor's Family," the first to bear the prefix "Chronicles of Carlingford," which was published in October 1861. Between that date and May 1866, three full-length novels and one story appeared in *Blackwood's*. "The Doctor's Family," in four parts, was succeeded by *Salem Chapel, The Perpetual Curate*, and *Miss Marjoribanks*. In between she kept up a steady stream of articles for the magazine, and wrote her biography of Edward Irving, a project with which she became increasingly engrossed as she went on.

The biography of Irving was published by Hurst and Blackett, as were the novels that immediately preceded and followed it. A further novel was first serialized in *Macmillan's Magazine* and then published in volume form by that firm.[2] But most of her work over the Carlingford years was done for Blackwood. As it progressed, John Blackwood became a kind of collaborator, constantly at her elbow, commenting on each number as it was written, making suggestions, proposing alterations, correcting details, excitedly asking what she had in store for particular characters and on one occasion intervening dramatically when he thought the story had taken a wrong turn.

The first mention of *The Curate* was made in December 1862 when *Salem Chapel* had only one more number to run. Part of the plot had been established in "The Rector" where the love affair between Lucy Wodehouse and the Perpetual Curate (he became Frank in the new story, retaining Cecil as his middle name) and the abortive romance between Mr. Proctor and Miss Wodehouse were hinted at. The ecclesiastical terrain was yet to be developed.

Salem ended with the January 1863 number. Oliphant took several months before beginning *The Curate*, filling in with a two-part story, "Mrs. Clifford's Marriage" in March and April and articles on Lacordaire (February), Savonarola (June) and "Marriage Bells" (April). She sent the first number to Blackwood in May, telling him that she could not at that stage say how long the story might be, preferring that to be decided by its "natural development," but adding that she doubted it could be shorter than *Salem Chapel*. She was "exhilarated" by his favorable opinion of "his Reverence," she told him, and had the materials in hand for a "little exhibition of all the three parties in the Church." The

Curate's brother was intended to go over to Rome, and she would not be neglectful of "the claims of Exeter Hall."[3]

This was the story as it stood in May 1863. During the spring and early summer various possibilities were germinating. "I am pondering much as to the character and amount of miseries to be inflicted upon the Perpetual Curate of Carlingford but I have not yet settled what they are to be," she wrote to Blackwood. It looked for a while as if the story might develop beyond the boundaries of the Established church. She announced at one point that she was thinking of having a try at "one of the Roman priests of the Manning school," but nothing more developed on that score. She had clearly taken pains with detail. She clarified the position of a Perpetual Curate in the early letter to Blackwood:

> A Perpetual Curate is independent, but it is because Mr. Wentworth is working in the parish with which he has nothing to do and which it is in reality high treason for any man even the Bishop to interfere that he comes under the Rector's displeasure. So good an Anglican would not have taken such a step but for the sanction of the late Rector which I think may be held to justify Mr Wentworth for carrying on his work until he is absolutely interdicted by the new incumbent.

When the Curate's brother Gerald's dilemma over whether to abandon his family and his living and join the Church of Rome was unfolded in the fourth number (September 1863), she was reassuring. "Make yourself quite easy about Gerald and his wife," she told Blackwood. "I never meant that he should succeed in getting free of her—but I am at present in expectation of the most definite information from headquarters, having appealed to a cardinal in Rome . . . but I have no intention of carrying out the sacrifice—though the process by which Louisa is wound up to consent will I hope tell well in the story." Here too her plans outstripped the actuality as Gerald's predicament does not get even this far in the final version.[4]

Unlike many midcentury writers of fiction, Oliphant thrived on the pressures of serial publication, and her enjoyment of her work was increased by the special relationship that developed with Blackwood. She preferred, as she put it, to let her stories "simmer" until it was necessary to put them on paper. She thought it preferable that what was read bit by bit should be written in the same way: "one looks to one's points and by dint of requiring to keep up one's own interest has a better chance of keeping up one's readers," she told him.⁵ The system had its hazards. Writing too close to a deadline was a constant problem and it had caused difficulties with *Salem Chapel*. It also threatened her plans for *The Curate*.

By September she was behind with the October number. After correcting the proofs she decided to change the last chapter and returned only a portion of the proofs, chapters 15 to 17, to Blackwood. The altered chapter 18 arrived at the eleventh hour and was set up in type immediately. Blackwood read the revised chapter and was appalled at the change of plot. The number dealt with the curate's arrival at Wentworth Rectory and his interviews with Gerald, Louisa, and his father, concerning Gerald's decision to leave the Church. Oliphant originally planned to delay Gerald's decision and to extend the Curate's time at Wentworth by the illness of Charley, their soldier-brother. She then thought better of it, and compressed the second round of conversations between the Curate, Louisa, Gerald, and the Squire, and brought forward a telegram introducing their reprobate brother Jack, and summoning the Curate back to Carlingford.

The magazine was due for despatch to London as soon as the missing chapter arrived. Blackwood peremptorily canceled the revised chapter and sent the number to press several pages short. He did so, he told Oliphant, because he feared she would regret the alteration later, and because he did not think it would "tell well" to hurry "the Perpetual" off in a train by special summons at the end of two numbers in succession. He was also concerned at the abrupt introduction of Jack Wentworth and the short time allowed for him to get to Carlingford, find out about the presence of his old friend Tom Wodehouse, and send a telegram off to the Curate. "Now why will you run yourself into such a corner as this," he expostulated. "It is not doing yourself justice, & I am sure you damaged Salem by the same sort of thing." The foreshortened number would not be a very striking part, but "very good of its kind," nonetheless, and "anything was better than to let you run the plot into a mess," he told her.⁶

Oliphant was unrepentant, and also angry at Blackwood's intervention. She had not hurriedly substituted Jack Wentworth's telegram in place of Charley's illness. The telegram had been in the plot from the beginning and was merely brought forward to add variety to a number that contained virtually no action at all. "I don't at all like the idea of this part breaking off so abruptly. We must make up for it next time," she insisted, and was as good as her word.[7] The sixth number in November expanded upon the Squire's distress, introduced his eldest son Jack, brought in his telegram to the Curate and sent him back to Carlingford to confront Elsworthy, distraught over the disappearance of his niece, Rosa, and to be told of Mr. Wodehouse's illness.

Blackwood was pleased with the number and harmony was restored. "I am very glad you like Jack Wentworth," she wrote to him with some relief. "I was in some doubt about it, thinking that the execution halted very lamely after the idea I had found—but I think I have now got all my materials very well in hand."[8] The monthly rhythm was quickly reestablished and for the most part she kept two months ahead of the magazine. The January number was dispatched at the end of November before she left for a holiday in Paris and the proof returned in December.

The Continental holiday was to culminate with an extended stay in Rome, accompanied by her children. Shortly after their arrival in January, Oliphant sustained yet another severe loss. Her eldest child, her much loved daughter Maggie, caught a fever and died, five years after her father's death in the same city. Oliphant was prostrate with grief. Blackwood wrote immediately to urge her not to disturb herself with work but only "when labour comes to you as a relief." She was fortunately well ahead with *The Curate*, which duly appeared in February and March. The gap occurred in April and then, almost miraculously, the story resumed in May, with no noticeable drop in the tempo of the comedy. The new number contained chapters 34 to 36 and concerned the revelation of Mr. Wodehouse's will, the existence of Thomas Wodehouse, and the opening of the investigations into Mr. Wentworth's character. The June number continued the comedy.

Blackwood once again was delighted. His entire family had read the June number in proof while visiting relatives in Derbyshire, he told her, and their enjoyment was compounded by the fact that his brother-in-law had been a member of a similar commission sitting on a clergyman in the next parish on a trumped-up charge of improper conduct toward a lady parishioner. Oliphant's description of the proceedings was "as like as possible" to the real thing, according to his brother-in-law. The clergyman was acquitted and the Blackwoods had dinner with him and his wife, "the most plain looking old gorgon I have seen for a long time.

Archie and I whispered to each other [that she was] ample justification & doubtless the origin of the report," he recounted with characteristic humor.[9]

The novel was due for completion some time in the summer of 1864. At the beginning of July it was not clear whether there would be two more numbers or three. Blackwood approved of the August number when she sent it to him, reporting that Lucy was more captivating than usual, and suggesting that Tom Wodehouse be made to say something even more offensive to justify her conduct. He thought this in some ways like a "winding-up" number but said that the story could stand another, and advised her not to compress this one into a conclusion, but to go on to September.

The ending of the story in the magazine affected the timing of its publication in three volumes. This was a crucial factor in the financial success of the book. Early in July Blackwood ordered a set of back numbers to be sent to Oliphant for revision. She reported that she could see very few necessary alterations, and made scarcely any changes, her customary practice on these occasions. Once it was settled that the serial would carry on into September, timing became a problem as Blackwood's staff were adamant that late summer was not a good time to bring out a new title and urged that it should be left until the beginning of October. In the end, the three-volume edition did not appear until late October, which distressed Oliphant, who thought the unusual interval between the completion of the story in the magazine and the appearance of the first edition would affect sales, the public "very reasonably" imagining that it was not to be republished at all.[10]

For whatever reason, the sales of *The Curate*, as Blackwood had anticipated, were less than those for *Salem Chapel*. By December 1864, 1,000 copies had been sold, but by April 1866 the number had risen only to 1,368. This figure was for the three-volume first edition. A cheap edition published later had by that time not produced "anything to speak of," Blackwood reported. Nevertheless his financial arrangements with Oliphant were generous. As early as November 1863, before leaving for the continent, she had suggested that if *The Curate* extended to three volumes in length and promised to be as successful as *Salem Chapel* she should be given one thousand pounds clear plus a share in the copyright. As was customary she agreed to leave the settlement until the completion of the story. In July Blackwood wrote that he thought her proposal too much and countered with an offer of one thousand pounds for the copyright, with the prospect of more if the reprint proved a success. Eventually he agreed to her original proposal, adding characteristically, "we have never had any discussion about these matters, and I care more about your books being good and successful on your account than I do on my own."[11] Oliphant received fifteen hundred pounds in total for *The Perpetual Curate,* the largest single sum in her career thus far.

The reviews were unanimous in declaring *The Curate* superior to *Salem Chapel,* and in noting with some relief the absence of a melodramatic subplot. *The Times* for 30 December 1864 was the most effusive, declaring it "one of the best pictures of clerical life that has ever been drawn." *The Spectator* (5 November 1864), the *Saturday Review* (12 November 1864) and the *Westminster* (January 1865) lamented the absence of a Mr. Tozer and his fellow dissenters, but found compensation in Mr. and Mrs. Proctor, Louisa, Miss Wodehouse, and the curate's three Evangelical aunts, all of whom were celebrated with affectionately lengthy quotations.[12]

It was the very ordinariness of the story, the quietness, even dullness of the life described and yet made interesting, which the reviewers emphasized. *The Times* declared Oliphant to be lady novelists what Trollope was to the men, in "the entire absence of high flown sentiment . . . a firm, unbending, grasp of things as they are." Only the *Athenaeum* (12 November 1864) demurred, suggesting that she had gone too far in her portrait of dullness, and would only appeal to those who required their fiction to be inoffensive, unexciting, and innocuous. The review saw Oliphant as an imitator of Trollope, without his humor, strength, and knowledge. As a painter of country life she was a Miss Mitford without that lady's genuine love of nature and sympathy with villagers. Most reviewers found the curate himself on the colorless side. *The Spectator* thought George Eliot would have painted the "speculative" side of his nature. Lucy, too, was a disappointment, as were the escapades of Jack Wentworth and Tom Wodehouse.

Nearly all the reviewers attacked Oliphant's penchant for epithets: "said the dauntless curate," "said the middle-aged lover," cried the trembling little woman," "declared the irreproachable solicitor." Most reviewers were also skeptical of her grasp of technical details. The *Saturday* and *Westminster* were worried by Mr. Proctor's translation from All Souls to Carlingford and then back to Oxford. Others picked on the circumstances of the Curate's working in the Rector's parish, the status of St. Roque's chapel and even the impromptu chapel at Wharfside. Some weeks after its original review, the *Athenaeum* (31 December 1864) printed a letter that declared Oliphant to have written a clerical novel that displayed "a wonderful ignorance" of the customs of the Church of England and even to be ignorant of the definition of a Perpetual Curate.[13]

In general Blackwood and Oliphant were pleased with the relatively wide coverage. All, apart from "those brutes in the Athenaeum" had helped sales and even Oliphant found herself amused at the latter, concluding that Blackwood must have done something to offend Hepworth Dixon, the editor, as she couldn't think of any reason why he should be personally so spiteful to herself.[14]

Her relationship with Blackwood reached a new level of intimacy and understanding as a result of *The Curate*. He was to remain an interested party to her publications as well as a scrupulous editor until his death in 1879. His recent experience of women novelists, including one in particular of extreme diffidence and sensitivity, had no doubt stood him in good stead. He had learned to be wary of excessive interference, and also to curb his instinctive caution when dealing with unusual talent.[15]

But the relationship with Oliphant was unlike the one that had developed between Blackwood and George Eliot. There was no intermediary, no G. H. Lewes, to protect her, nor was this particularly necessary. Oliphant had been writing for the magazine for many years. Blackwood undoubtedly sensed that her talent was of a different order to that of his star novelist, and sensed too, that with her professionalism and experience she could take criticism and even interference with a minimum of fuss. She bristled at Blackwood's suggestions or interference and was shameless in her demands for financial advances, but their relations were those of long-standing colleagues in the world of journalism and letters, rather than the more delicate and, it would seem, more deeply sympathetic relationship that developed between George Eliot and her first publisher.

George Eliot had published four major works with Blackwood by the time the "Chronicles of Carlingford" were mooted. At the point at which *Salem Chapel* was being published in the magazine she had decided, with some embarrassment, to publish *Romola* in George Smith's *Cornhill Magazine*, followed by republication by Smith, Elder. Blackwood had been generous in his response to the disappointment. He had also been left with more to time to devote to Oliphant.

His generosity to Oliphant is reinforced by a comparison of his financial arrangements with the two novelists. He could not hope to match Smith's offer of ten thousand pounds for *Romola*, he told Eliot, and he accepted defeat gracefully. His payments to her up to and including *Silas Marner* had totaled £8330. He had paid sixteen hundred pounds for *Silas Marner* and had offered two thousand pounds plus a 30 percent royalty for an edition of four thousand copies of *The Mill on the Floss*. The payment of fifteen hundred pounds for *The Perpetual Curate* therefore, given the respective reputations of the two women writers, was handsome.

Ironically, it was Eliot against whom Oliphant constantly measured herself, and found herself wanting for most of her career. The *Autobiography* poignantly reflects the mixture of admiration, envy, and self-pity with which the ever self-deprecating junior regarded this lioness of a senior novelist. But the writing of *The Perpetual Curate* strengthened her relationship with John Blackwood, and it was an association that was to be crucial to her career. Although Blackwood never adopted the deferential and protective air he assumed toward his newer, more emotionally fragile female author, by the end of the publication of *The Perpetual Curate* Oliphant would undoubtedly have endorsed wholeheartedly Eliot's compliment that he was "the most liberal and agreeable of editors, and ... the man of all others I would choose for a publisher."[16]

Notes

1. "The Executor" was, however, included in a one-volume American edition of the "Chronicles of Carlingford" published by Harper in 1863 and possibly in earlier American editions. It was eventually reprinted in Britain in 1986 in *The Doctor's Family and Other Stories*, ed. Merryn Williams, (Oxford: World's Classics).

2. *Lucy Crofton*, (1860), *The House on the Moor* (1861), *The Last of the Mortimers* (1862), and *Agnes* (1866), were published by Hurst and Blackett. *A Son of the Soil* came out under the Macmillan imprint in 1866 after being serialized in *Macmillan's Magazine* from November 1863 to April 1865.

3. MO-JB, 19 May [1863], NLS Blackwood 4184.42; *A&L* 191.

4. NLS Blackwood 4184.42, 58, 62, 102.

5. NLS Blackwood 4163.97; *A&L* 179.

6. JB-MO, 24 September 1863, NLS 23193.

7. NLS Blackwood 4184.56.

8. NLS Blackwood 4184.70.

9. JB-MO, 3 February 1864; 22 May 1864, NLS 23193.

10. It was standard practice when publishing novels in monthly numbers for the first two-or three-volume edition to coincide with the final double number. The practice presumably continued with serialization of fiction in monthly magazines from the 1850s onward. The Blackwood staff's reluctance to publish in late summer would be understood in publishing circles today, but Oliphant was right to be concerned that the nonappearance of a three-decker coincidentally with the final number would suggest that the novel was not being republished separately.

11. JB-MO, 6 and 11 July, 31 October and 5 December 1864, NLS 23193. The price of the three-volume edition was the standard 31s.6d. The cheap reprint cost 6s, again standard. See *The English Catalogue of Books for 1864* (London: Sampson, Low and Marston, 1865) 12, and for 1865 (1866) 13. See also John Sutherland, *The Longman Companion to Victorian Fiction* (London: Longman, 1988) 628.

12. "Novels," *Times*, 30 December 1864, 8; *Spectator*, 5 November 1864; *Saturday Review*, 12 November 1864; "Contemporary Literature," *Westminster Review*, O.S. 83, N.S. 27 (January 1865) 332–35; *Athenaeum*, 12 November 1864, 629.

13. A perpetual curate was nominated and licensed directly by a Bishop to officiate in a parish or an ecclesiastical district. The curacy was "perpetual" in that he could be removed only by revocation of the license. New ecclesiastical districts were created in areas of growing population in the nineteenth century, and were sometimes under the charge of perpetual curates. See *The Oxford Dictionary of the Christian Church*, ed. F. L. Cross and E. A. Livingstone, (Oxford, 1974). Mr. Wentworth's chapel of St. Roque's is anomalous in that it does not have an accompanying district and his pastoral work in Wharfside is technically irregular because Wharfside is part of the parish of Carlingford, under the care of the Rector. Perpetual curates with literary associations include the Reverend Patrick Bronte and the Reverend Josiah Crawley, the perpetual curate of Hogglestock in Trollope's *Last Chronicle of Barset* (1867).

14. JB-MO, 5 December 1864, NLS 23193; Blackwood 4191.187. Oliphant clearly assumed the *Athenaeum* review was by the editor, Hepworth Dixon. There is so far no contradictory evidence.

15. Blackwood's most important woman novelist was of course George Eliot. Others who published in the magazine or with the firm included Emily Jolly, Anna Eliza Bray, Amelia Gillespie Smyth, and Elizabeth J. Lysaght.

16. Gordon Haight, *George Eliot: A Biography* (Oxford: Clarendon, 1968) 318, 357. For a fuller description of Oliphant's association with the firm of Blackwood, see Colby, chapter 5, "Author and Publisher."

Absolute Commonplaces: Oliphant's Theory of Autobiography

LAURIE LANGBAUER

> The everyday escapes. Why does it escape? Because it is without a subject. When I live the everyday, it is anyone, anyone whatsoever, who does so.
> —Maurice Blanchot

> It is one of the paradoxes of which nature is full, that the more close we come to the absolute commonplace, the more difficult it is to understand it.
> —Margaret Oliphant

I

MARGARET Oliphant, perhaps still most familiar to us from her autobiography, was herself always interested in autobiography. In her insightful and self-questioning way, she was also intrigued by her own interest: just what was it about autobiography, she asked herself, that made it so interesting? Between 1881 and 1883, in *Blackwood's*, she published a series of essays on the form, a series that directly poses this question. In those essays, she reviews a range of autobiographical texts, written by figures including the obscure Alice Thornton, who lived in the time of the Commonwealth, as well as the more renowned Madame Roland and Edward Gibbon. Within the writings of such disparately everyday and extraordinary figures, she finds a common interest: they are all, to some extent, engaged in "thrusting their own little tale of events between [themselves] and the history of the world, finding their infant or their apple-tree of more importance than the convulsions of nations."[1] No matter their own status or part in the world's extraordinary affairs, what interests all these writers, she finds, are the most absolute commonplaces.

It is just such moments of engagement in these texts that engage Oliphant. She goes on to suggest that such self-consuming interest (common to us all) is more than foolish vanity. Oliphant implies that we are unthinkingly intrigued by such unimportant details in part because they are crucial to what we consider important; she makes a connection between commonplace details and the realm of politics, between the everyday lives of individuals and the momentous lives of nations. "Even an apple-tree," she writes, ". . . is of use in its way as revealing that undercurrent of peaceable life which streams serenely on, whatever storms may convulse the air, and which is the real secret of national continuance."[2] The supposedly trivial concerns of private history are the stuff of history itself, and are what draw us to it. Oliphant feels that "the gentle calm of ordinary life" that we find in "the narrowest domestic record" is "as interesting and instructive as any other part of the perennial drama" of social relations that make up what we call history proper.[3] Such commonplace details are useful in their own way, crucial in their very unimportance. The nation continues itself through them—through a calm bereft of signal import, an undercurrent secret if only because of its very obviousness: it is made up of everything that does not stand out. We find our interest in such an undercurrent, and, in it, we may really find our history.[4]

In pursuing this theme, and mulling over the trifling details that make up these particular private histories—"the strange scraps that a capacious memory hoards up," she calls them, "straws and rags like the materials of a bird's nest"[5]—the question of why each writer is drawn to particular (unimportant) details becomes transformed into different questions for Oliphant. In every one of these essays, she is intrigued with why each author writes his or her life at all, what reasons he or she gives for pursuing this interest, for undertaking autobiography. Why do they think their personal commonplace books would also interest us? In what do they ground their authority to speak? Such would be questions of particular interest for a writer herself engaged in autobiography at the time, as Oliphant was, of keeping a journal of what she saw as bits and scraps to record her own life.[6] In those autobiographical bits, Oliphant offers explicit reasons for her own undertaking: to leave a history for her sons, who might wish to know and preserve her memory—but then, after those sons both die before her, she continues the autobiography nonetheless, vowing to provide posthumous income for her other dependents, although she admits that they haven't as strong an interest in or claim on her story.

That Oliphant's reasons for pursuing her own (self) interests shift with her changing circumstances, and shift to whatever allows her to continue writing, suggests that those reasons—and her need to give them—are more complex than she is able, or willing, to acknowledge. I would like to push a little further her interest in reasons—in what authorizes the writing of private history—by considering it in terms of her other interest—the relation of the private—the commonplace and ordinary—to that public record we call history. Oliphant finds a paradoxical locus for her interest in autobiography—in that which resists interest altogether, the very things we cannot read because they are so commonplace as to be boring, to refuse our regard or interpretation. Yet such ordinary details, Oliphant's writing implies, are actually what constitute the form of autobiography, and our stake in it. They are the vehicle that carries whatever meaning resides in our sense of ourselves, and resides in history itself. And the first readers of Oliphant's own autobiography seem to have understood her message. *Blackwood's* review of that book suggested that those who expected lofty cant would be disappointed: "To them this must needs appear the eminently 'prosaic little narrative' which Mrs. Oliphant avows it to be. But over the more ordinary members of the human race, who have little taste for reasoning high on such matters, it will cast an irresistible spell."[7]

The relation of the everyday to the historical record—of how the lives of institutions such as nations are inscribed in and carried by the quotidian, which we ignore as trivial—has been the focus of recent attention by theorists of social history, such as historians of the *Annales* school, whose general influence is perhaps best known in literary criticism through the works of Michel de Certeau or Michel Foucault; it is as well an abiding concern of feminist theorists, who investigate the ways women have traditionally been kept out of the privileged sphere of great public events and relegated to the mundane.[8] For such critics, as for Oliphant, the relation of the banal to history revolves around the question of the creation of the subject—of the intimate connection between the everyday and how human beings turn themselves into subjects, turn themselves into that which is subject to such institutions and nations. Oliphant's attention to the commonplace in her writing of and about autobiography reveals too how the lives of nations are conducted at the level of our daily lives; our private and mundane moments, rather than being exempted from such history, actually carry it. But Oliphant's writing does not just record the connection of the public and private: it tells us something about that connection. By locating the emergence of the subject in its everyday record, she does not so much shift the ground of history's truth, as put that ground—and that truth—into question. The absolute commonplaces of our private and public histories make those histories—and history itself—ultimately unreadable.

II

Just what authorizes autobiography may be important to Oliphant because autobiography itself seems like an act of authorization to her, an act of self-authorization, a way to become or create one's self. What especially intrigues her about Madame Roland, for instance, is how she specifically figures her own self-creation. In describing Madame Roland's autobiographical method, Oliphant finds in it that creative role most intriguing but also most familiar (even routine and accustomed) to herself: that of a mother. Oliphant is intrigued with the way, in Roland's tale, Roland's infant intrudes between herself and great public events, but in this case that infant is actually Roland herself: in recounting her history, Roland becomes her own mother, giving herself birth. Oliphant focuses on the way that Roland says "'This child,' . . . [when describing herself], her spirit rising with her own description, and a curious tender pride, as if she were describing the feats of a child of her own, coming into the torn heart of the woman, older now than [her own] mother [was then]."[9] Roland dwells on insignificant details of her childhood because she finds in them the source of the public figure she has become: those details, rather than the revolutionary convulsions of her nation, have given birth to the self that writes her life. In looking back on herself, and recognizing herself in that child, Roland creates not just the figure of the child on the page but creates her very sense of herself as she writes, sees herself as a self, as a figure created by her own private history. Oliphant tells us that in describing these homely incidents of her infancy "her own character dawns upon her with wonder"; what Roland describes "is the revelation to her of herself."[10]

In her autobiography, too, Oliphant is engaged in reading and writing herself into existence, giving herself birth by interpreting, but also creating, the homely record of her life.[11] In fact, this split within history making—do we simply read or also create the events as we write them?—does not much bother her; in her autobiography, for example, she tells us with uncharacteristic pride (disclosing what she calls "the privatest thought in my mind") that, in thinking about her own writing, by connecting the acts of writing and reading, she has found "unawares an image that quite expresses what I mean—*i.e.*, that I wrote as I read, with much the same sort of feeling" (*A* 118). The writing of her history in a sense comes to stand in for it; her reading of herself (re)creates and authorizes it.

But in what does she ground her reading and writing? Near the beginning of her autobiography, Oliphant tells us that she has taken it up because she has no one to write to but herself. She has no one else to whom to write letters, no one who would be interested in them or know how to read them, to decipher their undercurrent—"no one to write to, of anything that is beneath the surface" (*A* 18). Oliphant especially associates reading past the surface of others with the literary—and public—part of her life. When attempting to describe the kind of literary gossip Oliphant thinks required of her in her autobiography, she describes literary parties—the sort that mix "every kind of lion and wonder, great and small" (*A* 41)—at which they all looked at each other "wondering ... whether the commonplace outside might not cover a painter or a poet or something equally fine—whose ethereal qualities were all invisible to the ordinary eye" (*A* 43). Part of what such attempts at reading hope to uncover is the difference between the commonplace and extraordinary, and Oliphant is impatient with such snobbery. She tells us that she herself is indisposed to being read by anyone at all, and resents as a pretension attempts to figure her out (*A* 43). Oliphant may be suspicious of the ability of others to recognize the fineness in her, but she may also be suggesting that the attempt to discover the uncommon beneath the surface misses the importance of the ordinary. She may feel that she has no one to write to of the undercurrent of her own life because everyone expects that undercurrent to be somehow extraordinary. The point of her autobiography (which she takes up to record the crucial but inconsequential facts of her life when no one else will listen to them) may be precisely what Oliphant claims it is again and again throughout its pages: that hers was an ordinary and uneventful life.

Moreover, Oliphant does not in its pages herself claim authority as a reader searching for uncommon details (and the kind of praise of her as a keen observer that we find in *Blackwood's* review of the *Autobiography and Letters,* for example, in this way misreads her purpose).[12] One of the happiest early memories this writer records, in fact, is just of her failure of keen insight, a failure to find something extraordinary past the surface. She remembers the giddy joy produced when her mind is checked and can go no farther—of lying on her back

> looking up into the sky. The depths of it, the blueness of it, the way in which it seemed to move and fly and avoid the gaze which could not penetrate beyond that profound unfathomable blue—the bliss of lying there doing nothing, trying to look into it, growing giddy with the effort, with a sort of vague realisation of the soft swaying of the world in space! I feel the giddiness in my brain still, and the happiness, as if I had been the first discoverer of that wonderful sky. All my little recollections are like pictures to which the meaning, naturally, is put long afterwards. (*A* 20)

The meaning Oliphant may be putting to this picture and to her life is her very inability to read them. This inability to read seems generative rather than frustrating to Oliphant; she records the bliss of her sensations as a first discovery, an originating moment. The ground from which Oliphant herself reads, rather than being stable, quite literally seems to sway and spin. Her reading (of herself) seems to be authorized by this lack of authority, by the very mystery that resists reading.

Perhaps it is not surprising that this author of ghost stories and meditations on the afterlife should value mystery as mystery, finding it interesting directly because it remains unfathomable. The pull of such mystery continues throughout her writing precisely to have to do with (the creation of) the subject. In "The Fancies of a Believer" (one of those essays to which Annie Coghill, the first editor of Oliphant's *Autobiography* refers us in her preface as supplementing that life history), Oliphant acknowledges the difficulties of accepting the unfathomable as such, our desire to continue to try to penetrate the surface, whether of the grand scale of events or our own small concerns: "We all form our theories to ourselves, whether great or small, whether as to the economy of the world or our own little private corner in it; and make out somehow our little standing-ground, and seek a certain coherence even amid the mysteries we cannot fathom."[13] Yet, she writes, despite our wants, the mystery of life is never fully dispersed, and, instead, the standing-ground on which we rest our theories can vanish from under us:

> we are all more or less acquainted with the phenomena of our own nature, and the great fact the most certain of all, that we have no certainty of anything even in the most intimate circle of our individual being, and are never sure that we may not in a moment, in the twinkling of an eye, change everything for ourselves, or have all changed for us by another—our circumstances, our personal happiness, what we call our fate. The vicissitudes of human life is the most trite and common of subjects.[14]

The "most intimate circle of our individual being" rests only on the certainty of uncertainty, a mystery unfathomable and yet, Oliphant emphasizes, "the most trite and common of subjects." It is in fact its triteness that creates its very unfathomableness.

The suggestion that it may be difficult to put a meaning to such commonplace pictures returns us to the connection between Oliphant's two concerns in the writing of autobiography: the ground on which autobiography rests and the relations between the private and the public. Oliphant, who feels that the interest of an autobiography may lie "in its simple pictures," finds mystery precisely in those everyday scenes, mystery that has everything to do with their meaning as history.[15] She is amazed that such banalities so satisfyingly make up the stuff of her own record, "this prosaic little narrative, all about the facts of a life so simple as mine"(A 99): "When I look back on my life, among the happy moments which I can recollect is one which is so curiously common and homely, with nothing in it, that it is strange even to record such a recollection, and yet it embodied more happiness to me than almost any real occasion as might be supposed for happiness" (A 63). And she proceeds to tell us a vivid, happy, meaningless memory from that life—how, as a young wife, she used to look in on her own infants each evening and then wash her hands before sitting down to her needlework. Such reminiscences of the everyday, and not of the great public events of the century that her life almost neatly spanned, make up all the history there is in the *Autobiography*. Even in attempting to review her own public history, her career as a writer at the height of her fame, Oliphant can only remember more about her infants: "Here is a pretty thing. I should like if I could to write what people like about my books, being just then, as I have said, at my high tide, and instead of that all I have to say is a couple of baby stories" (*A* 103). Some of Oliphant's surprise here is, of course, disingenuous. She quite seriously and consciously foregrounds in her life's story what the world may deem trivial, in part out of what we can recognize as the guilt of the working mother, downplaying her career, in part to adopt the proper role of the Victorian woman, removed from the public sphere, in part to insist that the facts of women's lives are in and of themselves important anyway, no matter how the world values them. But in locating her history in such banalities Oliphant is doing more than (what is important enough) just insisting, as feminist historians among others always have, that the personal is the political.

For Oliphant also insists that the personal may be the unreadable. In her review of the life of Mrs. Henry Wood as written by Wood's son, for instance, Oliphant locates the banalities of life as the very source of its mystery: anticipating Maurice Blanchot's statement that the everyday is "what is most difficult to discover," she writes that "the ideal commonplace is more inscrutable than all the mysteries," and it is "that mystery of the unmysterious, in face of which we must all gape and be silent."[16] Oliphant's emphasis on her own ideal commonplace, her infants more important to her than the convulsions of nations (or of the reading public), suggests that her meaning goes farther than the witty put-down of a competing writer whose books she found as ordinary as her life. The importance of those baby stories, as she calls them, suggests that the very story of life is generated from such details; it grows up out of the meaningless and unfathomable surface of the everyday, which points to nothing but itself.

Throughout her career as a writer, Oliphant was concerned with the tension between the exceptional and the ordinary subject, especially the exceptional or ordinary woman. In her reading of Lucy Hutchinson's autobiographical text, for instance, she returns repeatedly to Hutchinson's attempt to live up to her husband's last request: to conduct herself "'above the pitch of ordinary women.'"[17] In considering what prompts autobiographers to write, why they feel licensed to create themselves in print as subjects, Oliphant considers whether they are exceptional or not—whether they are great public figures like Madame Roland, for instance, part of the record of important times. Yet Oliphant, who characterizes herself in her autobiography as a "fat, little, commonplace woman," ultimately finds such distinctions immaterial, the public no more privileged, and less important to the creation of autobiography, than the private (*A* 17). She writes of Madame Roland herself that "human nature at its fiercest departs only by moments from the ordinary"[18]—and Madame Roland like Lucy Hutchinson may be most interesting in the very pitch of her ordinariness. It is in this light, perhaps, that we should read judgments of Oliphant's writing in her ability to conjure "the beauty in the essentially commonplace," or Oliphant's sharp rejoinder that she "is concerned about nothing except the most domestic and limited concerns," when John Blackwood tells her he sees her in "the first rank of novelists" (*A&L* 198).[19] She says of the little-known Alice Thornton (when compared to a more exceptional woman like Lucy Hutchinson) that "she has no share in the greater story of the nation, and her chronicle, besides a great deal of small-beer, is occupied with herself and her own affairs, to the exclusion of most other things.[20] Yet such a judgment is not a criticism, for Oliphant finds Thornton's obscure autobiography worthy of note precisely because it seems so ordinary. Indeed, Oliphant's own life's history makes it clear that she thinks suckling fools and chronicling small beer no mean feats, and she considers her achievements at each—as a capable mother of the most commonplace sons and a writer ready and able to turn out any amount of work on the most trivial of subjects—so worthy of note that "it may perhaps be suspected that I don't always think such small beer of myself as I say" (*A* 137).

Instead, by recognizing the importance of the commonplace in her own, and others' autobiographies, Oliphant has formed a theory of history to herself, one that adds to the most recent debate on the subject. Oliphant's emphasis that the everyday is exactly what we are unable to recognize or make out suggests that shifting our larger historical record to the subjects' relation to their daily lives will give us no more access to historical truth than our earlier attention to great events. The vast fretwork of the everyday, simply because it is everyday, remains ephemeral, meaningless, unplumbable. The self that emerges in recognition of its construction out of such a record is one that must ultimately give up claim to privilege, sense, to our usual notion of self at all. The close of Oliphant's own autobiography ("I cannot write any more" [*A* 154]) might be seen as the record of her own such recognition of her place as a subject in history, her invisibility in its record ("I am in very little danger of having my life written, . . . and that is all the better in this point of view—for what could be said of me?" [*A* 17]). It might be seen too, like the check to her attempts to read beyond the surface of the heavens, not as a frustration of her endeavors, but the very end toward which she writes. As she tells us of the rather commonplace private history left by the historian Edward Gibbon, "autobiography can go no further" because history cannot.[21]

Notes

1. "Autobiographies; No. I—Benvenuto Cellini," *Blackwood's* 129 (January 1881) 2.
2. "Benvenuto Cellini," 2. She makes a similar point in another essay on autobiography written before this series: "There is nothing more remarkable in all the contemporary histories of a troubled era than the quiet tenor of everyday, which, after all, public events agitate so little. . . . Daily human life, which can make nothing of the seven-leagued boots of history, but must tread on its ordinary pace with its prosaic ordinary footing, walks through revolutions blindfolded" ("Evelyn and Pepys," *Blackwood's* 76 [July, 1854] 41).
3. The first phrase comes from Oliphant, "Autobiographies; No. VII—Madame Roland," *Blackwood's* 133 (April 1883) 494; the rest, from "Benvenuto Cellini," 2. In fact, in "Evelyn and Pepys," she suggests it is more so: "when the broad and general story fails, it is rare that a bit of sun-bright daguerreotype— a homely clear succession of everydays threaded upon some individual life—is unsuccessful in catching the eye and rousing the interest" (37).
4. In "Jane Welsh Carlyle and Margaret Oliphant: An Unsung Friendship," *Carlyle Annual* 11 (1990) 31–40, D. J. Trela suggests that the friendship between Oliphant and both Carlyles had a cultural and intellectual basis, and that Oliphant especially may have been influenced by Thomas Carlyle's ideas on history and biography.
5. "Autobiographies; No. II—Lord Herbert of Cherbury," *Blackwood's* 129 (March 1881) 398.
6. For an intriguing discussion of these bits and scraps as a narrative strategy in Oliphant's *Autobiography*, see Elisabeth Jay's essay in this anthology.
7. J. H. Millar, "The Record of a Life," *Blackwood's* 165 (1899) 896.
8. See, for example, Michel de Certeau, *The Practice of Everyday Life*, trans.

Steven F. Rendall (Berkeley: University of California Press, 1984), or Michel Foucault, *Discipline and Punish: The Birth of the Prison*, trans. Alan Sheridan (New York: Vintage, 1979). For a discussion of the relation of (French) feminism to the Annales school, see Toril Moi, "Introduction," *French Feminist Thought: A Reader*, ed. Toril Moi (New York: Blackwell, 1988), 7–8; see also Annette Farge, "Women's History: An Overview," *French Feminist Thought*, 133–49.

9. "Madame Roland," 493. In her own autobiography, Oliphant several times confuses her (writing) self and her mother, telling us, for example, that her mother's memories had gotten so mixed up in her writing, that she can't separate whose memories they are (*A* 97).

10. "Madame Roland," 491.

11. For readings that discuss her act of creation, and the role of motherhood, in that autobiography, see Linda H. Peterson, "Audience and Autobiographer's Art: An Approach to the Autobiography of Mrs. M. O. W. Oliphant," in *Approaches to Victorian Autobiography*, ed. George P. Landow (Athens, OH: University of Ohio Press, 1979) 158–74, and Gail Twersky Reimer, "Revisions of Labor in Margaret Oliphant's Autobiography," in *Life/Lines: Theorizing Women's Autobiography*, ed. Bella Brodzki and Celeste Schenck (Ithaca: Cornell University Press, 1988) 203–20.

12. Millar, "The Record of a Life," 897.

13. "The Fancies of a Believer," *Blackwood's* 157 (February 1895) 237.

14. "Fancies," 243.

15. "Autobiographies; No. VI—In the Time of the Commonwealth: Lucy Hutchinson—Alice Thornton," *Blackwood's*, 132 (July 1882) 94.

16. Maurice Blanchot, "Everyday Speech," trans. Susan Hanson, *Yale French Studies* 73 (1987) 12; Oliphant, "Men and Women," *Blackwood's* 157 (April 1895) 646–7.

17. "In the Time of the Commonwealth," 93.

18. "Madame Roland," 489.

19. R. C. Terry, *Victorian Popular Fiction, 1860–80* (London: Macmillan, 1983) 72.

20. "In the Time of the Commonwealth," 94.

21. "Autobiographies; No. IV—Edward Gibbon," *Blackwood's* 130 (August 1881) 247.

Freed by Necessity, Trapped by the Market: The Editing of Oliphant's *Autobiography*

ELISABETH JAY

IN the process of getting to know the collected oeuvre of Margaret Oliphant Wilson Oliphant, a task involving the reading of ninety-eight novels, fifty or more stories, four hundred articles and numerous travel books and biographies, I became increasingly puzzled by her *Autobiography* (1899). I had first read it some twenty years ago and the memory of this bleak tale of loss had stayed with me. It tells the story of a woman whose husband took her to Italy, knowing that he was dying, but not preparing her. She was left in Rome, pregnant, with two other children to support and heavily in debt. Nevertheless she set to work and managed to give her two sons the most expensive education of the day. She then took on her bankrupted brother's family. Yet, as she wrote the final section of the account of her life, all her children had predeceased her, her two sons in their early thirties. When her literary executors came to publish her autobiography, which she had left as a money-raiser for her niece, they recorded that "a great disappointment befell them. It had no beginning; scraps had been written at long intervals and by no means consecutively." Moreover the last twenty years had gone unrecorded, "and possibly" they concluded, "in her last hours she forgot how great a gap was left" (*A&L* ix). So they set to work to produce a smooth narrative line for the market. The impetus of feminist criticism and particularly the interest paid to women's ways of viewing their own lives has prompted renewed attention to Oliphant's *Autobiography,* but the articles that have so far appeared have all been based on the assumption that the editors of the 1899 version merely tidied and rearranged the leaves of manuscript to provide a chronological thread to her tale.

Her editors' task was greatly facilitated by the notable continuity of style observable throughout Oliphant's long writing life; nevertheless, they could not wholly obscure certain dramatic points of disjunction. Linda Peterson attributes these disjunctures of tone and material to Oliphant's consciousness of a change of audience, when her last son to whom she had hoped to entrust her apologia died and a public audience alone remained.[1] This explanation, however, does not fully account for the more radical, pervasive, and self-conscious questioning of genre that takes place in portions written even before her son's death. Philip Davis, in his fascinating comments on Oliphant's autobiographical writings, suggests that the *Autobiography* seems almost an antinovel in its deliberate refusal of definitive structures and in Oliphant's sense of the obstinate resistance of real people to be transcribed in the manner to which her fictional writing had accustomed her, but his observations are directed to an understanding of her fiction.[2] How so professional a writer, who had reviewed numerous biographies and autobiographies, with keen attention to both content and structure, and who claimed biography as her preferred genre (Queen Victoria herself was reported to have wished Oliphant to be appointed as her official biographer) had left so curiously fragmentary, and in places repetitive a record, remained an enigma.

Consider then my pleasure when I found two small volumes in her own excruciatingly illegible hand and my surprise as I realized that the first few pages I read were new to me.[3] By the time I had finished my transcription well over a quarter consisted of previously unpublished material. Some of this new material takes the form of small cuts, deleted by her editors because they were potentially embarrassing to the living. One example will suffice here to suggest the anodyne effect of editorial intervention. Oliphant met Leslie Stephen on one of his Alpine expeditions, accompanied by his wife and his sister-in-law, Annie Thackeray, who was to become one of her closest friends. The ensuing portrait captures the fractious irritability, sometimes approaching cruelty, observed by others in Stephen's domestic relations, but it transcends the temptation merely to repay with a vicious epigram. (1899 version in italics.)

> *I made acquaintance with Mr. Leslie Stephen at that time, a man* I had some little prejudice against and *with whom I had had a slight passage of arms by letters about some literary work, he being the editor of the "Cornhill," a*

prosperous magazine in those days. Not an amiable man by any means, not thinking well of his neighbours, given to putting in a keen little stab as a penknife quietly, a penknife with a fine edge. *I fell into a chance talking with him one evening in front of the Bear, when the sky was growing dim over the Wetterhorn, and the shadows of the mountains drawing down as they do when night is coming on,* not liking him, nor intending to like him, with a small grievance in my own person and a greater one on another account. *I recollect we walked up and down and talked, I have not the smallest remembrance what about. But the end of it was that when I went in we had become friends, or so it was at least on my side.* I don't know why. There is no reason in these matters. The reason is if one was to put it in surprising language that the man has a great deal of charm. He is a cantankerous person and has not a good word for anybody, yet he has a fascination which is more effective than any amount of goodness. I don't mean that he is not good. I have always said of him that he is one of the men who are angry with God for not existing, and cannot get that irritation out of their mind or their eyes, but not in himself ungenerous or unnoble, though spoilt by that determined prepossession against the order of things and the course of life. There are some people to whom it seems to be easy enough to be without hope and without God—either by reason of an easy temper which takes anything lightly and does not trouble to think, or for other reasons. (Is it perhaps a theory to take into consideration that we are not all intended to be immortal, that some may always stop and cease when this world is over, thinking no more and wishing no more, and being taken by God, as it were, at their word?) But Leslie Stephen, I think, is not one of these. He is angry, always angry for that failure, never satisfied, restless and eager to put out this discontent on anybody or anything. I used to wonder what would be the effect on such a man of dying and finding out that he had been wrong—and think that the wonderful surprise and relief that there was some other Being regulating all things would more than make up to him for any personal suffering he might have to go through on account of his own perversity and obtuseness. (*A&L* 145; *A* 149–50)

The passage is characteristic of Oliphant's style of reminiscence that is devoid of all attempts at self-aggrandizement by contact with the great names of the day. Indeed, her sense of his "deal of charm" is made to stand both as a rebuke to her own petty prejudice and as a reproach to the novelist's reductive habit of "analyzing" or "making characters" (*A&L* 12; *A* 21) out of the irreducible human spirit. The dull sepia photograph of an Alpine encounter that might so easily have done duty for a memoir serves first as a stimulus to the eschatological speculation of which Oliphant had become increasingly fond, but then the professional writer's control asserts itself and we are returned to the task of capturing Stephen's paradoxical personality.

The larger and continuous portions of unpublished material, however, were all of a piece, and written in each case immediately after the deaths in 1864, 1890, and 1894 of her three surviving children at the ages of ten, thirty-three, and thirty-four, respectively. These passages are first and foremost remarkable for the intensity and integrity of the writing. However deep her grief the cadences of her lucid style never deserted her, but the significance of these passages is not limited to the purely personal. At each stage of the painfully direct attempt to log the daily agony or recollection, desolation and theological speculation, Oliphant made comparisons with other literary outpourings of personal loss, and, from the first, when the sons, whose affections by Peterson's account, she was trying to solicit by her autobiographical confessions, were only eight and five, she ponders the possible function of such writing.

The first page of writing that Oliphant left to stand was composed sometime between the writing of the earlier stories in the *Chronicles of Carlingford* series in the early 1860s and her daughter Maggie's death in Rome in 1864 and is obviously the tail end of a discussion with herself about the wisdom of her decision in 1860, after her husband's early death, to remain single.

> To return to the idea with which I started that it was better when I steadily made up my mind in Edinburgh to enter without any props upon my natural lonely life—I am not so sure that it was a good idea after all. This was the time when I got into the last deeps with my work. That time when John Blackwood sent me back paper after paper and driven half desperate I dashed at the first story of the Chronicles of Carlingford and wrote it in two or three days feeling as if it was my last chance. It was the turning point. How sore and wounded and humbled and unsatisfied I was—what hard work I had to keep the tears within my eyes that time when they told me they did not want any story from me, lest the hard men—who were very kind notwithstanding, and friendly and just—should see I was crying and think it an appeal to their sympathies. How much better off I am now than then. I remember going down the hill to Fettes Row with my heart swelling and moved to a kind of anguish of resistance and determination not to be overcome. I had not a soul to tell my trouble to or console me. I had to put all the anxious young heart into my work.

How well I recollect the wind that blew in my face going down the hill and how it dried the unshed tears and I said to myself, "The tear that gathered in his eye, He left the mountain breeze to dry" and the children's dear little faces when I got home who knew nothing about my trouble. It was bitter at the time, but it is not bitter to look back upon. I seem to think more kindly of myself after all the follies I know of when I remember such a trial. Poor heart of mine—it has had a good deal to go through one time and another—but I was not beaten that time after all and from that time as it happened to the giant who recovered strength every time he touched the earth, my fall was good for me and gave me a new start. Since then, but never mind what has come and gone since, always a little more experience and some hours very fanciful and some internal struggles which there is no comfort in recalling, but no harm to speak of. And now perhaps commences a graver era; more guarded and cautious than the past— if experience ever teaches—which, however, I have already concluded it does not. (*A* 3–4)

This opening fragment seems to encapsulate many of the themes, mannerisms, and tensions of the later pages: the relation between her writing and the private need that legitimated it for her; the ability to range back and forth between the subjective and objective view of her decisions; and the recognition she developed that she was best able to know herself in the act of writing. (Indeed in later troubled days it was her habit to write out prayers to carry in her purse "to read out when my broken cries were all exhausted and incoherent.")

The *journal intime* nature of this entry is continued in the ensuing pages logging her reactions to her daughter's death. What threatens very briefly to become an embarrassingly private display of grief is rescued almost immediately by the self-consciousness of the professional writer feeling her way toward appropriate form. Within a page or so she talks of Tennyson's *In Memoriam,* which a theologian friend, Principal Tulloch, who was with her during the first days of her ordeal, had described to her as "an embodiment of the spirit of this age, which he says does not know what to think, yet thinks and wonders and stop itself, and thinks again; which believes and does not believe, and perhaps, I think, carries the human yearning and longing farther than it was ever carried before" (*A&L* 93; *A* 6). Personal experience had opened her eyes to the innovative nature of *In Memoriam* that she had initially reviewed harshly, seeing it as an excuse for philosophizing rather than a spontaneous and bitter cry of pain.[4] Tennyson had supplied her with a mode for putting "the long musings of my agony into words" and helped her to acknowledge the potential of this type of writing as an epistemological act. Such an acknowledgement was disconcerting because it abruptly raised the issue of the place of writing in her life. Her mother had encouraged her daughter's talent (in this Oliphant was unlike so many of those motherless female novelists of the nineteenth century out to prove themselves to their fathers) and Oliphant had taken pleasure in writing fiction from an early age, but it had always been considered "an admirable joke" (A&L 24; A 30) that was permissible as long as it accommodated itself to the demands of family life. This in Oliphant's case it had by 1864 already and quite remarkably done, since it had enabled her to bolster the ego and finances of an alcoholic brother by permitting him to claim her work as his own, augmented the finances of her idealistic but unsuccessful artist husband and achieved the single-handed support of her three children. Yet now she became aware that although she had been able to see these external demands as legitimating her professional activities as novelist and reviewer, writing was in fact for her a deeply self-centered activity. One of the greatest disservices her editors did her was to extract and transfer the following passage discussing this problem from the 1864 period to stand in the last portion of her *Autobiography* composed in the 1890s.

> I was reading of Charlotte Bronte the other day, and could not help comparing myself with the picture more or less as I read. I don't suppose my powers are equal to hers—my work to myself looks perfectly pale and colourless beside hers—but yet I have had far more experience and, I think, a fuller conception of life. I have learned to take perhaps more of a man's view of mortal affairs,—to feel that the love between men and women, the marrying and giving in marriage, occupy in fact so small a portion of either existence or thought. When I die I know what people will say of me: they will give me credit for courage (which I almost think is not courage but insensibility), and for honesty and honourable dealing; they will say I did my duty with a kind of steadiness, not knowing how I have rebelled and groaned under the rod. Scarcely anybody who cares to speculate further will know what to say of my working power and my own conception of it; for, except one or two, even my friends will scarcely believe how little possessed I am with any thought of it at all,—how little credit I feel due to me, how accidental most things have been, and how entirely a

matter of daily labour, congenial work, sometimes now and then the expression of my own heart, almost always the work most pleasant to me, this has been. I wonder if God were to try me with the loss of this gift, such as it is, whether I should feel it much? If I could live otherwise I do not think I should. If I could move about the house, and serve my children with my own hands, I know I should be happier. But this is vain talking; only I know very well that for years past neither praise nor blame has quickened my pulse ten beats that I am aware of. This insensibility saves me some pain, but it must also lose me a great deal of pleasure. (A&L 67; A 10)

By relocating the passage we can see that from the early period of her writing career it had been her habit to compare her work with that of the best novelists of her day and her lot in life with other women novelists. Charlotte Bronte became a yardstick for her at this period because Oliphant saw *Jane Eyre* as a literary landmark whose passionate strength had unleashed a spate of inferior imitations, known as "novels of sensation," in which, in Oliphant's view, women novelists capitalized on revealing women's feelings while using morality as a literary fig leaf.[5] Two aspects of her own thinking combined to make this tendency repellent to her: her innate dislike of such immodesty and her growing conviction that such novels created a market for a type of fiction wholly at odds with her fundamental vision of life. Experience "if it had taught her anything" convinced Oliphant that "the love between men and women, the marrying and giving in marriage, occupy in fact so small a portion of either existence or thought."

Yet her temperamental aversion to self-revelation, combined with the tyranny of the marketplace, increasingly hedged her in as a novelist. John A. Sutherland claims as an important distinguishing feature between Victorian novelists of the first rank and lesser artists the ability of the former group to use their autobiographical experiences to break the mold of the public's suffocating demand for more of the same. Exploring new territory, however, had economic implications: reprints of *Pickwick Papers*, for instance, always outsold Dickens's other novels.[6] By 1864 Oliphant had in fact experimented widely within available fictional genres. She had tried the *roman a thèse* form popular in her earliest days as a writer, adapted Scott's popularization of all things Scottish to the more domestic framework of her own vision and tried her hand at historical novels, before hitting her best-selling formula in the *Chronicles of Carlingford*, which clearly owed much to George Eliot and Trollope in the choice of an imagined provincial setting, though the handling of the material was distinctively her own. Yet she had not dared the full "expression of her own heart" and the iron hand of the market clenched itself even more firmly on her work in 1868 as she undertook the further burden of supporting the family of her middle brother who fled the country on his bankruptcy only to return a broken man on his wife's death in 1870 and to live out the next five years in a life of childlike dependence on his sister.

For twenty-one years Oliphant committed no more to her autobiographical musings and then a combination of circumstances seems to have prompted her once again to explore versions of her self. Between March 1881 and November 1884 she had completed a series of eight review articles on famous autobiographies,[7] during which she suggested that the function of the autobiography was to amuse and to maintain one's dignity in old age by finding a wider sympathetic audience to listen to one's experience.[8] Two further publications of this period spurred her to further self-evaluation. Although she herself was only fifty-seven, her writing career had begun early so that the deaths of George Eliot and Trollope, who had been her writing contemporaries, aroused a fin de siècle atmosphere within her. The monumental dullness of Cross's biographical account of George Eliot's life, with its total absence of self-directed irony, appalled her[9] and she reported herself "astonished . . . beyond measure" (*A&L* 4; *A* 14) by Trollope's intimate chat about his characters in his posthumously published *Autobiography* (1883). She had accustomed herself to laughing good-naturedly about "the systematic way in which Mr. Trollope grinds out his work" (*A&L* 258) and the imaginative intimacy he seemed to have shared with his characters combined with the extreme reticence about his domestic life suggested values and priorities wholly alien to her own, for, as she remarked in the last phase of her *Autobiography*, "it is exactly those family details that are interesting,—the human story in all its chapters" (*A&L* 122; *A* 130).

Without the human story, which natural reticence and good taste alike forbade her noising abroad, her own life, she felt would be incomprehensible. For she could not, of course, appeal to the single-mindedness of commitment to the artistic life that might produce an autobiography shaped according to the myth of progress that Avrom Fleishman has demonstrated to be so beloved by nineteenth-century male writers.[10] Over and above the sense of deterioration or aging rather than maturing that Cynthia Pomerleau[11] has suggested as typical of the female autobiographical perspective, Oliphant had a sense of diversity, diffusion, and even dissipation of energy as she reviewed her different selves. For honesty compelled her to admit that her work might not necessarily have been of greater literary merit had her circumstances been easier. More unsettling still was the acknowledgement that her ever extending family had been her alibi for the temerity of asserting herself as a writer and had provided a satisfaction compensating for her sense of opportunities and visions unrealized as a writer. Private circumstances now combined to reveal that the mutually sustaining interests of motherhood and writing were not, as she had striven to believe, interdependent but had become alternative standards by which the success or failure of her life might be judged. A nephew whose expensive education she had financed died at the start of his career in India and her sons, respectively twenty-eight and twenty-four, were turning at best into harmless parasites. Missing from the 1899 version of her *Autobiography* is the bitter reflection that if she does not herself put down "a few autobiographical bits" (*A&L* 7; *A* 16), "No one belonging to me has energy enough to do it, or even to gather the fragments for someone else." Despite her desire, after the death of both her sons, to convince herself that the work had been intended for them they seem at this stage to have been an irritant rather than an audience. The case of Browning's Andrea del Sarto repeatedly provoked sympathetic recognition from Oliphant,[12] but the comparison could be extended beyond her explicit reading of the relation of her life and her work: for Lucrezia's greatest betrayal is not perhaps her adultery, but her indifference to her husband's self-disclosure. Nevertheless it is Lucrezia's felt absence, her silence, that creates the necessary condition for his self-appraisal. In Oliphant's case, her sons' indifference created the necessary "weight of things unsaid," in Tillie Olsen's phrase, which allowed her to explore her hidden silences and to examine the way in which "Not to be able to come to one's truth or not to use it in one's writing, even in telling the truth having 'to tell it slant,' robs one of drive, of conviction; limits potential stature, results in loss to literature and comprehensions not previously admitted to literature and the comprehensions we seek in it. Compounding the difficulty is that experiences and comprehensions not previously admitted into literature—especially when at variance with the canon—are exceedingly hard to come to, validate, establish as legitimate material for literature—let alone shape into art."[13] Seen in the light of Olsen's remarks, Oliphant's repeated use of such synonyms as "bits" and "fragments" to describe her method as she embarked upon the main body of her self-inscription is not merely self-deprecation or a charm against the uncertainties of time and death, but a declaration of intent and narrative strategy. Differing "points of view," subjective and objective, varied genres: personal lament, prayerful meditation, public memoir, and family anecdote are all essential to her enterprise and are equally necessary to enable her self-deconstruction and hesitant self-recreation. Elegy discountenances a sense of linear progress; the fervency of her desire to believe in a divine final chapter to the human story is constantly challenged by a structure that underlines her accompanying sense of life's random plotlessness. Memory and recalled emotion are shifting sands, for in the very act of recall the signification of previous images changes as those moments of being are tinged with the ironies of time or serve merely to deepen the sense of present numbness that alone makes the process bearable. Here in her act of self-discovery and recovery Oliphant could take risks to achieve the ideal condition to which a later woman writer believed that fiction should aspire, "so that, if a writer were a free man and not a slave, if he could write what he chose, not what he must, if he could base his work upon his own feeling and not upon convention, there would not be plot, no comedy, no tragedy, no love interest or catastrophe in the accepted style."[14] After her last son's death two factors combined to force her autobiography back into the "accepted style." Her will to live and therefore her desire for self-reconstruction disappeared and she welcomed writing only as a distraction from her pain and a means of earning an inheritance for her remaining spinster niece. Her attempts at self-discovery had depended on her need to convince herself that she was more than a disregarded mother or the "fat, little, commonplace woman, rather than tongue-tied" (A&L 8; A 17) of her perceived public persona. Some of the anecdotes included in the more conventional memoir of the last portion do, as Peterson's article so persuasively argues,[15] present her own case obliquely in the manner to which her fiction had accustomed her, but now she shrank from "making pennyworths of myself" (A&L 75; A 95) and judged harshly contemporary autobiographies like that of J. A. Symonds, which indulged in "elaborate self-discussions" (*A&L* 80; *A* 99) in the belief "that the human document he left behind him would make up for the partial successes or failures which he had accomplished during his life."[16] Her reviews of this period, however, constantly privilege biography and autobiography over other genres and are at times equally dismissive of the "feeble memoir writers of our time."[17] The editors of her *Autobiography* entirely missed the self-directed irony of her repeatedly expressed conviction in these last years that most people would rather read a cheerful tale of "a simple, busy, happy life" and set to work to delete as much as they could of the most agonizingly self-questioning material since they were unable to see that it was precisely in these passages that she had attempted something new. Ironically the Mrs. Oliphant who had been freed by financial necessity into the life of a writer, then trapped by her commercial success, was in death once again trapped by a market that the necessity of her grief and need for a sense of self-identity had helped her to transcend.

Notes

Portions of this essay appear in my 'Introduction' to *The Autobiography of Margaret Oliphant: The Complete Text* and are reprinted by permission of Oxford University Press.

1. "Audience and the Autobiographer's Arts: An Approach to the 'Autobiography of Mrs. M. O. W. Oliphant'" in *Approaches to Victorian Autobiography*, ed. G. P. Landow (Athens: Ohio University Press, 1979) 158–74.

2. *Memory and Writing from Wordsworth to Lawrence* (Liverpool: Liverpool University Press, 1983) 273–96, 312–31, 343, 382.

3. The MS is now lodged in the NLS (23218/9). I am grateful to Oliphant's heirs and to the NLS for their permission to reproduce those portions of the hitherto unpublished autobiographical MS that remain in copyright.

4. "Modern Light Literature—Poetry," *Blackwood's* 79 (February 1856) 129–31.

5. "Novels," *Blackwood's* 102 (September 1867) 257–80.

6. *Victorian Novelists and Publishers* (Chicago: University of Chicago Press; London: Athlone Press, 1976) 153.

7. "Autobiographies. No.1.—Benvenuto Cellini," *Blackwood's* 129 (January 1881) 1–30; "Autobiographies. No. 2.—Lord Herbert of Cherbury," *Blackwood's* 129 (March 1881) 385–410; "Autobiographies. No. 3.—Margaret, Duchess of Newcastle," *Blackwood's* 129 (May 1881) 617–39; "Autobiographies. No. 4. Edward Gibbon," *Blackwood's* 130 (August 1881) 229–47; "Autobiographies. No.

5—Cardinal Goldoni," *Blackwood's* 130 (October 1881) 516–41; "Autobiographies. No. 6—In the Time of the Commonwealth: Lucy Hutchinson—Alice Thornton," *Blackwood's* 132 (July 1882) 79–101; "Autobiographies. No. 7.—Madame Roland," *Blackwood's* 133 (April 1883) 485–511; "An Artist's Autobiography," *Blackwood's* 136 (November 1884) 614–31.

8. "Benvenuto Cellini," 1–2.

9. Oliphant's review of *George Eliot's Life as Related in Her Letters and Journals*, 3 vols., ed. J. W. Cross (Edinburgh, 1883) appeared in the *Edinburgh Review*, 161 (April 1885) 514–53.

10. "Personal Myth: Three Victorian Autobiographies," *Approaches*, 215–34.

11. "The Emergence of Women's Autobiography in England," in *Women's Autobiography: Essays in Criticism*, ed. Estelle C. Jelinek (Bloomington: Indiana University Press, 1980) 21–38.

12. *A&L* 5–6 makes deliberate comparison of her own lot with Andrea's. The pervasive use of Browning's poem in *At His Gates: A Novel* (London: Tinsley, 1872) has normally been interpreted as a comment on Oliphant's frustration in her own marriage to an artist whom she recognized as second-rate, but the novel would repay a reading that focused upon her self-imaging in the artist who achieves his greatest work only at the expense of total alienation from his family.

13. *Silences* (New York: Delacorte, 1978) 44.

14. Virginia Woolf, "Modern Fiction," in *The Common Reader: First Series* (London: Hogarth, 1975) 189.

15 "Men and Women," *Blackwood's* 157 (April 1895) 620–50.

16. "The Looker On," *Blackwood's* 157 (January 1895) 168.

17. Cf. "Men and Women," 641 with "The Looker On," 159.

The Cry That Binds: Oliphant's Theory of Domestic Tragedy

DALE KRAMER

ONE of Margaret Oliphant's many literary activities by which she earned her family's and retainers' keep was reviewing books, in large part for *Blackwood's Edinburgh Magazine.* Her judgments of books often centered on their qualities as tragedy. Writing and evaluating contemporary tragedies were frequent concerns of persons of letters during the Victorian era. Victorian writers saw tragedy as an attractive genre, and unlike many twentieth-century writers were neither fearful of its aesthetic challenges nor perplexed by a sense of their own or their society's moral or ethical unworthiness. It is impossible to ascertain how directly influential Oliphant herself was, but her expressions of ideas about the centrality of morality in literary evaluations, about the significance of humble lives and ambitions, and about the dominant role of domesticity in readers' motives for reading are part and parcel of our present definition of "Victorianism." Beyond whatever institutional force they may have gained from their appearance in the magisterial and widely read *Blackwood's,* Oliphant's reviews comprise in themselves a long-continuing practical commentary on tragedy, and they also reflect the transition in critical consciousness during the Victorian period from the dominant awareness of Classical precedent to a less rigid but articulate grounding in community values, in particular Christianity, and in the inherent significance of the individual.

It seems fair to suggest that she was not an ambitious aesthetician whose primary concern was theory itself; but she participated in, and may have led, the shift away from the previous stress in *Blackwood's* (as in most literary journals) upon ideals inspired by Greek tragedy. Standards in Victorian book reviewing were never uniform, and reviewers even in the journals strongly controlled by their editors or publishers had a degree of independence; nonetheless, as would be expected, Classical precedent and academic conservatism encouraged reviewers to look to the Greeks—and in certain contexts to Shakespeare—for parallels and exemplars.[1] Admiration for Classical writing remained strong throughout the century, and indeed down to the present; but political and scientific developments in the Victorian age inspired novelists to locate tragic dilemmas and emotions in less austere, more "open" frameworks. Oliphant found more to admire than to criticize in the aesthetic and emotional effects of this shift. Her contribution was to give an extensive and consistent valorization of a subject matter and a treatment whose syncretic manner she termed "domestic tragedy" (using the concept frequently enough that it acquires at least retrospectively a defining quality). Herself a novelist of not inconsiderable skill with reflective awareness of private and actual as opposed to assumed motivations for behavior, as a judge of others' works she applied her pragmatic and sentiment-oriented standards to novels, poetry, and printed drama. Although in fiction like *Kirsteen*, to which I shall return, she was clearly capable of employing "tragedy" to define the context in a quite traditional sense, this is not customary in her novels. More crucially, the point to be kept in mind in looking at Oliphant's *reviews* concerning tragedy is the deliberate imprecision of terminology, the avoidance of strain, and the setting of limitations. Although she became well read through the course of her life, neither the pathos in her stories nor the concept of tragedy in her reviews or her novels relied upon abstract concepts. She was not interested in assessing artistic success by formula or learnedness. But while her use of the words "tragic" and "tragedy" may occasionally seem casual in its implicit refusal to draw distinctions, as if everybody *knows* what the words mean (in this she was typical of Victorian—and modern—reviewers) her usage seldom diverges from her sense of the poignancy of ordinariness, the pain and anguish in lives of decency and frustration and cross-purposes.

Although *Blackwood's* had a powerful reputation, which was enforced by its editors and publishers, Oliphant's criticism in *Blackwood's* represents not just the journal's position but her individual opinion. Nor was she merely a wind vane responding to currents in nineteenth-century life and thought. Independent-minded from the start of her writing career, she had firm ideas about life that allowed her to respond directly and efficiently to the many books that came into her hands. On both principled and *ad hoc* grounds, for example, she was at once critical of certain aspects of the women's movement while sensitive to and bitter about the difficulty of women's lives in and out of marriage.

Her firmness included an almost prototypically Victorian religious security, which remained stronger in her than it did in the larger society. In the larger sphere, as belief systems decayed, creating widespread anxiety, domestic emotions gained a power and aura resembling nostalgia, compensating for the sense of desolation and anxiety. Oliphant was not immune to these moods; indeed they were often her own responses to life, although in her case the domestic emotions complemented religious feelings rather than compensated for their inadequacy. That the situation was thus perhaps contributed to her being an ideal reviewer for *Blackwood's*. Although the late-Victorian *Blackwood's* is notable for its publication of some of Joseph Conrad's most innovative fiction (including *Lord Jim* and *Heart of Darkness*), its market appeal was to persons not given to intense analysis. Oliphant's way of viewing life—a cool appraisal of conventional behavior in terms of the actualities and necessities of life rather than romantic idealism—dominated her reviews for decades in the *Magazine,* and was comfortable for her audience, although her editors by no means accepted all she offered. Still, her forty-five years with *Blackwood's* attests that the journal's readers were not unreceptive to her standards and tastes.

To put the comments in this essay into perspective they need to be situated by a number of provisos. First, I deal here with her reviews almost exclusively; arbitrarily I am not attempting a canvass of her entire range of novels, essays, biographies, and the like. Second, as I have suggested, the topic of the writing and evaluation of tragic writing during the Victorian era is a massive one, and space permits no more than a superficial sketching of Victorian tragedy as it pertains to Oliphant's periodical criticism. Third, I don't wish to suggest that Oliphant was the only important shaper of ideas about tragedy during the Victorian era. I do not even contend that she created the concept or the term "domestic tragedy." Other writers for *Blackwood's* also used it in reviews—for example, A. Innes Shand implies it is a mode that mixes well with humor, characters drawn from the commercial class (not usually seen in Classical tragedies, of course), and mundane details of living.² The term has been used in relation to George Eliot's early fiction, and general studies of Victorian fiction deal with "domestic" writing. Oliphant could have learned of it while reviewing Lessing's "Dramaturgie," or during some other period of reading. "Domestic tragedy" is an umbrella term of widespread usage; plays as early as George Lillo's have been thus categorized. Nonetheless, it appears in Oliphant's reviews frequently enough to suggest it conveys a central element of her conception of tragedy. For Oliphant, and evidently for others, "domestic tragedy" was an identifiable kind of writing. Put briefly—and paraphrasing Vineta Colby on "domestic realism"—domestic tragedy can be described "in its narrow sense as simply a literary manner and, in its larger sense, as a whole artistic conception or vision of life," which has, like "the major Victorian novel," an "essentially bourgeois orientation. It is antiromantic, unaristocratic, home- and family-centered. Its values, its subjects, and its principal characters are drawn from middle-class life."³

I

Oliphant began to review in *Blackwood's* in the 1850s. Her early reviews involve considerations not of tragedy but of morality and decorum, concerns that she holds to throughout her career (with tolerance and increased breadth). Although she is not considering these early books as tragedies, the comments are relevant, especially in view of her much later revulsion from tragedies by such French writers as Balzac: she says that English novelists have tacitly agreed to avoid "all noxious topics," so that anyone can pick up a novel—a young girl, a lady, someone seeking relaxation—and read and discuss it with anyone, never having to hide the book. Oliphant sees this agreement as positive; she criticizes books (mostly "lurid" love stories) that transgress that principle.⁴

Her first review in *Blackwood's* employing comments about tragedy I have located was printed in 1870, where she comments on *Ginx's Baby: His Birth and Other Misfortunes* (shades of Thomas Hardy). The baby in question is the thirteenth, whose father threatens to drown him because he cannot take care of him. Oliphant notes that "The tale is told with a pathetic humour which is very effective, and now and then reaches the border of tragic power—which probably it would have reached altogether, had it not been necessary for the author's plan to bring in a variety of interlocutors" who object to killing the baby but offer no solution. (The novel portrays bureaucrats and supposed philanthropists who lament the lot of the poor but are ineffectual and self-serving in behavior.) The narrative ends years later with the child, now grown and still destitute, throwing himself off a bridge.[5]

The interplay of the values of tragedy and morality dominates one of *Blackwood's* famous attacks on Dickens, written by Oliphant. Even though Dickens's works are "of the purest morality," and even though his genius makes a whole range of unattractive characters well-loved, he has been unable to create one noble, truly good, exemplary, elevating man or woman: he has "not added one to that lofty rank where dwell the best of humanity." Even at his best (showing true knowledge of London street life and tolerance and understanding for the evil characters), Dickens is superficial. "His instinct leads him to keep on the surface." For example, "Sam Weller is not only true, but original. There is no tragic side to him. There is no real tragic side, indeed, to any of the Dickens characters." Probably Dickens is the only great artist for whom this is true, "for to most creative minds there is a charm indescribable in the contact of human character with the profounder difficulties of life." She thinks *Pickwick Papers* is more cynical (Dickens laughs at everything) than *Vanity Fair,* which is "full of deep and tragic meaning, of profound feeling and sentiment. . . . [Thackeray] sneers sometimes, but it is because his heart grows hot as he watches the pranks that men play before high heaven." In *Pickwick,* on the other hand, Dickens laughs at everything rather than assign blame, revealing a callow youthful attitude.[6]

About this time, the early 1870s, Oliphant began fairly often to employ the "tragic" aspect of life as one of the criteria of satisfactory fiction. It needs to be remembered that she had no university education, and gained her knowledge through wide reading— much of which was conducted while writing book reviews. It is evident that she was aware, or became aware, of what Greek tragedy amounted to, and rejected it in a deliberate, conscious fashion in preference for something more satisfactory—the sense that profound feelings are not restricted to a cultural or social elite. That preference dovetailed with her practicality, which scorned elaborate but useless learning.

Before Oliphant's reputation declined in her later years she held a respected position in the reviewing world, and there is a representativeness in her ideas about tragedy. As I have mentioned, her stress on morality falls in with expectations of the times; similarly, her perception of an ultimate dignity in the humble is individually characteristic as well as reflective of the political and social evolution taking place during her lifetime. But if Oliphant's views reflected these shifts, they had their own source and took their own form. They were not always expressed in terms consistent with the views of other major critics or of the creative writers themselves. For example, contributions to the Victorian revaluation of individuality made by such writers as Newman, Arnold, Ruskin, Hopkins, and Pater are founded in ontological anxieties and theoretical syntheses, Oliphant's in the lived experience of a parent, spouse, and friend who labored incessantly to support her numerous dependents.

But however empirical in their origin, these aspects of her outlook shaped the drift of her remarks about tragic qualities of non-dramatic poetry. In a long piece on William Wordsworth, Oliphant says that Wordsworth's point is that "the feelings of Betty Foy while her boy was lost were as deep and tragical, and as worthy of revelation" to the world as a queen's; "and there is no doubt that this is perfectly true."[7] In an essay on Robert Burns, Oliphant says, "All lives are tragedies," and refers to "the supremely tragic character of the lives of poets." An additional index to the broad relevance of Oliphant's ideas in perhaps unexpected quarters is that although her practical approach to life causes her to be more concerned with mundane reality than with generalized synthesis, her commentary can remind one of the handling of tragic themes by a more poetic and speculative writer like Hardy; for example, in this essay on Burns she observes that life is worthy and noble "so long as it remained in its natural channel,"[8] a sentiment close to many assertions in Hardy's stories.

In such comments one sees how alive Oliphant was to the democratization of tragedy, one of the major shifts of emphasis during the nineteenth century. An instance of her awareness is her identifying Margaret as the tragic victim of the Faust-devil struggle, arguing that this makes the struggle more immense. "The tragedy of Margaret brings the drama into a region accessible to those who have neither insight nor patience enough to follow that unending tragedy of Faust." A "universal and sovereign poetry must confine itself within the limits of common human perception and feeling"; a proof of this is that the majority of readers are interested primarily in Margaret.[9]

Oliphant's typicality as a Victorian in thinking the success of a piece of writing as tragedy depends on the morality of the protagonist is evident in "Percy Bysshe Shelley." She says that not only is the subject of *The Cenci* too horrible for tragedy, but that in the end Beatrice's allowing Marzio to lie, thus dying for her while she saves her life by her own lie to him, "is the negation of moral qualities which brings Beatrice down from all the advantages of her tragic position." The poet has preferred his "bigot-dogma of resistance at all hazards . . . to the far higher principle of personal truth and honour." Shelley's failure is great, a "wilful throwing away of a very noble tragic opportunity."[10]

To many twentieth-century readers Oliphant's moral criteria may seem to approach a fanaticism of perfection if it is unable to allow more sympathy for Beatrice than this, if it is unable to allow an empathy beyond primer-level religiosity. But her concern that tragic sufferers be innocent or guiltless makes her quite at one with her own time. She appears to be contradictory about whether Fate should be operative in satisfactory tragedy; and she tends to equate tragedy with nobility of personality and principles, maybe even religion and morals, more than with the complexities of Fate and volition, or with the paradox of nobility mixed with weakness. As do many other Victorian critics, Oliphant seems to prefer the tragic heroes and heroines who perish innocently, rather than the ones who bring about their own downfall, a preference that perhaps helps account for the peculiar sentiment (or sentimentality) that has since seemed a less than heroic quality in much of Victorian "tragedy."

II

These features of Oliphant's thinking are implicated in her ideas about "domestic tragedy." When she specifically alludes to "domestic tragedy" she stresses the manner in which it justifies a concern quite other than those traditionally associated with tragedy. Among other points, she notes its particular application to fiction and the novel. In 1873, in her earliest use in *Blackwood's* of the term "domestic tragedy" I have located, she contrasts this quality with the "great heroic tragedy of the drama." She cites the "very simple ... narrative" and "the melancholy completeness of that gentler form of domestic tragedy, which moves the heart almost more, by its greater resemblance to ordinary life, than does the great heroic tragedy of the drama." She believes that "novel-readers have an instinctive dread of sad endings, though almost all young artists delight in them."[11] In the novel being reviewed, *Alcestis,* the protagonist's success as a composer is made possible by a dreadful self-sacrifice of the heroine, although he never becomes aware of it. An opera-producer of despicable character forces the heroine to marry him before he will stage the composer-protagonist's opera (named *Alcestis,* after the Greek story of the wife who offers to die in place of her husband). She agrees, despite the composer's illness and impending death, so that he will not have to die thinking he had lived in vain. This feature draws the tone close to that of pathetic and sentimental "tragedy," and it provides an interesting variation of what is perhaps the most pervasive of all Victorian themes, that of self-sacrifice, especially a female's self-sacrifice for others' emotional needs. (The culmination of this theme is *Tess of the d'Urbervilles,* raising the thought that although Hardy customarily is believed—including by Oliphant—to treat harshly Victorian sentimentalities and conventions, his success was subsidized in part by his ability to exploit them.)

The more explicitly conscious idea of tragedy that Oliphant seemed to be developing at this time in her writing career, the early 1870s, stresses sentiment arising from non-elevated situations, the best ones being domestic trials. For instance, she presents Victor Hugo both in more-or-less traditional terms and also as a purveyor of those qualities she especially admired. Oliphant praises highly the portrayal of the three fatherless children adopted by a battalion of soldiers at the beginning of *Quatre-Vingt-Treize*—she says they take the place of the traditional love interest. "The episode is beyond praise. It is the purest poetry in its absolute simplicity—a picture at once so lovely and so true, so tragically and pathetically trivial, so heart rending in its playfulness." The association of "trivial" with "tragical" underscores a refusal to limit tragedy to grand contexts, and she uses the word "tragical" in at least two more constructions: "vulgar tragical conclusion"; and "Michelle Flechard is ... a pitiful tragical impersonation, never rising for a moment above the low level of nature, yet grand in the one overwhelming sentiment which possesses her."[12]

"Tragical" serves here as a deliberate approximation, imparting little more than "sad," or "something like tragedy." Paradoxically, the function of "tragical" here is to serve as a marker of imposed sentiment—so that, oddly enough, in this context "tragical" identifies an aesthetic quality whose merit in Oliphant's eyes is precisely that it refrains from higher and grander (and more traditional) tragic ambitions.

In short, Oliphant seems to be advocating a didactically anti-intellectual, pro-sentiment theory of tragedy. In 1874 she remarks that it's curious how all European nations agree on the preeminence of the Greeks, that they are firmly entrenched in the culture even though "rules of Art have changed," as have habits, thinking, and morality. Athenian drama included "the most gloomy and appalling tragedies that man has ever ventured to shape and give utterance to." There is not much "variety in these primitive little dramas"; and she notes further that the Chorus is not the "happiest of inventions" and that moderns can remain unmoved during presentations of Greek plays. Elsewhere she hints it could be debated whether reverence for Greek writers is a good thing, complaining that everyone is prejudiced by education. The Greeks deal always with the action of Fate, depending on a dread of "unseen influence which leads to crime" and a "whirlwind of ruin." Despite the approbation in her customary use of "tragic," she objects to the quality in Greek drama that is conveyed through the sense of impending disaster, or Fate (she thus engages another Victorian concern: approval of innocence made to suffer, but disapproval of attributing the cause of innocent suffering to a final Authority). Everything is in "gloom"—no bright light and shade such as are demanded by modern audiences. Oliphant comments that *Antigone* is "full of gloom so unbroken, that the reader trembles and shrinks as he reads"—only the sunny land of Greece, and the brightness of Greeks' real lives, could counteract such gloom. She objects to the theme of attributing evil tendencies and crimes to the curse of ancestry; she says too many hold that idea now.[13]

From what I have said so far critics or readers may think they have grounds to deduce that Oliphant's rejection of Classical precedent implies a lack of stringency of standards. But they will need to accommodate the fact that in the midst of writing reviews containing formulations of the concept of "domestic tragedy" she also reveals an appreciation of works written according to other standards. For example, she comments favorably on Arnold's *Merope,* saying it is a "sustained and powerful study of one passion. . . . Variety has been entirely sacrificed to intensity, and with reason," supporting the view that concentrated literary form arouses the most profound emotions. While she praises Arnold's imitation of Greek drama for its "severely-guarded unit of sentiment," her endorsement is guarded, tempered by the seemingly reluctant concession that she is "far from asserting . . . that [such] tragedies are unworthy of admiration." She seems to feel that with *Merope* as with Voltaire's dramas the impact provided by their "concentration and regularity" is of a lesser sort than that developed through Shakespeare's soliloquies. Thus even her praise for Classical qualities conveys again that closeness to actual life that is her predominant standard.[14] Oliphant also notes that it is praiseworthy to adhere to rules for tragedy "splendidly laid down upon the noblest of foundations, the theories of Aristotle, and the example of the Greek dramatists"—at least, so I conjecture skeptically about Oliphant's assumptions, if the writers are German. Her approval of Lessing's essay "Dramaturgie" depends squarely on its assertion of Aristotelian principles. She notes that the essay's "laying down of the highest laws of art and setting up of its highest standard is an educational agenc[y] of the highest kind in the development of German literature."[15]

Her own creative works are not written to conform to or illustrate a set of "rules" of this sort; indeed, occasional passages in her novels make obvious that what she does her best work with—the concentration on the subtleties of interactions between individuals within a family—is a conscious selection of material. For example, a comment on tragedy in *Kirsteen* is evidence that she could have analyzed "tragedy" along Classical lines had she wished. The passage is the climax in the mind of Douglas of Drumcarro after he has killed Lord John, having come upon him and his daughter Jeanie and overhearing his intention to seduce her to a relationship with no thought of marriage. His thoughts were not "specially about Lord John. They were the bewildered circling of a mind suddenly driven into tragic self-consciousness, about the entire chapter of his [Douglas's] life now perhaps about to be brought to an end." This is in line with traditional tragic self-awareness, a concatenating moment of recognition, for Douglas is thinking not so much about his killing Lord John as similar, but more corrupting acts he had committed as a slave owner in the

West Indies, including, evidently, murder of slaves: "Something within from which even if they should hang him [for the murder of Lord John] he knew he would not get free" (328). Such passages enrich the novels, here the characterization of Douglas, communicating the horribleness of his life in the West Indies that fitted him to be in his own person the most potent force in the novel. But although Douglas is a father, and indeed kills Lord John as a father full of passion, enraged at the danger and insult to his daughter it is the non-"domestic" aspect of his identity as the reestablisher of his hereditary family position—that is, in his depredations upon a slave society—that is at the back of the resonance of this passage. To put it this way suggests that the tactic of implying close ethical interrelationships may have an impact in terms of achieving tragedy that Oliphant's characteristic domestic concerns do not match. I am not sure this is actually so; but it would be curious to know how Oliphant would have developed an entire novel along a line of comparable density (dense at least in comparison with her usual direct lucidity presenting ordinary, "domestic" dilemmas).

Modern admirers of orthodox academic aesthetics may ask why Oliphant did not write more tragic stories with traditionally evocative rhetorical connections like this. My suspicion is that Oliphant's need to make money with her books was greater than university dons' with their books, and she knew that abstract ethical or psychological connections were neither as interesting, finally, nor as saleable, as is an emphasis on basic human issues that refrains from distancing generalizations.

But the matter is not just money and rejection of intellectual endeavor. Instead of manifesting intellectual flaccidity, Oliphant's frequent rejection of the notion of Greek models and her scorn of authors evoking Classical contexts can be laid to the fundamentally straightforward way she conducted her life and analyzed characters' situations in her own novels. Quite simply, in the matters actual and fictional she felt most strongly about, Classical precepts and hearkenings were beside the point. In one review, she asks why Lady Elliott, the author of the volume under consideration, chose Classical fables. There are too many of these. "What is Medusa to us or we to Medusa that we should weep for her? when there are as many tender and tragic scenes around us as ever were enacted in Greece, and all the passions that ever moved humanity are still in force in England?" Oliphant's firm verdict is that relying on classical myths is "one of the affectations of the age."[16]

In tandem with her applying an explicit concept of domestic tragedy, during the 1870s Oliphant further honed her sense of the tragic as a quality of individual works and oeuvres. For example, she continues to correlate the sublimest tragedy with the most moral feelings, and queries the importance of stature or worldly greatness as a prerequisite for tragedy. One of her statements indicates that a tragedy can be "not noble, . . . not sublime, . . . but yet heart-rending in its pathos and force of indignant reality"; and she argues for due restraint in plotting, saying that "extravagant means . . . beyond the range of legitimate art" cannot be allowed, "however necessary it may be to the tragical intention of the drama." She expresses admiration for a genius like Balzac, who in *Père Goriot* creates an "awful tragedy" that can "weave every combination of folly and wickedness into its somber web, without losing the higher force of fate and misery in it"; but she objects (in terms common in Victorian reviewing of French writing) to "monstrous," "sickening," and "nauseous" scenes such materials result in at the hands of less capable writers than Balzac and Daudet.[17] (In 1887, as if to underscore an abiding preference for domestic rationales, Oliphant's reason for admiring *Père Goriot* is "that horrible, tragical *self-sacrifice* of paternal love" that throws away everything, including morals, for daughters.)[18]

Oliphant's preference for domestic tragedy was not restrictive or blinkered. She recognized that special cases like Hamlet ignore boundaries of a scheme: "No other tragic creation . . . has the same hold upon us. . . . [Hamlet] is a part of our intellectual training, of our higher being, of all the mysteries that move within us, and so often burst into unconscious expression in his very words."[19] Of course she may be parroting common wisdom of the nineteenth century about the uncircumscribable vigor of this play, but this passage also goes against her ordinary emphasis upon commonly felt domestic feelings in tragedy. She is able to incorporate the complexity of an unprecedented (and rationally inexplicable) response. This is in keeping with one of the essential merits of Oliphant's reliance on common sense, that it allows her to elide the formal constraints of a genre. She was one of the several Victorian critics (but, and this is the point, they are probably still in the minority) who discount one of the most traditional aspects of tragedy of all, its basis in stage representation. As I've already noted, and as is obvious from her comments on novels of domestic tragedy, she rejects the idea that drama is the necessary medium for the effects she describes as tragic. Honoring the Queen's Jubilee, Oliphant in a survey of half a century's writing cites no dramatic tragedies but several prose pieces and poems for their "tragic" writing—including Carlyle's *French Revolution* ("the one mad and horrible moment of modern history in which all that was permitted to the ancient drama, the pity and the terror of solemn fate, is overpassed in the horror of that tragedy of real life which knows no limits"),[20] George Eliot's *Adam Bede* (Hetty Sorrel's quest for her lover and betrayer), and several novels by Trollope ("touches in the tragic history of Mr. Crawley; . . . Lady Mason's . . . crime; . . . that ludicrous tragedy of the unfaithful Crosbie").

It seems obvious that Oliphant has, if not a formal definition, a *concept* of tragedy, one that arises out of the context of the literary work she is reviewing and that focuses her attention. The phrase "domestic tragedy" is employed in usually evaluative references to hearth and home, a steady concern of Oliphant in her fiction as well. Writing about Turgenev, Oliphant discusses "domestic tragedy" concerning the scene in *Fathers and Sons* in which Bazarof returns to his home and dislikes being around his parents: "This is the truest and tenderest strain of domestic tragedy—the poetry of our day which is not involved in great catastrophes or alarming events, but which finds in the commonest incidents of life all those elements of pity and of terror that the poet requires."[21]

III

These concerns shape several of her reviews written in the decade of the 1880s. She does not have to employ directly the term "domestic tragedy" for us to identify what interests her. Commenting in "The Old Saloon" (the name given to the commentary column she frequently wrote) on de Maupassant's *Pierre and Jean*, Oliphant makes points very close to those she made about Turgenev in 1880. In de Maupassant's story, an older brother discovers his younger brother is the result of their mother's affair with a family friend. The tragedy is his awareness of his mother's shame, and her awareness of *his* awareness. De Maupassant's story is "one of those mute tragedies, which may be carried on sometimes within the closest enclosure of a family circle." Pierre has the "tragic certainty" that his mother guesses his suspicions, but is unable to desist from his enquiry in spite of his love for his gentle mother. There are no grand scenes of revelation, no "self-sacrifice": "Great scandals are not in the way of the ordinary and commonplace people among whom, all the same, the greatest tragedies may be enacted." There is no exposure of the secret, "only how to go on, and spread a decent veil over the tragedy, and continue to live." "The very environment of ordinary existence" (the sea, his father's shop, the widow he loves who prefers his brother) "enhance[s] the tragic effect."[22]

Several observations in these reviews have bearing upon Oliphant's own life. In one, Oliphant becomes quite enthusiastic about a story (in a book she found otherwise boring) about a wife whose tragedy is a husband who did not do as well as expected; she had to behave publicly as if all were well, to support the family by translating books and articles, to bear with disappointments and to accept him as he was—all of which of course closely parallels Oliphant's own marital history. "This domestic tragedy, so silent, so covered over with shields of affection and respect, and all the decorums of life, is by far the most interesting thing in this book"; this story has the "highest elements of tragedy."[23] A similar review deals with a novel, *Grania* by Emily Lawless, whose heroine supports a smooth-talking Irishman who doesn't work. "Her silence as she labours on, listening to the vapouring of the lout whose thoughts are all on himself; her sudden impatiences and revolts, the quick uprisings of again another and another hope, embody the whole tragedy of womankind in perhaps its deepest phase."[24] While here Frank Oliphant may not be in his widow's mind, possibly she could have been thinking of her brothers Willie or Frank, who after failing to find and keep jobs devolved upon her without evident lamentation or regret, or of her older son Cyril.

Until near the end of her life Oliphant continued to write reviews, with no indication that her views of the tragic once established by the mid-1870s changed significantly. She always preferred to reflect on the pains endemic to everyday life rather than on those endemic to specialness or eminence. And she always had her doubts about the ethical and moral value of a supposedly ennobling art form. "Tragedy is no doubt the highest art, but it is painful to have in a novel nobody of whom we can approve, nor any incident upon which the mind can rest with pleasure."[25]

An implicit challenge to much of what I have written here is that—despite the similarity between Oliphant's idea of tragedy in the ordinary humdrumness of life and the experiments in fiction over several decades climaxed by Hardy's *Tess of the d'Urbervilles*—she makes no reference to this novel's tragic qualities in her review of the book. One might take this as an indication that Oliphant was not able to recognize tragedy without more direct authorial guidance than even Hardy gives; but I suspect—in addition to acknowledging that reviewers are not required to force every review to turn on the linchpin of a "theory"—that the absence of such comment reflects her view that at the core of this controversial novel is a profound confusion. Assessing the novel's quality as tragedy was not relevant for her as long as Hardy did not know what were his strengths, and what was fanciful, in his plot events and characterizations. The novel simply did not come up to the mark. This, in spite of her approval of Hardy's "good brown soil and substantial flesh and blood, and the cows . . .—which he makes us smell and see. Here is the genuine article at last." Her preference for plausibility and her insistence that fiction adhere to common procedures are evident in her disclaiming any belief in Angel, either in reacting as he does initially to Tess's confession or in accepting her "without a moment's hesitation" as she comes to him straight from Alec's bed at the end of the novel; and in her skepticism that an intelligent girl, as Tess is presented, would have either ridden away with Alec on horseback at night to escape the teasing of her fellow-servants, gone back to Alec, or killed him. "It is no use making men and women for us, and then forcing them to do the last thing possible to their nature."[26] An ironic aspect in her review is that she thinks Hardy's "indignant anti-religion" is droll and even amusing, since, if he doesn't believe in God, with whom is he so angry?

This kind of wryness or tolerance, so characteristic of Oliphant's reviews and indeed of her approach to life, was exhausted by the time Hardy's next novel appeared, and she is barely able to control her feelings in her review of *Jude the Obscure*, whose tack is clearly indicated in its title, "The Anti-Marriage League."[27] It is again ironic that as with *Tess of the d'Urbervilles* she does not consider tragedy in relation to *Jude*, so that we have the strange situation in which a principal theorist and practitioner of "domestic tragedy" did not recognize the deep appropriateness of this approach to two of the century's most ambitious expressions of the tragic possibilities in ordinary individuals. Perhaps, wearied almost literally to death by her family griefs and the deterioration of her literary reputation, she took refuge in the ironic (and perhaps bitter) derision of Hardy's poor scholarship, implausibilities, and artificially elevated tone in *Tess*. On all these points she has a great deal of fun, and indeed her criticisms are still amusing. But there are no openings for levity in her comments on *Jude the Obscure*. Her misapprehension of Hardy's aims in *Tess*, and the complete rejection of *Jude* with Hardy's resulting contemptuous dismissal of her as a prolix and unselfcritical hack, make for a poignant ending of a productive and resourceful career. (For an alternative reading of this incident, see Merryn Williams's essay and D. J. Trela's "Introduction.")

It is particularly regrettable that this one essay, which attacked *Jude* only as one of several recent novels whose morality and effect she detested and resented, has had a greater impact on Oliphant's standing in literary history than the number and quality of novels she wrote and greater than the massive commonsensical and generally sensitive commentary on literature she compiled in the pages of *Blackwood's* and elsewhere. A fairer appraisal would note that in her literary commentary in *Blackwood's*, Margaret Oliphant took considerable care in giving substance to a theory of tragedy—that is, a standard for judging "tragedy," which in its wider application was a standard for judging literature, and in its more personal ramifications a description of what she herself attempted to perform in her novels.

Notes

1. Two essays relevant to this point, particularly because they show the flexibility with which Greek precedent could be applied, are Thomas De Quincey, "Theory of Greek Tragedy," *Blackwood's* 47 (February 1840) 145–53, and Archibald Alison, "The Greek and Romantic Drama," *Blackwood's* 59 (January 1846) 54–73.

2. Shand, "Balzac," *Blackwood's* 121 (March 1877) 300–23; especially 314. For the identification of authorship of this and other reviews discussed in this essay I am indebted to the *Wellesley Index to Victorian Periodicals, 1824–1900*, ed. Walter E. Houghton (University of Toronto Press, 1966), vol. 1. I am also indebted to my research assistant, Mary Jane Brown, for her many astute com-

ments and her close attention to detail during the preliminary stage of this project.

3. Vineta Colby, *Yesterday's Woman: Domestic Realism in the English Novel* (Princeton University Press, 1974) 3–4. This definition I think would not be rejected by Oliphant. See also Harold Orel, *Victorian Literary Critics: George Henry Lewes, Walter Bagehot, Richard Holt, Leslie Stephen, Andrew Lang, George Saintsbury, and Edmund Gosse* (London: Macmillan, 1984) 162: George Saintsbury concerning Elizabeth Gaskell.

Oliphant had for much of her career an idea about her audience, as defined by the Colbys, that confirms the general direction of her observations about domestic tragedy: "All in all, Mrs. Oliphant stood by her conviction, first voiced in disparagement of Hawthorne, that 'the novelist's true audience is the common people of ordinary comprehension and everyday sympathies, whatever their rank may be'" (190). She also held to her own literary standards: another observation in the Colby's study would support a contention that Oliphant's judgments of writings aspiring to tragedy could be stringent: "Praise for Joanna Baillie's fine delicacy and gentility is followed by this shaft: 'Perhaps, however, we must add, such a one is very inadequately qualified for the composition of tragedies, especially those that deal with the passions'" (194).

What Oliphant refers to as "feminine cynicism" could be correlated with "domestic tragedy" as another way of measuring her aesthetic/literary quality. Merryn Williams quotes one of Oliphant's definitions of feminine cynicism: "It is something altogether different from the rude and brutal male quality that bears the same name. It is the soft and silent disbelief of a spectator who has to look at a great many things without showing any outward discomposure, and who has learned to give up any moral classification of social sins, and to place them instead on the level of absurdities. She is not surprised or offended, much less horror-stricken or indignant, when her people show vulgar or mean traits of character, when they make it evident how selfish and self-absorbed they are, or even when they fall into those social cruelties which selfish and stupid people are so often guilty of, not without intention, but yet without the power of realising half the pain they inflict. . . . This position of mind is essentially feminine" (Williams 55).

4. A strong example is "New Novels," *Blackwood's* 102 (September 1867) 257–80, Cf. also *Blackwood's* 160 (December 1896) 822–46; especially 841–42.

5. "New Novels," *Blackwood's* 108 (November 1870) 607–31; especially 622–24.

6. "Charles Dickens," *Blackwood's* 109 (June 1871) 673–95; especially 675, 678, 679.

7. "William Wordsworth," *Blackwood's* 110 (September 1871) 299–326; especially 312.

8. "Robert Burns," *Blackwood's* 111 (February 1872) 140–68; especially 140, 149.

9. "Johanne Wolfgang Goethe," *Blackwood's* 112 (December 1872) 675–97; especially 693–94.

10. "Percy Bysshe Shelley," *Blackwood's* 111 (April 1872) 415–40; especially 437–38.

11. "New Books," *Blackwood's* 114 (November 1873) 596–617; especially 614.

12. "Victor Hugo's Quatre-Vingt-Treize," *Blackwood's* 115 (June 1874) 750–69; especially 755, 758, 762.

13. "The Ancient Classics," *Blackwood's* 116 (September 1874) 365–86; especially 365, 372, 376–77.

14. "Voltaire," *Blackwood's* 111 (March 1872) 270–90; especially 283.

15. "New Books," *Blackwood's* 123 (March 1878) 305–27, especially 309.

16. "New Books," *Blackwood's* 123 (June 1878) 681–702; especially 701.

17. "The Novels of Alphonse Daudet," *Blackwood's* 125 (January 1879) 93–111; especially 104, 110, 93.

18. "The Old Saloon: French Contemporary Novelists," *Blackwood's* 141 (May 1887) 683–710.

19. "Hamlet," *Blackwood's* 125 (April 1879) 462–81; especially 462.

20. "The Old Saloon: The Literature of the Last Fifty Years," *Blackwood's* 141 (June 1887) 737–61; especially 747–48.

21. "Russia and Nihilism in the Novels of M. Tourgenief,' *Blackwood's* 127 (May 1880) 623–47; especially 634. There seems to be a correlation between Oliphant's views of "domestic tragedy" and her theory of the everyday and ordinary in autobiography. See Laurie Langbauer's essay in this collection.

22. "The Old Saloon," *Blackwood's* 144 (September 1888) 419–43; especially 441, 443.

23. "The Old Saloon," *Blackwood's* 144 (December 1888) 874–99; especially 895.

24. "The Old Saloon," *Blackwood's* 152 (October 1892) 574–96; especially 595.

25. "The Old Saloon," *Blackwood's* 146 (December 1889) 857–78; especially 878.

26. "The Old Saloon," *Blackwood's* 151 (March 1892) 455–74; especially 473–74.

27. "The Anti-Marriage League," *Blackwood's* 159 (January 1896) 135–49.

Feminist or Antifeminist? Oliphant and the Woman Question

MERRYN WILLIAMS

ON 16 August 1866 Margaret Oliphant wrote to her publisher John Blackwood:

> I send you a little paper I have just finished about Stuart Mill and his mad notion of the franchise for women. . . . Probably you will find it too respectful to Mr Mill, but I can't for my part find any satisfaction in simply jeering at a man who may do a foolish thing in his life but yet is a great philosopher. (A&L 211)

This has often been used against her by people who have read neither the article nor much else she wrote. Until quite recently, when her novels began to come into print again, most knowledge of her was based on the *Autobiography and Letters* from which this quotation is taken. The "fact" that she thought women's suffrage a "mad notion" has passed into literary history, and she has not been admired by feminist critics, one of whom, Patricia Stubbs, writes:

> The superficially emancipated heroines of novelists like . . . Mrs Oliphant. . . remain well within the limits of moral and social convention. Their independent-minded young ladies have shed the fragility and insipidity so admired by Wilkie Collins, but they are in no way a serious challenge to patriarchal stereotypes of feminine character or behaviour. . . . She maintained a consistently conservative attitude towards the emancipation movement.[1]

The truth is, though, that her views were neither conservative nor, over a career of nearly fifty years, consistent. "I suppose the ideas of the time do get into one's head," she wrote privately in 1895, "however much one may disapprove of them."[2]

The *Autobiography and Letters,* published in 1899 and reprinted without corrections four times, most recently in 1974 and 1988, is a flawed text. The Colbys and I discovered this in research on our respective biographies. As Elisabeth Jay noted in preparing her recently published scholarly edition, several passages in Oliphant's record of her life were struck out by the original editor, her cousin Annie Coghill. Mrs. Coghill was basically a stupid woman who presented the novelist as much more conformist than she really was. Out of thousands of letters she selected only a few, and these not always interesting or representative. The antisuffrage letter of 1866 went in, but not one of ten years later that shows that her views had changed. It refers to a story, "The Lady Candidate," which had been appearing in *Blackwood's* and that made fun of the suffragists: "This sort of glib nonsense has by degrees brought me round to the conviction that however indifferent I may be personally to political privileges the system which supposes me incapable of forming a reasonable opinion on public matters is very far from a perfect one."[3]

If we read more letters and articles, and especially her novels, a more complex picture emerges. Oliphant was not reactionary; she had much to say about the condition of women in her time. Yet it would be a mistake to typecast her as a forerunner of present-day Women's Liberationists.

"The woman question" was debated with great intensity during the second half of the nineteenth century. Briefly, in the years while Oliphant was growing up, women had no votes and few rights. Their education was poor (except in her birthplace Scotland); the professions were closed to them; married women could not own property or claim custody of children. It was almost impossible to leave a bad husband or father. A double standard of morality existed. Women were trained to think that their aim in life was to get a husband, and be despised if they did not.

Several things changed in her lifetime. The Infants' Custody and Married Women's Property Acts passed; some women got the municipal vote and others succeeded in becoming doctors; good schools for girls opened as did women's colleges at Oxford and Cambridge. The demand for the vote, which would not succeed until after World War I, was heard more often in respectable circles. The "women's movement" became a real force.

Yet not all women were struggling against the system. If we look only at novelists, who had greater opportunities than most of their sex to speak their minds, we find Charlotte Yonge declaring her "full belief in the inferiority of woman,"[4] Charlotte Bronte and George Eliot refusing to identify with the suffrage movement, and Mrs. Humphrey Ward and Eliza Lynn Linton signing the well-known "Appeal Against Female Suffrage" of 1889. This last group believed women should be educated, and should be encouraged to be responsible citizens, but were not competent to risk their lives in war or be politically active.

Oliphant took an interest in women's issues from an early stage—indeed, before most English people could have heard of it. Writing in *Merkland* (1850), only two years after the Women's Rights Association was founded in the United States, the twenty-two year old author made her heroine say: "We are one-half the world—we have our work to do, like the other half—let us do our work as honourably and wisely as we can, but for pity's sake, do not let us make this mighty bustle and noise about it . . . no one gains respect by claiming it" (2:40).

The three articles that she wrote on this subject for *Blackwood's* during the 1850s and 1860s are all critical of the women's movement, although she made it clear that she did not want to defend injustice or thwart anyone's aspirations. "This idea, that the two portions of humankind are natural antagonists to each other, is, to our thinking . . . a monstrous and unnatural idea."[5] Yet only a few pages later she refers ironically to the cherished belief that men had better brains. "Let us not enter upon the tender question of mental inferiority. Every individual woman, we presume, is perfectly easy on her own account that she at least is not remarkably behind her masculine companions."[6]

Her best-known statement is "The Great Unrepresented," the 1866 article in which she took issue with Mill. He had presented a petition to Parliament, signed by several eminent women, which demanded the vote for female householders, "lone women who pay their own rent and taxes,"[7] like Margaret herself. She admitted that this was logical, but claimed that ordinary women did not want the vote and felt rather insulted when it was thrust at them. Indeed, she was somewhat critical of the "exceptional women" who had proved that they could do good work in "masculine" spheres. "By chance now and then a woman may be found who is capable of any or all these things; but if she gives up her own existence to it, then God's purpose is defeated in her . . . and she is of no more use than if she were a man."[8]

There is some ironic ambiguity in this last clause, as there is in the letter to her publisher that acknowledged that Mill was a great thinker. However, she concluded:

> Twenty literary and other exceptional women in London may speak for a hundred or two more of their like, scattered over the kingdom; but we speak for the mass, which is not exceptional, which writes no books, and paints no pictures, and wants no votes.... We decline Mr Mill's proposal totally, and without equivocation.[9]

This article appeared anonymously; if her readers had known that she was a literary woman who had written thirty books they might have thought the article a piece of breathtaking hypocrisy. Yet she was often diffident about her talent and level of achievement, noting in one letter that she was "a poor soul who is concerned about nothing except the most domestic and limited concerns."[10]

The tension between her role as a self-supporting writer, and what she felt to be her more important role as the mother of a family continued. Three years later we find her again writing about Mill, in a review of his *Subjection of Women*. Here, although she does not accept his picture of one sex cruelly oppressing the other, she does agree with many of the reforms he suggests. She concedes that if female householders really want the vote, they should have it. She says that the marriage law conveys "a stinging sense of humiliation and insult," and that while the average wife is not mistreated, a Married Women's Property Act is necessary to prevent a husband taking "the bread out of her mouth and the children out of her arms."[11] She now believed that women were quite capable of doing men's work, and was especially sympathetic to the campaign for women doctors.

Yet she doubted whether, in the end, changes in the law would make much difference. Women who chose to be celibate might indeed compete on equal terms with men, but she pointed out that no man was asked to make that kind of sacrifice. Those who married and had children would always fall behind their male contemporaries.

> This is the inevitable course, known only too well to every woman who has endeavoured to combine professional exertions with the ordinary duties of a man's wife.... Her children born amid these cares, and

injured before their birth by the undue activity of brain which weakens their mother's physical powers, come into the world feeble or die in her arms, quenching out her courage in the bitterest waves of personal suffering. This is no fancy picture.[12]

So far as she was concerned, it certainly was not. During her marriage when she was writing continuously, two of her babies died of heart problems, which she believed were "connected with too much mental work" (*A* 40).

The Minister's Wife (1869), a minor but interesting novel, sheds more light on her attitudes. She did not wish, like some feminists, to be liberated from children; on the contrary, she said that the ordinary woman found, in looking after her baby, "a delight more exquisite than can be given her by all the arts and all the pleasures of the world" (3:41). The heroine becomes deeply disillusioned with her husband, who does not believe in her love for her child and expects her to think only of him:

> What he exacted was that she should have no rights, no independence of action, but should flatter him into granting all her desires . . . making herself sweet for his eyes, and submissive for his pleasure, looking up to him with anxious desire to please him, with wistful waiting upon his looks, as a slave to a Sultan. . . . Was this what she was reduced to? (3:238–39)

This women ends up, like Margaret herself, with a child but no husband. In her *Autobiography*, recalling her own seven years' marriage that had been faithful and affectionate, but perhaps not really happy, she wrote that "the love between men and women, the marrying and giving in marriage, occupy in fact so small a portion of either existence or thought" (*A* 10). Claims such as these make all the more extraordinary Patricia Stubbs's observation that "In [Oliphant's] novels the relationship between hero and heroine adheres strictly to the conventions which impose dominance on the man and submission on the woman."[13] For, as other critics have noted, Oliphant's work is full of strong, responsible women and men good for very little. We see this pattern clearly in the two best of the Carlingford novels, *The Doctor's Family* and *Miss Marjoribanks*, which were written not long before her critique of Mill.

The "hero" of *The Doctor's Family* is a weak and selfish man (whose brother is an alcoholic and dead weight), who is outclassed by the tough young heroine, Nettie. Although she marries him in the end, she is aware that she will have to make allowances:

> Nettie looked at him with a certain careless scorn of the inferior creature—"Ah, yes, I daresay, but then you are only a man," said Nettie. (116)

Patricia Stubbs has read *Miss Marjoribanks* but does not seem to have grasped its point. Here again the heroine is superior to the men she meets, most of whom are frightened by her and prefer more conventional women. When she eventually marries her kind, but not very intelligent cousin Tom, she has no intention of retreating into domesticity because "I have always been doing something, and responsible for something, all my life" (484). Yet Stubbs asserts that "Ultimately the novel still implies that the proper place for a talented young woman is in queening it over the dinner or tea table and in gracefully dispensing charity to the agricultural poor. There is no suggestion that Lucilla is in any way wasted, or that she could become bored or frustrated with the social whirl."[14] This really is perverse. Although the novel is a comedy, the author makes the serious point that no talented young woman can go on amusing herself with dinner parties forever:

> she had come to an age at which she might have gone into Parliament herself had there been no disqualification of sex, and when it was almost a necessity for her to make some use of her social influence.... When a woman has an active mind, and still does not care for parish work, it is a little hard for her to find a "sphere." And Lucilla, though she said nothing about a sphere, was still more or less in that condition of mind which has been so often and so fully described to the British public—when the ripe female intelligence, not having the natural resource of a nursery and a husband to manage, turns inwards, and begins to "make a protest" against the existing order of society, and to call the world to account for giving it no due occupation—and to consume itself.... Lucilla had become conscious that her capabilities were greater than her work. (394–95)

It is clear from this and other passages that Oliphant was well aware of the raging argument about the "woman question." Lucilla *is* wasted; there can be no question of her going into Parliament, nor will she be allowed to take over her father's medical practice as a young man could do:

But somehow it struck the Doctor more than ever how great a loss it was to society and to herself that Lucilla was not "the boy." She could have continued, and perhaps extended, the practice, whereas just now it was quite possible that she might drop down into worsted-work and tea-parties like any other single woman. (400)

At the same time, her cousin Tom is not half so gifted. Life for a spinster without money seems likely to be "limited and unsatisfactory" (435). The other single woman in the book, the artist Rose who has given up her cherished career, suggests that Lucilla found a House of Mercy, and although this is inappropriate Lucilla has "no intention of sinking into a nobody, and giving up all power of acting upon her fellow-creatures" (435). Marriage, children, active philanthropic work, and thorough management of her husband's career offer her by far the best chance of a happy and useful life, as Linda Peterson discusses in her essay.

Although she ended most of her novels with a marriage, Oliphant herself never remarried. For most of her adult life she saw herself primarily as a mother, and noted rather sadly in *Madonna Mary* (1866) that she had little to look forward to:

> The boys *must* go away and would probably marry . . . and the mother who had given up the best part of her life to them *must* remain alone . . . her occupation over, her personal history at an end. (2:184)

She identified with older women, and noted men's scornful attitude to them. (An original objection of hers to early feminists was that they exposed other women to ridicule.) While she insisted she did not regard men as the enemy, and that most of them meant well, she bitterly resented the "ungenerous sentiment" of men toward women, and "the strong sense of superiority which exists in the male bosom from the age of two upwards."[15] These words are from the most overtly feminist piece of nonfiction she wrote, "The Grievances of Women," which appeared in 1880. There is a strong undertow of deep personal feeling here. She did not go to feminist meetings, she said, but

> We are so weak as to be offended deeply and wounded by the ridicule which has not yet ceased to be poured upon every such manifestation. We shrink from the laugh of rude friends, the smile of the gentler ones. . . . Fair and honourable criticism is a thing which no accus-

tomed writer will shrink from . . . but to be met with an insolent laugh, a storm of ridiculous epithets, and that coarse superiority of sex which a great many men think it not unbecoming to exhibit to women is a mode of treatment which affects our temper."[16]

She stated that widows like herself who brought up families and paid taxes, ought to be allowed a vote, and that women who wished to enter the professions were entitled to do so. But she felt that the real grievance was men's basic attitude, which was beyond the reach of legislation.

> Whatever women do, in the general, is undervalued by men in the general, because it is done by women. How this impairs the comfort of women, how it shakes the authority of mothers, injures the self-respect of wives, and gives a general soreness of feeling everywhere, I will not attempt to tell.[17]

That "soreness of feeling" is evident in many apparently casual remarks scattered through her novels and other works. It comes out in her comment on Mary Wollstonecraft, that the demand for women's rights has "risen almost invariably from women compelled by hard stress of circumstances to despise the men about them"; in *Within the Precincts,* where the heroine's male relatives want to make money from her singing; in her comment to Principal Tulloch who had been suffering from depression and was unable to work that she would have no wife to look after her if she became ill.[18] Yet one reason she kept away from reform movements was that she did not believe they would achieve anything.

> I admit for my part the superiority of sex. It is not a pretty subject, nor one for my handling. Yet it is a fact. As belonging to the physical part of our nature, which is universal—whereas the mental and moral part is not so—that superiority must always tell. It will keep women in subjection as long as the race endures.[19]

This is the main conclusion of "The Grievances of Women," and it is this essentially tragic view that colors her great novels of the 1880s.

Even these works contain uninteresting young couples who have no problems, who are only there to pad the story or provide the happy endings that Victorians liked. Indeed, Oliphant had written, "I believe nothing can be more certain than the large predominance of happiness over unhappiness in married life."[20] Yet it is the tragic or imperfect marriages that she describes with most conviction.

The Ladies Lindores (1883) gives a haunting picture of marriage based on mental cruelty. It is a novel about male domination. Lady Caroline (a natural victim, who will rush into another unsuitable marriage at the end of the book) is compelled by her father to marry the rich but boorish Pat Torrance. Both are excellent character studies. He is a brutal man who sees her as his "proudest and finest possession" (2:188) and a "servant whom he need not fear bullying" (1:182); she an overrefined woman whose nerves are worn to shreds by his "rude fury, and ruder affection." She has "nothing but a little discussion about Wordsworth or Shelley to stand in place of happiness to her heart" (2:144). Yet it is noted other women would marry him because he is "such a cluster of worldly advantages" (1:91). Her sister believes that she should leave him rather than submit to what is virtually rape, but she will never have the strength to take such an unconventional step. She prefers to think of herself as a martyr to "duty." Yet when her husband is killed, she feels no sympathy, but cries out in a powerful and disturbing scene:

> To think I shall never be subject to all *that* anymore—that he can never come in here again—that I am free—that I can be alone. Oh, mother, how can you tell what it is? Never to be alone: never to have a corner in the world where—some one else has not a right to come, a better right than yourself. . . . It is so sweet to sit still and know that no one will burst the door open and come in. (2:265)

But Caroline is obviously not fated to be happy, partly because of her weakness, partly because she has two children who do not take after her family and are "pieces of Torrance" (3:171) who will be with her for life. Even motherhood cannot be a full consolation. Her own mother, Lady Lindores, has to watch her daughter suffer and is disenchanted with the men of her family. "Her husband was not a perfect mate for her—her son had failed to her hopes" (3:333). She must accept that "with all the relationships of life still round her, mother and wife, she, for all solace and support, was like most of us virtually alone" (3:50).

A similar type of older woman appears in another remarkable and neglected novel, *A Country Gentleman and His Family* (1886). Mrs. Warrender, mother of the "hero," has no real role in the plot but impresses one as a woman more perceptive than those around her and who has accepted that "her own being was an undiscovered country for her children" (2:218). Oliphant had much the same feeling in the 1880s, as she watched her own sons turn out so different from herself.

Theo Warrender, a depressingly convincing young man with an "extremely impatient temper and fastidious, almost capricious temperament" (2:79), becomes head of the family over his mother and older sisters after his father dies. Having been unsuccessful in the larger world, because others will not put up with his whims, he is determined that he will at best dominate his own household. He can turn his sisters out, they discover because "we are only daughters, and you are the boy" (1:96). Soon he falls in love with an older widow Frances, who with her son is in a much higher social position than he is. Theo bears down her opposition and marries her although she warns him she is "not only older in years, but so much older in life" (2:111). "I am a woman who have had to act for myself. I am Geoff's mother. I must think of him and what has to be done for him" (2:130).

The author is sympathetic to Frances's natural longings. "A woman in the flower of her life does not necessarily centre every wish in the progress of a little boy" (2:142). Yet the marriage is doomed because Theo will never accept his wife's child (and Oliphant seems to feel this is not only because he is an intolerant man but also because the situation is unnatural), and because she is not a pliable young girl but a woman of more experience than himself. She does not take his name or live in his house when they are married—more wounds to his self-esteem. Indeed, the whole novel could be called a study of "the wounds which people closely connected in life so often give to each other" (1:231). Theo not surprisingly becomes miserable.

> He was jealous of his wife, not in the ordinary vulgar way, for which there was no possibility, but for every year of additional age, and every experience, and all the life she had led apart from him. He could not endure to think that she had formed the most of her ideas before she knew him; the thought of her past was horrible to him. (3:152)

Frances attempts to make herself a lesser person for his sake. "She seemed to have one eye upon Theo always, whatever she was doing, to see that he was pleased, or at least not displeased" (3:141). But in the end, when he orders her to give up her child and seeks to enforce the conventional Victorian view of the man-woman relationship, saying "Can any one doubt what is your first duty? It is to me. It is I that must settle what our life is to be. It is you who must yield and obey" (3:216), she rebels and breaks with him. Her marriage—which has brought her two more children—becomes "a strange dream, a dream full of fever and unrest, of fugitive happiness but lasting trouble" (3:225).

Oliphant suggests in this novel that marriage "almost always makes trouble; it breaks as well as unites" (2:194). Her fine short story, "Queen Eleanor and Fair Rosamond," first published in 1886, also shows a marriage that breaks down because of the man's conduct. A middle-aged couple appears to be contentedly married; when the husband goes away his wife cannot guess the real reason. "How could it mean anything except business, or the good of the children, or some other perfectly legitimate desire?"[21] In fact, he has illegitimate desires and has "married" a young girl in another town. The wife copes without self-pity, indeed with some heroism, while her husband is eventually seen as a commonplace and rather silly man, points Margarete Rubik makes in her discussion of this story in her essay.

Kirsteen is probably Oliphant's masterpiece. Here, most unusually, the heroine remains a spinster, although that does not free her from family ties. She has a fiance who dies in India; her feeling for him is the "golden thread" running through her life. But this relationship is not studied in detail. Her real links are with her sisters and the women who help her break away from home and become independent; her real fulfillment is in being a dressmaker and creating "beautiful manufactured things . . . with much of the genuine enjoyment which attends an artist in all crafts (165). When the author looks closely at marriage relationships, her picture is much darker. Kirsteen's father, a former slave trader and future murderer treats his wife and daughters with thorough contempt, which proves intolerable for Kirsteen with her "quick temper and high spirit and lively imagination." She will "make a story for" herself (36).

It is Kirsteen who makes the family's fortune, fulfilling the pattern of success normally reserved for men, as Linda Peterson demonstrates. Yet it is done at a price, and, like her creator, she ends up a breadwinner, but also celibate with many poor relations needing her help and others upset with her because she has worked for a living. Thus Oliphant treats, not only Kirsteen, but the several spinsters in the novel, with respect and dignity.

Another novel that shows a husband as less than a great prize is *The Marriage of Elinor* (1892), in which the heroine has too much spirit to put up with her husband's infidelity, but makes a fairly happy alternative home with her mother and child. Although Oliphant's tone is cautious, she distances herself from the view that a woman should hang on to her marriage at any price:

> Had Elinor fulfilled what would appear to many her first duty, and stood by Phil through neglect, ill-treatment, and misery, as she had vowed, for better, for worse, she would by this time have been not only a wretched but a deteriorated woman, and her son most probably would have been injured both in his moral and intellectual being. What she had done was not the abstract duty of her marriage vow, but it had been better—had it not been better for them both? In such a question who is to be the judge? (3:70–71)

In this novel, the relationship between mother and adult daughter is a deep one that lasts throughout their lives, while men come and go.

During the 1880s and 1890s, while Oliphant wrote these remarkable works, a "singular and scarcely recognised revolution" had "taken place in the position and aspirations of women." These are her own words, from an article of 1889 in which she noted that many young girls were now trying to work out "their own career and destiny."[22] She sympathized, taking great trouble with the education of her two nieces so they could eventually get suitable work. Emancipated young women come into her novels too, usually in small parts like the girl in *The Railwayman and His Children* who says that "work is not the thing to make a fortune by. But I am of opinion that it is the first thing in the world (397). *The Marriage of Elinor* contains girls who play music seriously, climb mountains and do social work in hospitals and the East End of London.

I do not for a moment mean to imply that the Miss Gaythornes did their good work because it was the fashion: but the fact that it is the fashion has liberated many girls, and allowed them to carry out their natural wishes in that way, who otherwise would have been restrained and hampered by parents and friends, who would have upbraided them with making themselves remarkable, if in a former generation they had attempted to go to Whitechapel or St Thomas's with any active intentions. (2:230)

More women now wanted votes, held responsible jobs, and perhaps did not wish to live as their mothers had. New novels by Olive Schreiner, James, Moore, Hardy, and Gissing among others examined the position of women and the ideal relationship between the sexes. On the whole Oliphant was not impressed. In a review of *Tess of the d'Urbervilles* she acknowledged the book's greatness, and showed sympathy for the central character, but still preferred to read about "a world which is round and contains everything, not 'the relations between the sexes' alone."[23] In an article of 1894 she sensed a certain narcissism in "the much talk about women, and their rights and disabilities, with which the air is full":

> Whether they agree or disagree, women, in this generation at least, love to read about themselves; and the subject, though beginning, we hope, to pall upon the better intellects, is always attractive to the mass which. . . is more than anything else drawn to the consideration of its own gifts and graces, as specially seen in its attitudes towards its partner in life. All this is no doubt part of the defective education of the past, and of the fact that a generation or two ago women had many real and galling disabilities, and were held under an actual subjection (by law, if only now and then in fact) which was sometimes very cruel and unjust, and always highly offensive to feminine pride.

Yet some writers, she thought, had gone too far. "They grow hot over wrongs that have long ceased to be, and argue as they might have done before there was any Married Women's Property Act or other amelioration."[24]

She returned to this subject in 1895, arguing as she had done years before that feminists had not fully addressed their minds to the question of children.

> The women who work should be . . . celibates, who make up their minds to the other line of life, and do not marry. The functions, especially of a mother, are not easily combined with any other trade

> or profession. We have seen very melancholy spectacles in the attempt to carry out both well. . . . But work of itself is really at bottom often more agreeable to women than it is to men.[25]

It is likely that among the "melancholy spectacles" she had seen were her own life and career. She had tried to be a good mother as well as an artist, but she knew that she had been forced to write a great deal of rubbish to get an income, and her last child had died only a few months before. It would have been simpler—she may have felt—if she had had a clearer, easier choice.

She might seem extremely hostile to the "New Woman" in her now infamous review of *Jude the Obscure,* which Hardy called "the screaming of a poor lady in *Blackwood* that there was an unholy anti-marriage league afoot."[26] Titled "The Anti-Marriage League," the review discussed *Jude* and Grant Allen's *The Woman Who Did,* both of which were hostile to marriage and featured sexually emancipated heroines.

Aware of the novels' popularity, Oliphant nonetheless protested against the tendency "to place what is called the Sex-question above all others as the theme of fiction":

> Its result is to select, as the most important thing in existence, one small (though no doubt highly important) fact of life, which natural instinct has agreed, even among savages, to keep in the background. . . . To make this the supreme incident, always in the foreground, to be discussed by young men and women, and held up before boys and girls, and intruded upon those from whom circumstances or choice have shut it off, or who have outlived the period in which it is interesting, seems to me an outrage for which there is no justification. . . . It puts life out of focus altogether, and distorts hopelessly its magnitudes and its littlenesses.

To the charge that these novelists were sex-obsessed she added that if marriage were to be downgraded, it would be women who would suffer. "It makes the woman not the helpmeet of the man according to the noble and beautiful conception of that relationship in the first description of it ever given in literature—but his accomplice. . . in a certain act common to men and beasts, and no more sacred in one case than in the other from this point of view."[27]

She had realized that men might turn certain feminist demands to their own advantage. "The desire of women for work," she had warned in *Within the Precincts,* "is apt to be supported from an undesirable side" (326). Probably most contemporary feminists shared her distrust of male novelists who, they felt, only wanted women to be sexually emancipated. The president of the National Union of Women Suffrage Societies, Millicent Fawcett, had written in her review of *The Woman Who Did* that "Mr. Grant Allen has never given help by tongue or pen to any practical effort to improve the legal or social status of women. He is not a friend but an enemy, and it is as an enemy that he endeavours to link together the claim of women to citizenship and social and industrial independence, with attacks upon marriage and the family."[28]

Oliphant also raised the "great insoluble question of what is to be the fate of children in such circumstances." Were they to be killed, as in *Jude the Obscure,* or alternatively "hang on to their mother's second honeymoon?" "Mr Hardy knows," she insisted, "that the children are a most serious part of the question of the abolition of marriage."[29] Reading this review today, one sees Oliphant overstated her case and may also have been insensitive to the quality of Hardy's writing. Nevertheless, she raised issues that are still highly relevant.

To sum up, Margaret Oliphant is a complex figure, typecast as antifeminist, yet concerned throughout her life with the problems of women and the author of several novels that are rooted in this concern. Some of her opinions have dated; much of worth remains.

She would not have liked modern feminists. Their attitudes to sex and children would have been deeply alien to her, as would be their stridency and frequent self-pity. It is more helpful and fairer to see her as one of a long and honorable line of women who were known in England between the wars as the Old Feminists. They did not concentrate on women's "special" or biological problems, although of course they were aware of them (and might even write about them as Margaret did). Ultimately all they asked was that men and women be equal before the law and that no persons should be forbidden to make their contribution because they were the "wrong" sex. Above all, they were aware, as was Oliphant, that the world "is round, and contains everything."

Editions of Out-of-Print Novels Used

A Country Gentleman and His Family. London: Macmillan, 1886.
The Ladies Lindores. London: Blackwood, 1883.

Madonna Mary. London: Hurst and Blackett, 1866.
The Marriage of Elinor. London: Macmillan, 1892.
Merkland. London: Henry Colburn, 1850.
The Minister's Wife. London: Hurst and Blackett, 1869.
The Railwayman and His Children. London: Macmillan, 1892.
Within the Precincts. London: Smith, Elder and Co., 1885.

Notes

1. *Women and Fiction: Feminism and the Novel 1880–1920* (Brighton: Harvester, 1979) 39–40.
2. Oliphant-Madge Valentine, 2 December 1895, NLS Acc.5678/4.
3. Oliphant-JB, n.d. 1876, NLS Blackwood MS 4349.
4. In *Womankind* (London, 1876) 1.
5. "The Laws Concerning Women," *Blackwood's* 79 (April 1856) 379.
6. "Laws" 381.
7. "The Great Unrepresented," *Blackwood's* 100 (September 1866) 369.
8. "Great," 376.
9. "Great," 379.
10. Oliphant-JB, 8 March 1865, NLS Blackwoods MS 4202.
11. [Review of Mill and Josephine Butler], *Edinburgh Review* 130 (October 1869) 580.
12. [Review] 597.
13. Stubbs, 43.
14. Stubbs, 42.
15. "The Grievances of Women," *Fraser's,* 21 (May 1880) 707.
16. "Grievances," 698.
17. "Grievances," 710.
18. *The Literary History of England in the End of the Eighteenth Century and the Beginning of the Nineteenth Century* (London: Macmillan, 1882) 2:248; Oliphant-John Tulloch, September 1881, A&L 300.
19. "Grievances," 698.
20.. "Grievances," 705.
21. In *A Widow's Tale and Other Stories* (London: Blackwood, 1898) 67.
22. "The Old Saloon," *Blackwood's* 146 (August 1889) 257.
23. "The Old Saloon," *Blackwood's* 151 (March 1892) 465.
24. "The Looker-On," *Blackwood's* 156 (August 1894) 289–90.
25. "The Looker-On," *Blackwood's* 159 (January 1896) 137.
26. See Hardy's postscripts in the New Wessex Edition (London: Macmillan, 1975) 30.
27. *Blackwood's* 159 (January 1896) 137, 144–45.
28. "The Woman Who Did," *Contemporary Review* 67 (May 1895) 630.
29. "Anti-Marriage," 141, 147, 142.

Contributors

John Stock Clarke has published *Margaret Oliphant (1828–1897). A Bibliography* (Queensland, Australia, 1986), and articles on Oliphant and Victorian periodicals. He is co-author, with D. J. Trela, of a forthcoming secondary bibliography of Oliphant (Locust Hill Press).

Elisabeth Jay, Head of English at Westminster College, Oxford has edited *The Autobiography of Margaret Oliphant: The Complete Text* (Oxford, 1990). Her full-scale study of Oliphant's oeuvre, *A Fiction to Herself: Mrs. Oliphant, a Literary Life*, will also be published by Oxford. She is presently editing a new Penguin edition of Elizabeth Gaskell's *Life of Charlotte Bronte*.

Dale Kramer is a professor of English at the University of Illinois. He has edited *The Woodlanders* and *The Mayor of Casterbridge* for Oxford, has written extensively on Thomas Hardy and also serves as editor of the *Journal of English and Germanic Philology*.

Laurie Langbauer is an associate professor of English, teaching critical theory at Swarthmore College (Pennsylvania). Her book *Women and Romance: The Consolations of Gender in the English Novel* was published by Cornell in 1990. She is working on Oliphant as part of her next book, a study of women writers and the category of the everyday.

Linda Peterson is professor of English at Yale University. She has written *Victorian Autobiography: The Tradition of Self-Interpretation* (Yale, 1986).

Margarete Rubik is associate professor of English and American Literature at the University of Vienna, Austria. She has published widely on modern British drama and the Victorian novel, especially on the works of Oliphant. Her study of Oliphant's novels will be published by Peter Lang in 1994.

Contributors

Esther H. Schor is associate professor of English at Princeton University. She has co-edited two books, *Women's Voices: Visions and Perspectives* (McGraw, 1990), and *The Other Mary Shelley: Beyond 'Frankenstein'* (Oxford, 1993). Her book, *Bearing the Dead: The British Culture of Mourning from the Enlightenment to Victoria* will be published by Princeton in 1994.

Joanne Shattock is director of the Victorian Studies Centre in the Department of English at the University of Leicester. She has published *The Oxford Guide to British Women Writers* (1993), *Politics and Reviewers* (1989), has edited *Dickens and Other Victorians* (1988) and co-edited *The Victorian Periodical Press* (1982). She is currently editing the nineteenth century volume of the third edition of *The Cambridge Bibliography of English Literature* and writing a book on literature and journalism in the nineteenth century.

D. J. Trela is associate professor of English and Director of the School of Liberal Studies at Roosevelt University, Chicago. He has published *A History of Carlyle's 'Oliver Cromwell's Letters and Speeches'* (Mellen, 1992) contributed to *Victorian Scandals* (Ohio University Press, 1992) and published widely on Carlyle and Oliphant. Associate Editor of *Carlyle Studies Annual* and Executive Secretary of the Midwest Victorian Studies Association, his current research includes a study of Oliphant's literary criticism and critical editions of Carlyle's *Past and Present* and *Historical Sketches*.

Merryn Williams is a poet and critic who published *Margaret Oliphant: A Critical Biography* in 1986 (Macmillan). She has also edited *Kirsteen, The Doctor's Family, A Beleaguered City and Other Stories* and *The Curate in Charge*. She lives in Bedfordshire, England. Her latest work is *Wilfred Owen* (1993).

Index

Abel, Elizabeth, 87 n. 1
Academy, 36
Alcestis (novel), Oliphant on, 154
Alison, Archibald, 162 n. 1
Allen, Grant: *The Woman Who Did*, Millicent Fawcett on, 178–79, 180 n. 28
Arnold, Matthew, 152; Oliphant on *Merope*, 156, 164 n. 14
Athenaeum, 36, letter about *Perpetual Curate* in, 123 n. 12; review of *Perpetual Curate* in, 120
Auerbach, Nina, 89 n. 23, 109 n. 3
Austen, Jane, 16, 83; Oliphant on, 85.

Baillie, Joanna: Oliphant on, 163 n. 3
Balfour, Lady Francis: Oliphant's letter to quoted, 14
Balzac, Honoré de, 150; Oliphant on *Père Goriot*, 158, 164 n. 17
Barrie, J. M., 13
Baruch, Elaine, 75, 82 nn. 2 and 13
Bendixen, Alfred, 108 n. 3
Bildungsroman, 66–89; female, 66–67, 87–88 nn. 1–4; male, 66
Blackett, Henry, 113
Blackwood, John, 12, 19; and George Eliot, 122, 132; letter to Oliphant, 22; opinion of *Miss Marjoribanks*, 69; on *The Perpetual Curate*, 113–23; rejection of Oliphant's articles, 138
Blackwood, Major William, 19
Blackwood's Edinburgh Magazine: *Autobiography and Letters* reviewed in, 129, 133 n. 7; "Chronicles of Carlingford" published in, 113–23; "The Lady Candidate" serialized in, 166; Oliphant's articles on autobiography in, 124–34; Oliphant's first appearance in, 18–19; theory of tragedy in, 147–50, 162–63 nn. 1 and 2; mentioned, 14, 20, 26 n. 2, 27 n. 13, 46 n. 3, 47 n. 20, 48 nn. 22 and 23, 64 n. 14, 70, 109 n. 7
Blanchot, Maurice, 124, 131, 134 n. 16
Bleiler, E. F., 108 n. 1
Braddon, Mary Elizabeth: Oliphant's on, 88 n. 12
Bray, Anna Eliza, 123 n. 15
Briggs, Julia, 108 n. 1
Brontë, Charlotte: characters in novels of, 69, 84; Oliphant on, in *Autobiography*, 140–41; Oliphant's criticism of, 88 n. 12; Oliphant on *Jane Eyre*, 141, 145 n. 5; mentioned, 66, 167
Brontë, Emily, 93
Brown, Peter, 102
Browning, Robert, 110 n. 13, Oliphant on "Andrea del Sarto," 143, 146 n. 12
Buckley, J. H., 87–88 n. 1
Bulwer-Lytton, Edward: *Ernest Maltravers*, 18, 20; *A Strange Story*, 90; *Zanoni*, 90
Burns, Robert: Oliphant's review of, 152, 163 n. 8

Calder, Jenni, 51, 52, 64 n. 6
Carlyle, Jane Welsh, 13, 21, 133 n. 4
Carlyle, Thomas: *The French Revolution*, 159, 164 n. 20; mentioned, 13, 21, 133 n. 4
Certeau, Michel de, 126, 133–34 n. 8
Chapman and Hall, 21
Chodorow, Nancy, 80, 86, 89 nn. 17 and 21
Clarke, John Stock: articles on Oliphant, 25–26 n. 2, 26 n. 4
Coghill, Annie (Mrs. Harry), 129–30, 166
Colby, Robert and Vineta: *The Equivo-*

183

cal Virtue, 12, 24, 25 n. 2, 46, 108 n. 3, 109 n. 4, 110 n. 16, 123 n. 16, 166; on *A Beleaguered City,* 110 n. 13
Colby, Vineta: *Yesterday's Woman,* 150, 163 n. 3
Coleridge, Samuel Taylor, 95
Collins, Wilkie, 96, 110 n. 13, 165
Conrad, Joseph: publications in *Blackwood's,* 149
Cornhill Magazine, 37, 39, 121, 136–37
Cunningham, Gail, 88–89 n. 15
Cunningham, Valentine, 43, 47 n. 19

Dante Alighieri, *Purgatorio,* 96–97
Daudet, Alfonse: Oliphant on, 158, 164 n. 17
Davis, Philip: on *Autobiography and Letters,* 136, 145 n. 2
Dent, J. M., 24
De Quincey, Thomas, 162 n. 1
Dickens, Charles: Oliphant's reviews of, 151, 163 n. 6; *Great Expectations* as *bildungsroman,* 79, 84–85, compared to *A Son of His Father,* 62, 65 n. 22; *Hard Times,* 26 n. 5; mentioned, 141
Dixon, Hepworth, 121, 123 n. 14
Douglas, Ann, 90

Eliot, George: and *bildungsroman,* 67, 69; compared to Oliphant, 26 n. 2, 46, 48 n. 25, 121–22; Oliphant on *Adam Bede,* 26 n. 5, 159, 164 n. 20; on *Romola,* 26 n. 5, 54, on Cross's *Life of Eliot,* 142, 146 n. 9; *Mill on the Floss* compared to *Joyce,* 56–57; mentioned, 84, 150, 167
Elliot, Lady, 157

F. V. White (publisher), 21
Farge, Annette, 134 n. 8
Fawcett, Millicent, 179
Felski, Rita, 87 n. 1
Fernando, Lloyd, 89 n. 15
Fitzgerald, Penelope: on Oliphant, 25
Foucault, Michel, 126, 133–34 n. 8
Friends in Council, 68

Galt, John, 65 n. 20
Gaskell, Elizabeth: *Wives and Daughters,* 56; mentioned, 84, 163 n. 3

Gibbon, Edward, 133, 134 n. 21
Gilbert, Sandra, and Susan Gubar, 109 n. 3
Ginx's Baby, Oliphant's review of, 150–51, 163 n. 5
Gissing, George, 177
Goethe, Johann Wolfgang von: Oliphant's review of, 152–53, 163 n. 9
Grand, Sarah: Oliphant's review of *Ideala,* 44
Graves, C. L.: on Oliphant, 43
Gray, Margaret K.: on Oliphant's supernatural fiction, 90

Hardy, Thomas: Oliphant's opinion of, 13–14, 26 nn. 2 and 4, 88–89 n. 15, 152, 177, 179; *Jude the Obscure,* 13, 45, 46, 88–89 n. 15, 161–62, 164 n. 27, 178, 179, 180 nn. 27 and 29; *Tess of the D'Urbervilles,* Oliphant's review of, 13, 88–89 n. 15, 161–62, 177; tragedy in, 154
Harper and Brothers, 21
Haythornethwaite, J. A.: article on Oliphant, 26 n. 2
Henry Colburn (publisher) 18
Holman, C. Hugh, 88 n. 14
Hopkins, Gerard Manley, 152
Houghton, Walter E., 162 n. 2
Hugo, Victor: Oliphant's review of *Quatre-Vingt-Treize,* 154–55, 164 n. 12
Hurst and Blackett, 21, 113, 115, 122 n. 2
Hutchinson (publisher), 21

Illustrated London News, 39
Infants' Custody Act, 166

James, Henry: on *Kirsteen,* 47 n. 11; on Oliphant, 13, 38
Jeffrey, Francis, Lord, 13
Jolly, Emily, 123 n. 15

"Lady Candidate, The," 166
Landow, George P., 134 n. 11
Langbauer, Laurie, 164 n. 21
Lawless, Emily: Oliphant's review of *Grania,* 160, 164 n. 24

Index

Leavis, Q. D.: on Oliphant, 12, 25 n. 2, on Oliphant's supernatural fiction, 106–7; mentioned, 46
Lessing, Gotthold Ephraim: Oliphant on *Dramaturgie* of, 150, 156, 164 n. 15
Lewes, G. H., 121
Lillo, George, 150
Linton, Eliza Lynn, 167
Longmans (publisher), 21
Lysaght, Elizabeth J., 123 n. 15

Macaulay, Thomas, 20
Macmillan (publisher) 21, 91, 122 n. 2
Macmillan's Magazine, 115, 122 n. 2
Married Women's Property Act, 166, 168, 177
Martineau, Harriet: Oliphant on, 83–84; mentioned, 70
Maupassant, Guy de: Oliphant's review of *Pierre and Jean,* 159–60, 164 n. 22
Methuen (publisher), 21
Mill, John Stuart: Oliphant's article on, 167–68; Oliphant's letter about, 165, mentioned, 14
Mitford, Mary Russell: Oliphant's article on, 85; mentioned, 20
Moers, Ellen, 90, 108–9 n. 3
Moi, Toril, 134 n. 8
Moore, George, 177
Moretti, Franco, 66, 88 n. 4
Morley, John, 63–64 n. 2
Morse, Deborah: unpublished essay on Oliphant, 64 n. 7
Mudie's Library, 18, 46
Musset, Alfred de, 23

New Quarterly Magazine: serialization of *A Beleaguered City* in, 109 n. 7
"New Woman," 78, 82, 85, 88–89 n. 15, 178
Newton, Judith Lowder, 51–52, 64 n. 7
Noble, James Ashcroft: review of *A Poor Gentleman,* 36, 37, 40, 47 n. 8

Oliphant, Cyril (son, known as "Tiddy"), 20, 23, 27 n. 16, 160
Oliphant, Francis (husband) 18, 19, 20, 160
Oliphant, Francis Romano (son, known as "Cecco"), 20, 23–24, 27 n. 16
Oliphant, Margaret (daughter), 20, 23, 118, 138
Oliphant, Margaret
—Biographical information: alcoholism of brother William Wilson, 19; birth, 17; and *Blackwood's,* 19, 22–23, 113–23; death, 24–25; deaths of children, 23–24; death of husband, 20; early critical articles of, 20; early novels of, 18; early reading of, 18; edits "Foreign Classics for English Readers," 23; influence of mother on, 17; marriage of, 18–20; religion, 18, 24–25, 90, 103, 108, 108 n. 2, 149; supports brother's family, 23; travel of, 24
—Literary life of: Penelope Fitzgerald on, 25; James Ashcroft Noble on, 36; modern reputation of, 12–17; reputation as reviewer, 147–50; reputation in 1890s, 36–38; reputation of supernatural fiction, 90–91, 108; James Payn on, 39, 42; reviews of: *see* Oliphant, Margaret: Nonfiction, *and also under authors' names;* Travor Royle on, 12–13, 26 n. 3; George Saintsbury on, 34–35; serial publication and, 116–18; Leslie Stephen on, 33–34; G. S. Street on, 38–39; Patricia Stubbs on, 165, 169, 170; Howard Overing Sturges on, 38; themes of death, 60–62; themes of poetic justice, 59–60; themes of subversiveness, 12–17, 25, 87; theory of autobiography, 124–43; theory of domestic tragedy, 147–64; Jennifer Uglow on, 89 n. 16; Hugh Walker on, 35; William Wallace on, 45–46; Oscar Wilde on, 38; Virginia Woolf on, 34–35
—Women and marriage in fiction of: *Agnes,* 45; *A Beleaguered City,* 103–4; *A Country Gentleman and His Family,* 45, 174–75; *The Doctor's Family,* 169–70; *Hester,* 78–81; *A House Divided*

186 INDEX

Against Itself, 45; *Kirsteen,* 81–87; *Lady Car,* 45; *The Ladies Lindores,* 45, 173; *Madonna Mary,* 171; *The Marriage of Eleanor,* 45, 176–77; *Merkland,* 167; *The Minister's Wife,* 169; *Miss Marjoribanks,* 59–60, 67–73, 170–71; *Old Mr. Tredgold,* 58; *Phoebe, Junior,* 73–78; "Queen Eleanor and Fair Rosamond," 52–53, 175; *The Railwayman and His Children,* 32–33, 52, 55, 176; *Sir Robert's Fortune,* 45; *Sir Tom,* 56; *A Son of the Soil,* 57–58; *Within the Precincts,* 178–79
—Women's rights and, 13–15, 44–45, 165–79

Oliphant, Margaret: Fiction
—*Agnes,* 41, 45, 122 n. 2
—*At His Gates,* 42, 43, 45, 146 n. 12
—*Beleaguered City, A,* instability of signs in, 97–107, 110 n. 11; reprintings of, 91; serialization in *New Quarterly Magazine,* 109 n. 7; R. L. Stevenson on, 13
—*Caleb Field,* 35
—*Carità:* death in, 61; negative review of, 47 n. 18, 48 n. 26
—*Christian Melville,* 18
—*Chronicles of Carlingford.* See individual novels and short stories
—*Country Gentleman and His Family, A:* Julia Wedgwood's negative review of, 43, 45; women and marriage in, 174–75
—*Cuckoo in the Nest, The:* death in, 61; women and marriage in, 51
—*Curate in Charge, The:* egotism in, 62; women and marriage in, 52, 55
—*Days of My Life, The,* 42
—*Diana Trelawney:* women and marriage in, 52, 64 n. 7
—*Doctor's Family, The:* women and marriage in, 169–70; mentioned 21, 115
—"Dr. Barrère," 41
—"Earthbound:" interpretive and sexual mastery in, 91–97; mentioned, 99, 107, 109 n. 7, 109–10 n. 10
—"Executor, The:" first of *Chronicles of Carlingford,* 113–14, 122 n. 1; writing of, 21
—*For Love and Life:* men in, 42; women and marriage in, 55–56
—"Girl of the Period, A," 41
—*Harry Muir:* alcoholism in, 16
—*Hester:* compared to *Kirsteen,* 82, 83, 86, 87, 88–89 n. 15; as *female bildungsroman,* 67, 78–81; men in, 43; unity of, 42; Victorian conventions in, 16; mentioned, 41, 58, 65 n. 16
—*House Divided Against Itself, A:* compared to *Wives and Daughters,* 56; mentioned, 45
—*House on the Moor, The,* 122 n. 2
—"Isabel Dysart," 41
—"John," 41
—*John Drayton,* 35
—*Joyce:* women and marriage in, 56–57
—*Katie Stewart:* appearance in *Blackwood's,* 18–19; John Blackwood's disapproval of, 65 n. 23
—*Kirsteen:* as female *bildungsroman,* 81–87; Henry James on, 47 n. 11; tragedy in, 156–57; women and marriage in, 175–76; mentioned, 52, 67
—*Ladies Lindores, The:* women and marriage in, 173; mentioned, 45
—*Lady Car:* women and marriage in, 55; mentioned, 45
—*Laird of Norlaw, The:* death in, 60–61
—*Last of the Mortimers, The:* 122 n. 2
—"Land of Darkness, The," 91
—"Library Window, The," 41, 107–8
—*Little Pilgrim in the Unseen, A:* popularity of, 91
—*Lucy Crofton:* 44, 122 n. 2
—"Mademoiselle," 41
—*Madonna Mary:* women and marriage in, 171; mentioned, 41
—*Marriage of Elinor, The:* women and marriage in, 176–77; mentioned, 45
—*Merkland:* women in, 64 n. 7; mentioned, 35, 167
—*Minister's Wife, The:* women and marriage in, 169

—*Miss Marjoribanks:* as female *bildungsroman*, 67–73; John Blackwood on, 22; mock heroic in, 72; modern criticism on, 26 n. 2; women and marriage in, 170–71; mentioned, 12, 21, 41, 49, 53, 88 n. 10, 115
—*Mr. Sandford:* review of, 39; serialization and publication of, 47 n. 15
—"Mrs. Clifford's Marriage," 115
—*Mystery of Mrs. Blencarrow, The,* 40
—"Old Lady Mary," 41, 91
—*Old Mr. Tredgold:* poetic justice in, 59, 65 n. 18; women and marriage in, 58
—*Oliver's Bride,* 40
—*Passages in the Life of Mistress Margaret Maitland,* 18
—*Perpetual Curate, The:* book publication of, 119–20, 123 n. 10; John Blackwood and, 113–23; payment for, 119–20; poetic justice in, 59–60, 68; reviews of, 120–21; serialization of, 116–18; mentioned, 21, 55
—*Phoebe, Junior:* as female *bildungsroman*, 73–78, 88 n. 11; negative review of, 64 n. 4; similarity to Trollope's *Last Chronicle of Barset,* 50–51; mentioned, 55
—"Portrait, The," 41
—*Poor Gentleman, A:* review of, 37, 40, 47 n. 8
—*Primrose Path, The,* 48 n. 26
—"Queen Eleanor and Fair Rosamond": negative review of, 43; women and marriage in, 52–53, 175; mentioned, 41
—*Railwayman and His Children, The:* women and marriage in, 52, 55, 176
—"Rector, The," 67, 114, 115
—*Rose in June, A:* death in, 60
—*Salem Chapel:* as *bildungsroman,* 67, 68; mentioned, 21, 48 n. 26, 115, 117, 119, 121
—*Second Son, The:* death in, 61; poetic justice in, 59
—*Sir Robert's Fortune:* women and marriage in, 45; mentioned, 41, 43

—*Sir Tom:* women and marriage in, 56; mentioned, 44
—*Son of His Father, The:* men in, 51, 62–63
—*Son of the Soil A:* women and marriage in, 57–58, 65 n. 19; serialization of, 122 n. 2
—*Sons and Daughters,* 42–43
—*Sorceress, The:* women and marriage in, 55
—*Stories of the Seen and Unseen. See* individual novels and stories of the series
—"Story of a Wedding Tour, A," negative review of, 43; mentioned, 41
—*Two Strangers,* 41
—*Unjust Steward, The,* 41
—*Whiteladies,* 42
—"Widow's Tale, A," women and marriage in, 54; mentioned, 41
—*Within the Precincts:* women's rights in, 178–79; mentioned, 48 n. 26, 172
—*Wizard's Son, The,* 41
Oliphant, Margaret: Non-Fiction
—"Ancient Classics, The," 155, 164 n. 13
Annals of a Publishing House, 24, 26 n. 9, 27 n. 15
—"Anthony Trollope," 11, 25 n. 1
—"Anti-Marriage League, The," 13–14, 48 n. 23, 161–62, 164 n. 27, 180 nn. 27 and 29
—"Artist's Autobiography, An," 146 n. 7
—"Autobiographies; No. I—Benvenuto Cellini," 124, 125, 133 nn. 1 and 2, 145 n. 7
—"Autobiographies; No. II—Lord Herbert of Cherbury," 125, 133 n. 5, 145 n. 7
—"Autobiographies; No. III—Margaret, Duchess of Newcastle," 145 n. 7
—"Autobiographies; No. IV—Edward Gibbon," 124, 133, 134 n. 21, 145 n. 7
—"Autobiographies; No. V—Cardinal Goldoni," 145–46 n. 7
—"Autobiographies; No. VI—In the

Time of the Commonwealth: Lucy Hutchinson—Alice Thornton," 131–32, 134 n. 15, 146 n. 7
—"Autobiographies; No. VII—Madame Roland," 124, 125, 127–28, 132, 133 n. 3, 134 n. 9, 146 n. 7
—*Autobiography and Letters* (edited by Coghill): inaccurate editing of, 15, 26 n. 2, 135–45; modern criticism of, 134 n. 11; reviews of, 38–39, 129, 133 n. 7; mentioned, 12, 46, 106, 165
—*Autobiography* (edited by Jay): editing of, 135–45; theory of autobiography in, 128–33, 133 n. 6; mentioned, 12, 15, 18, 24, 110 n. 15, 122, 169
—"Condition of Women, The," 47 n. 20
—"Evelyn and Pepys," 133 nn. 2 and 3
—"Fancies of a Believer, The," 129–30, 134 n. 13
—"Great Unrepresented, The," opposition to Mill in, 167, 180 n. 7; mentioned, 47 n. 20
—"Grievances of Women, The," 14, 48 n. 20, 171–72, 180 n. 15
—"Hamlet," 158, 164 n. 19
—"Harriet Martineau," 89 n. 19
—"Lacordaire," 115
—"Laws Concerning Women, The": women's rights in, 167, 180 n. 5; mentioned, 47 n. 20
—[Letter to *The Spectator* on women's rights], 44
—*Life of Edward Irving, Minister of the National Scotch Church, London*, 13, 21, 115
—"Looker-On, The" (August 1894): women's rights in, 177, 180 n. 24
—"Looker-On, The" (January 1895): 146 n. 16
—"Looker-On, The" (January 1896): women's rights in, 177–78, 180 n. 25
—"Marriage Bells," 115
—*Memoir of the Life of John Tulloch, D.D., LL.D.*, 26 n. 10
—"Men and Women," 146 n. 15
—"Miss Austen and Miss Mitford," 85, 89 n. 20
—"Modern Light Literature—Poetry," 139–40, 145 n. 4
—"New Books" (November 1873), 153–54, 163 n. 11
—"New Books" (March 1878), 156, 164 n. 15
—"New Books" (June 1878), 157–58, 164 n. 16
—"New Novels" (September 1867), 70, 88 nn. 8 and 12, 145 n. 5, 150, 163 n. 4
—"New Novels" (November 1870), 150–51, 163 n. 5
—"Novels" (1863), 89 n. 18
—"Novels of Alfonse Daudet, The," 158, 164 n. 17
—"Old Saloon, The: French Contemporary Novelists" (May 1887), 158, 164 n. 18
—"Old Saloon, The" The Literature of the Last Fifty Years" (June 1887), 158–59, 164 n. 20
—"Old Saloon, The" (September 1888), 160, 164 n. 22
—"Old Saloon, The" (December 1888), 160, 164 n. 23
—"Old Saloon, The" (August 1889), 176, 180 n. 22
—"Old Saloon, The" (December 1889), 160–61, 164 n. 25
—"Old Saloon, The" (March 1892), 161, 164 n. 26, 177, 180 n. 23
—"Old Saloon, The" (October 1892), 160, 164 n. 24
—[Review of Cross' *George Eliot's Life*], 142, 146 n. 9
—[Review of Grand's *Ideala*], 44, 48 n. 22
—[Review of Mill and Josephine Butler], women's rights in, 47 n. 20, 168–69, 180 n. 11
—"Russia and Nihilism in the Novels of M. Tourgenief," 159, 164 n. 21
—"Savonarola," 115
—*Victorian Age in English Literature, The*, 24, 26 n. 4

—"Voltaire," 156, 164 n. 14
Oliphant, William (brother), 19, 160
Olsen, Tillie, 143–44
O'Mealy, Joseph H.: article on Oliphant, 26 n. 2
Orel, Harold, 163 n. 3

Pall Mall Gazette, 38
Pater, Walter, 152
Payn, James: on Oliphant, 39, 42
Perpetual curate: defined, 123 n. 13
Peterson, Linda H.: on *Autobiography and Letters,* 134 n. 11, 136, 144, 145 n. 1
Phelps, Elizabeth Stuart: *The Gates Ajar,* 108 n. 3
Pigott, Edward: letter of Oliphant's to, 23, 27 n. 16
Pomerleau, Cynthia, 143, 146 n. 11
Porter, Mrs. Gerald (Mary), 27 n. 15
Pratt, Annis, 87 n. 1

Reed, John: on Oliphant's supernatural fiction, 90, 108 n. 2; mentioned 62, 63 n. 2
Reimer, Gail Twersky: on *Autobiography and Letters,* 134 n. 11
Ritchie, Anne Thackeray: Oliphant's review of *The Story of Elizabeth,* 83, 89 n. 18; mentioned, 13, 136
Rosowski, Susan J., 66, 88 n. 3
Royle, Trevor: on Oliphant, 12–13, 26 n. 3
Rubik, Margarete (formerly Holubetz): article on Oliphant, 26 n. 2
Ruskin, John, 152

Saintsbury, George: on Oliphant, 35–36, 39, 47 n. 3; mentioned, 46, 163 n. 3
Saturday Review: review of *Perpetual Curate* in, 120, 123 n. 12; mentioned, 64 n. 5
Schreiner, Olive, 177
Scottish Review, The, 45
Shand, A. Innes, 149–50, 162 n. 2
Shaw, Marion: on Oliphant, 14, 26 n. 6
Shelley, Percy Bysshe: Oliphant's review of, 153, 163 n. 10

Showalter, Elaine, 109 n. 3
Slater, Gertrude: on Oliphant, 59, 165 n. 18
Smith, Elder, 21, 121
Smythe, Amelia Gillespie, 123 n. 15
Sontag, Susan, 97, 109 n. 9
Spectator, The, Oliphant's letter to on women's rights, 44; reviews of Oliphant in, 37, 51, 64 n. 5, 64 n. 7; review of *Perpetual Curate* in, 120, 123 n. 12
Stebbins, Lucy Poate, 43, 46
Stephen, Leslie: on Oliphant, 33–34, 39, 46 n. 1; Oliphant on in *Autobiography,* 136–38
Stevenson, Robert Louis: on *A Beleaguered City,* 13
Street, George Slythe: on Oliphant, 38–39
Stubbs, Patricia: on *Miss Marjoribanks,* 165, 169, 170
Sturges, Howard Overing: on Oliphant, 38
Sullivan, Jack, 108 n. 1
Sutherland, John A., 141
Symonds, J. A.: Oliphant on, 145, 146 n. 16

Tennyson, Alfred, Lord: Oliphant on in *Autobiography,* 110 n. 15, 139–40
Terry, R. C., 134 n. 19
Thackeray, William Makepeace: Oliphant on *Vanity Fair,* 151, 163 n. 6; *The Newcomes,* 56; *Vanity Fair,* 72; mentioned, 20
Times, The: review of *Carità* in, 43; review of *Perpetual Curate* in, 120, 123 n. 12
Townsend, Meredith: letter of Oliphant's, 47 n. 7; mentioned, 36
Tragedy. See *Blackwood's Edinburgh Magazine:* theory of tragedy in; Oliphant, Margaret, literary life of: theory of domestic tragedy
Trela, D. J.: articles on Oliphant, 26 n. 2, 27 n. 13, 133 n. 4, 162
Trollope, Anthony: Oliphant's article on, 11; Oliphant on Trollope's *Auto-*

biography, 142, 159, 164 n. 20; mentioned, 38, 50–51, 57, 120, 123 n. 13
Tuchman, Gaye, 26 n. 2
Tulloch, John, 110 n. 15, 139
Turgenev, Ivan: *Fathers and Sons,* 159, 164 n. 21

Uglow, Jennifer: on Oliphant, 89 n. 16

Vargish, Thomas, 59
Victoria, Queen, 136

Walker, Hugh: on Oliphant, 35–36, 39, 47 n. 5
Wallace, William: on Oliphant, 45–46, 48 n. 25
Ward, Mrs. Humphry, 167
Wedgwood, Julia: negative review of Oliphant, 43

Westminster Review: "The Grievances of Women" published in, 14; review of Oliphant in, 59; review of *Perpetual Curate* in, 120, 123 n. 12
Wilde, Oscar: on Oliphant, 38
William Blackwood and Sons (publishers), 21, 26 n. 2
Williams, Merryn, 26 n. 2, 162, 163 n. 3
Wilson, Frank (brother), 23, 160
Wilson, Frank, Jr. (nephew), 23
Wilson, Margaret (mother), 17, 140
Wilson, William (brother), 19, 35, 160
Wood, Mrs. Henry, 131
Woodfield, Malcolm, 64 n. 7
Woolf, Virginia: on Oliphant, 33–34, 39; mentioned, 144, 146 n. 14
Wordsworth, William: Oliphant's article on, 152, 163 n. 7

Yonge, Charlotte, 167